Joomla! 1.5 Templa~~te~~ ~~Desig~~

Create your own professional-quality templates with this fast, friendly guide

Tessa Blakeley Silver

[PACKT] PUBLISHING

BIRMINGHAM - MUMBAI

Joomla! 1.5 Template Design

First published: June 2009

Production Reference: 1120609

Published by Packt Publishing Ltd.
32 Lincoln Road
Olton
Birmingham, B27 6PA, UK.

ISBN 978-1-84719-716-0

www.packtpub.com

Cover Image by Vinayak Chittar (vinayak.chittar@gmail.com)

Credits

Author
Tessa Blakeley Silver

Reviewers
Harry B. Reinhardt
Niko Kotiniemi

Acquisition Editor
David Barnes

Development Editor
Siddharth Mangarole

Technical Editor
Mithun Sehgal

Indexer
Hemangini Bari

Editorial Team Leader
Abhijeet Deobhakta

Project Team Leader
Lata Basantani

Project Coordinator
Zainab Bagasrawala

Proofreader
Lynda Sliwoski

Production Coordinator
Aparna Bhagat

Cover Work
Aparna Bhagat

About the Author

Tessa Blakeley Silver's background is in print design and traditional illustration. She evolved over the years into web and multi-media development, where she focuses on usability and interface design.

Prior to starting her consulting and development company hyper3media (pronounced hyper-cube media: http://hyper3media.com), Tessa was the VP of Interactive Technologies at eHigherEducation, an online learning and technology company developing compelling multimedia simulations, interactions, and games, which met online educational requirements such as 508, AICC, and SCORM. She has also worked as a consultant and freelancer for J. Walter Thompson and The Diamond Trading Company (formerly known as DeBeers), and was a Design Specialist and Senior Associate for PricewaterhouseCoopers' East Region Marketing department.

Tessa has authored a few books fro Packt Publishing, including WordPress Theme Design.

I send a huge "thank you" to the Packt team who has made this title possible, and whose help in getting it out into the world has been invaluable. Special thanks to Mithun as well as Niko, Harry, and Siddharth, for their editing work. I'd also like to thank the large and wonderful Joomla! community and all who participate and power the open source world and strive to improve the accessibility of the Web for all. Additional thanks go out to my very patient family who spent quite a few evenings without me while I worked on this title.

About the Reviewers

Harry is a long time Joomla! community member, and has been knocking around the IT industry since the days of punched cards and magnetic tapes. He has spent most of his career as a network systems engineer, fooling around with stuff such as protocols, routing, flow control, and other just as boring networking arcania.

In the real world, Harry has a more-than-passing interest in pickup trucks, country music, open source software, and genealogy. He, his first wife, and two terrible terriers live in Northern Virginia about 20 miles west of Washington, DC.

You can learn more about Harry and what he's currently up to at `www.hrpr.com`.

You can find him on Twitter as "harryb_hrpr" and on the Joomla Forum as "HarryB".

Niko Kotiniemi is a web developer and web/mobile technology enthusiast living in Jyväskylä, in central Finland. He has worked on developing and maintaining web sites professionally as a freelancer for over three years. Lately, he has also reviewed three Joomla! books for Packt Publishing: *"Joomla! E-Commerce with VirtueMart"*, *Suhreed Sarkar, Packt Publishing*; *"Joomla! Accessibility"*, *Joshue O Connor, Packt Publishing*; and *"Joomla! Cash"*, *Brandon Dawson, Tom Canavan, Packt Publishing*.

Niko Kotiniemi is currently employed as a web designer at the Guidance and Counseling Services for Adults—National Coordination Project (`www.opinovi.fi`). Over the past few years, he has been employed by the Federation of Special Service and Clerical employees, ERTO (`www.erto.fi`)—a labor union whose membership, among others, includes those who work in the private sector in the IT-service industry.

He continues his lifetime computer hobby by studying a Bachelor's degree in software and telecommunications engineering at the Jyväskylä University of Applied Sciences, JAMK. In his spare time, he enjoys the outdoors with his family and friends, or delving into that next ultimate solution or API that will allow applications and web sites to interlink and share information.

Table of Contents

Preface

The goal of this title is to explain the basic steps of creating a Joomla! 1.5 template, then walk you through some more advanced techniques that can be used to enhance your template. This book's approach is different than my previous Joomla! 1.0 template book's approach ("*Joomla! Template Design: Create your own professional-quality templates with this fast, friendly guide*", *Tessa Blakeley Silver, Packt Publishing*). I've reviewed a lot of feedback on the previous 1.0 book, via email exchange, Packt's site, and book reviews. It's clear that I and my publisher were a bit off on our target readers' needs. I had attempted to write a book on creating Joomla! templates for someone who was not as familiar with standard web development techniques. This approach made for a book that was a little awkward to write, as it took me away from my own standard design and development process in order to focus on "Photoshop slice n' dice"/ WYSIWYG techniques that, of course, required me to spend more time explaining why those antiquated development methods don't work for dynamic Joomla! templates and the mundane basics of XHTML/CSS development.

I'd like to thank all of you in the Joomla! community who took the time to read the first book and email me with comments and post book reviews. This is your book. While it still discusses some helpful design approaches, tips and tricks, in *Chapter 2* and *Chapter 9*, this book focuses squarely on the development, creation, and enhancement of Joomla! 1.5 templates and, therefore, does not cover general "how to" information about Joomla's basic features and capabilities and assumes you have some level of understanding about the basics of web development.

Joomla! 1.5 has excellent online documentation, which can be found at `http://docs.joomla.org`. There is also a large community of supporters who host all sorts of helpful articles and forums about Joomla. I do not try to replace or duplicate those sources or Joomla's documentation, but intend this book to be a companion to them.

My motive is to save you some time searching the Web, Joomla.org's extensive documentation, and various forum boards, trying to find relevant information on how to create and modify templates. This book should help you understand how Joomla! 1.5 templates work, and show you how to design and build a rich, in-depth web site interface on your own. Throughout the book, wherever applicable, I'll point you to the relevant Joomla! 1.5 documentation, along with many other useful on-line articles and sites.

I've attempted to create a realistic Joomla! template example that anyone can take the concepts from and apply to their own standard web site, while at the same time, show how flexible Joomla! 1.5 and its template capabilities are. I hope this book's case study example shows that Joomla! can be used to create truly unique and beautiful web sites.

What this book covers

Chapter 1 introduces you to the Joomla! CMS by making sure you know what you'll need to be aware of about the Joomla! 1.5 template project that you're ready to embark on. The chapter also covers the development tools that are recommended and the web skills you'll need to begin developing a Joomla! 1.5 template.

Chapter 2 takes a look at the essential elements you need to consider when planning your Joomla! template design. It discusses the best tools and processes for making your template design a reality. I explain my own **rapid design comping** technique and give you some tips and tricks for developing color schemes and graphic styles for your Joomla! template. By the end of the chapter, you'll have a working XHTML- and CSS-based "comp" (or mockup) of your template design, ready to be coded up and assembled into a fully-functional Joomla! template.

You say you're not that creative? The upside of this process means that you don't have to design your own XHTML/CSS mockup to move on to *Chapter 3*. You can use any basic, static XHTML/CSS design (though you'll need to understand the XHTML and CSS used in it) and convert it into a Joomla! template using the methods explained in *Chapter 3*.

Chapter 3 uses our final XHTML and CSS mockup from *Chapter 2* and shows you how to add Joomla's 1.5 jdoc tags to it. Along the way, this chapter covers the essentials of what makes a Joomla! template work. At the end of the chapter, you'll have a working Joomla! template.

Chapter 4 discusses the basic techniques of debugging and validation that you should be employing throughout your template's development. It covers the W3C's XHTML and CSS validation services and how to use the Firefox browser and some of its extensions as a development tool, not just another browser. This chapter also covers troubleshooting some of the most common reasons "good code goes bad", especially in IE 6 and IE7, and best practices for fixing those problems, giving you a great-looking template across all browsers and platforms. We'll also take a look at some SEO enhancements you can make to your site.

Chapter 5 discusses how to properly set up your Joomla! template's templateDetails.xml file and package up your files using the ZIP file format, so that they install into Joomla! correctly. It also discusses running some test installations of your template's package in the Joomla's Administration panel so you can share your Joomla! template with the world.

Chapter 6 covers key information about easy-to-look-up headers that will help you with your Joomla! template development—from the many CSS id and class styles that Joomla! itself outputs, to Joomla's jdoc tags and their controlling attributes. It also covers key 1.0 to 1.5 update information for those of you trying to update a Joomla!1.0 template to a native 1.5 template. The information in this chapter is listed along with key links to bookmark, to make your template development as easy as possible.

Chapter 7 dives into taking your working, debugged, validated, and properly-packaged Joomla! template from *Chapters 3, 4*, and *5*, and starting to enhance it with a dynamic layout that has collapsible columns, using Joomla's PHP code. We'll then spruce up our main menu using the Suckerfish CSS-based method and Adobe Flash media.

Chapter 8 continues showing you how to enhance your Joomla! template, by taking a look at the most popular methods for leveraging AJAX techniques in Joomla! using extensions. I'll also give you a complete background on AJAX and when it's best to use those techniques or skip them. The chapter also reviews some cool JavaScript toolkits, libraries, and scripts that you can use to simply make your Joomla! template appear "Ajaxy".

Chapter 9 covers how to enhance your template by adding a params.ini file, so that your template's users have more dynamic control over your template's configuration right from the Administration panel. For you PHP gurus out there, we'll also cover the basics you need to know to get started with creating your own "module chrome" and "template override" files. We'll also review the main tips from the previous chapters and cover some key tips for easily implementing today's coolest CSS2 and CSS3 tricks into your template. Finally, we'll go over a few final PHP tips to help you enhance your template's usability, so that it can handle right-to-left languages.

What you need for this book

We'll cover more of this in detail in *Chapter 1*, but essentially, you'll need an HTML or text/code editor, a graphic editor such as GIMP, Photoshop or Fireworks, the latest Firefox browser, plus any other web browsers you'd like your template to display well in (IE6 or IE7, Safari, Google Chrome, Opera, and so on). Most importantly, you'll need an installation of the latest, stable version of Joomla! 1.5.

Joomla! 1.5 requires the following to be installed:

- PHP Version 4.3.10 or greater (**PHP 5.2** and above is recommended)
- MySQL Version 3.23 or greater (**MySQL 4.1** and above is recommended)

For more information on Joomla! 1.5's requirements, please browse to:

```
http://www.joomla.org/about-joomla/technical-requirements.html
```

Who this book is for

This book is aimed at web designers who want to create their own unique templates for Joomla! 1.5. The readers should have a basic knowledge of Joomla! 1.5 (*"Building Websites with Joomla! 1.5"*, *Hagen Graf, Packt Publishing* will help you with this) and table-less CSS and XHTML techniques, as well as using Dreamweaver or other text/code editors for coding purposes.

Conventions

In this book, you will find a number of styles of text that distinguish between different kinds of information. Here are some examples of these styles, and an explanation of their meaning.

Code words in text are shown as follows: "I added `class="menu"` to my `ul` inside my `top_navlist div`".

A block of code is set as follows (Code and markup preceded and ended with ellipses "..." are extracted from the full context of code and/or a larger body of code and markup. Please reference the downloadable code packet to see the entire work.):

```
...
#container {
    font-family: "Trebuchet MS", Arial, Helvetica, sans-serif;
}
...
```

When we wish to draw your attention to a particular part of a code block, the relevant lines or items are set in bold:

```
...
#container {
  font-family: "Trebuchet MS", Verdana, Arial, Helvetica, sans-serif;
  font-size: 12px;
}

...
```

New terms and **important words** are shown in bold words that you see on the screen, in menus or dialog boxes for example, appear in the text like this: "In your Joomla! 1.5 Administration panel, go to **Extensions | Template Manager**. There, you'll be able to select the new template you just created".

> Warnings or important notes appear in a box like this.

> Tips and tricks appear like this.

Reader feedback

Feedback from our readers is always welcome. Let us know what you think about this book—what you liked or may have disliked. Reader feedback is important for us to develop titles that you really get the most out of.

To send us general feedback, simply send an email to feedback@packtpub.com, and mention the book title via the subject of your message.

If there is a book that you need and would like to see us publish, please send us a note in the **SUGGEST A TITLE** form on www.packtpub.com or email to suggest@packtpub.com.

If there is a topic that you have expertise in and you are interested in either writing or contributing to a book on, see our author guide on www.packtpub.com/authors.

Customer support

Now that you are the proud owner of a Packt book, we have a number of things to help you to get the most from your purchase.

Downloading the example code for the book

Visit http://www.packtpub.com/files/code/7160_Code.zip to directly download the example code.

The downloadable files contain instructions on how to use them.

Errata

Although we have taken every care to ensure the accuracy of our content, mistakes do happen. If you find a mistake in one of our books—maybe a mistake in the text or the code—we would be grateful if you would report this to us. By doing so, you can save other readers from frustration and help us to improve subsequent versions of this book. If you find any errata, please report them by visiting http://www.packtpub.com/support, selecting your book, clicking on the **let us know** link, and entering the details of your errata. Once your errata are verified, your submission will be accepted and the errata added to any list of existing errata. Any existing errata can be viewed by selecting your title from http://www.packtpub.com/support.

Piracy

Piracy of copyright material on the Internet is an ongoing problem across all media. At Packt, we take the protection of our copyright and licenses very seriously. If you come across any illegal copies of our works, in any form, on the Internet, please provide us with the location address or website name immediately so that we can pursue a remedy.

Please contact us at copyright@packtpub.com with a link to the suspected pirated material.

We appreciate your help in protecting our authors, and our ability to bring you valuable content.

Questions

You can contact us at questions@packtpub.com if you are having a problem with any aspect of the book, and we will do our best to address it.

1
Getting Started as a Joomla! Template Designer

Welcome to Joomla! 1.5 template design. This title is intended to take you through the intricate details of creating sophisticated professional templates for Joomla! 1.5's CMS. In the summer of 2007, I wrote a book for creating Joomla! 1.0 templates. You wouldn't think that much has changed since then, but it has.

With Joomla's official stable release of 1.5 comes a completely reworked and greatly improved administration panel and all new template construction methods. In addition to Joomla's enhancements, the release of IE8 has brought CSS2.1 and a bit more CSS3 support for all major browsers. This means between Joomla's improvements and advances in web standards, the approach and techniques we can use to create our templates is remarkably different from just two years ago. While we all will still need to support IE6 and IE7 for some time further, where applicable, I'll discuss the use of some CSS3 techniques and any graceful degrading methods they might have (just a few samples—this is a book about Joomla! templates, not just CSS, after all).

In these up coming chapters, we'll walk through all the necessary steps required to aid, enhance, and speed up your Joomla! template design process. From design tips and suggestions to packaging up the final template, we'll review best practices for the following range of topics: designing a great template, rapid template development, coding markup, testing, debugging, and taking it live.

The last three chapters are dedicated to additional tips, tricks, and various cookbook recipes for adding popular site enhancements to your Joomla! template designs by using third-party extensions, as well as creating your own solutions.

Joomla! 1.5 perks

Since you're interested in generating custom templates for Joomla! 1.5, you'll be very happy to know (especially, all you "web standards evangelists") that Joomla! does separate content from design, as has always been the case. What's new is our control as template developers over what Joomla! outputs from its "core" (or, how it displays our CMS content).

A few of Joomla! 1.5's newest and most important template features include:

- The removal of bulky PHP-wrapped mosLoadModule tags in place of more XHTML-markup-friendly jdoc tags (which are similar to XHTML, but are part of Joomla's template system). Jdoc tags give you much cleaner template code (and much less syntax to accidentally mess up). If you're not a PHP developer, you can now develop a template with essentially no PHP code (though, as we'll discover, some PHP is still used and quite helpful in enhancing a template).

- Template positions are easily defined and handled through your template's jdoc tags and templateDetails.xml file. No need to use predefined module position names or worry that your template user must set up special positions in the administration panel.

- Full, easy to implement control over what's known as **module chrome** (that is, how your modules are wrapped in XHTML). You can just simply assign one of the built-in style selectors to your jdoc tags, or if you've got a handle on PHP, you can create your own custom module chrome and implement it through jdoc tags. (We'll touch on that advanced technique in *Chapter 9*)

- The introduction of **template overrides**, which allow you to bypass Joomla's table-heavy core output in favor of table-less output. Joomla! provides us with a great set of accessible, table-less overrides in the **Beez** template, which we'll work with in *Chapter 3*. However, if you're an XHTML and PHP wiz, you can create any custom output you can dream of, which we'll cover the basics of in *Chapter 9*.

- There's also an exciting addition of template parameters. Joomla! lets you set up params.ini file and construct your template in such a way that users can change settings from *within* the administration interface. This is a great perk to add to your templates that your users will appreciate.

- Of course, there are more new features than the above, and I'll be pointing them out as we come across them in the following chapters of the book.

Pick a template or design your own?

My approach to template design can be from one of two angles: The first is *Simplicity*, and the second is *Unique and Beautiful*.

- For the *Simplicity* route, sometimes it suites the client and/or the site to go as bare bones as possible. If that is the case, it's just quick and easy to take a very basic pre-made template and modify it. This does not have to be a Joomla! 1.5 template! This book will teach you how to take *any* basic XHTML/CSS markup that you understand and turn it into a working Joomla! 1.5 template.

- Occasionally, you'll need to take the *Unique and Beautiful* route and create the site's template from scratch, so that everything displayed caters to the specific kind of content the site offers. This ensures the site is something eye-catching and completely unique. This is often the best route when custom branding is a priority, or when you just want to show off your "Hey, I'm hot stuff" design skills.

There are many benefits to using or tweaking pre-made templates, some of which are:

- You can potentially save a lot of time getting your site up with a nice template design
- You don't need to know as much about CSS, XHTML, or PHP

This means, with a little web surfing, you can have your Joomla! site up and running with a stylish look in no time.

Drawbacks to using a pre-made template

A drawback to using a pre-made template is that whether it's another Joomla! template or just a static XHTML/CSS template, it may not save you as much time as hoped for. Even with your new header text and graphic, several other sites have downloaded and/or purchased them for themselves, and you don't stand enough apart.

Perhaps your Joomla! site needs a special third-party extension for a specific type of content; it might not look quite right in your template without a lot of tweaking. Moreover, while we're discussing tweaking, I find every CSS designer is different and sets up his/her design's layout and stylesheet accordingly. While it makes perfect sense to them, it can be confusing and time-consuming to work through.

Your approach may have started out as *Simplicity*, but then, for one reason or another, you find yourself having to dig deeper and deeper through the template, and pretty soon it doesn't feel like quick tweaking anymore. Sometimes you realize, for simplicity's sake (no pun intended), it would have been a whole lot quicker to start from scratch.

Before trying to cut corners with a pre-existing template, make sure your project really is as simple as it claims to be. Once you find a template, check that you are allowed to tweak and customize it (such as an open source GNU/GPL or Creative Commons license or royalty free purchase from a template site) and that you have a look at the stylesheet and template files. Make sure the template's assets seem logical and make sense to you.

This book's approach

The approach of this book is going to take you through the *Unique and Beautiful* route with the idea that once you know how to create a template from scratch, you'll be able to understand what to look for in other people's XHTML/CSS markup and/or Joomla! templates. You'll then be able to assess when it is really better or easier to use a pre-made template versus building up something of your own from scratch.

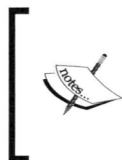

> **Updating 1.0 templates**? If you're looking to update a legacy Joomla! 1.0 template to a native Joomla! 1.5 template, you'll find reading through this book's overall process helpful before sitting down with Chapter 6's Reference Guide, which details how to update major 1.0 template code to 1.5 template code.

Things you'll need to know

This book is geared toward visual designers with no server-side scripting or programming experience who are used to working with common industry standard tools, such as Photoshop and Dreamweaver, or other popular graphic, HTML, and text editors.

Regardless of your web development skill set or level, you'll be walked through clear, step-by-step instructions, although there are many web development skills and much Joomla! know-how you'll need to be familiar with to gain maximum benefit from this book.

Joomla! 1.5

Most importantly, you should be familiar with the most current, stable version of Joomla! 1.5. This includes a general understanding of the Administrative Panel's layout and basic functions.

> **What version of Joomla! 1.5 does this book use**? While this book's case study was developed using versions 1.5.7, 1.5.8, and 1.5.9, any newer version of Joomla! 1.5 should have the same core capabilities, enabling you to develop templates for it using these techniques. Bug fixes and new features for each new version of Joomla! are documented at `http://docs.joomla.org/Special:RecentChanges`.

You should understand how to add content to the Joomla! CMS and how its modules and components work. Understanding the basics of installing and using module and component extensions will also be helpful (though we will cover that to some extent in the later chapters of the book as well). *Chapter 3* will give you some great resources for installing your Joomla! 1.5 development **sandbox**.

Even if you'll be working with a more technical Joomla! administrator, you should have an overview of what the Joomla! site you're designing for entails and what, if any, additional extensions will be needed for the project. If your site does require additional extensions, you'll want to have them handy and/or installed in your Joomla! development installation (your sandbox—a place to test and play without messing up a live site). This will ensure that your design will cover all the various types of content the site intends to provide.

> **First time with Joomla!**? I recommend you read *"Building Websites With Joomla! 1.5"*, Hagen Graf, Packt Publishing.

CSS

I'll be giving detailed explanations of most of the CSS rules and properties used in this book, along with the "how and why" behind those decisions. I won't cover every minor detail of the more basic CSS styles and rules, as, after all, this is not a book about CSS or general web development. We'll be focusing more on what you need to know about Joomla! 1.5 in terms of templating.

You should know a bit about what CSS is and the basics of setting up a cascading style sheet and including it as an external file within an XHTML page. CSS is an essential part of today's web development process. You'll find that the more comfortable you are with CSS markup and how to use it effectively with XHTML, the better your experience creating a Joomla! template will be. Where applicable, I'll point you towards some great resources for better understanding CSS techniques and adding to personal tricks and code arsenal.

XHTML

You don't need to have every markup tag in the XHTML standard memorized (yes, if you really want to, you can still switch to the **Design** view in your HTML editor to drop in those markup tags you keep forgetting—I won't tell). However, the more XHTML basics you understand, the more comfortable you'll be working with the markup in the **Code** view of your HTML editor or with a plain text editor. And, the more you can work directly with the markup, the quicker you'll be able to create well-built templates that are quick loading, semantic, expand easily to accommodate new features, and are search engine friendly.

PHP

You definitely don't have to be a PHP programmer to get through this book. Joomla! 1.5 has gone through great pains to ensure PHP is not needed in your base template. However, be aware that Joomla! does run on PHP and certain template enhancements are still made using PHP code.

If you at least understand how basic PHP syntax is structured, you'll be much less likely to make mistakes while re-typing or copy-pasting code snippets of PHP into your `index.php` file. You'll be able to more easily recognize the difference between your template's XHTML markup and PHP code, so that you don't accidentally delete or overwrite anything crucial.

If you get more comfortable with PHP, you'll have the ability to change out variables and call new functions, template overrides, and module chrome on your own. In later chapters, we'll touch on getting you started with those endeavors.

> **Beef up those web skills**
>
> I'm a big fan of the W3Schools site. If you'd like to build up your XHTML, CSS, and PHP understanding, this site walks you through everything, from basic introductions to robust uses of top web languages and technologies. All the lessons are easy, comprehensive, and free (`http://w3schools.com`).

Not necessary, but helpful

If your project will be incorporating any other special technologies such as JavaScripting, AJAX, or Flash content, the more you know and understand how those scripting languages and technologies work, the better it is for your template-making experience (again W3Schools.com is a great place to start).

> The more web technologies you have a general understanding of, the more likely it is to intuitively make a more flexible template that will be able to handle anything the site's administrators and authors may want to incorporate in the future.

Tools of the trade

In order to get started in the next chapter, you'll need the following tools to help you out.

HTML editor

You'll need a good HTML editor. Dreamweaver is good (`http://www.adobe.com/products/dreamweaver/`); I prefer to use Coda for Mac (`http://www.panic.com/coda/`). When I was on a PC, I loved the free text/code editor HTML-kit (`http://www.htmlkit.com/`). Any HTML or text editor that lets you enable the following features will work just great. (I recommend you enable *all* of the following):

- **View line numbers**: This comes in very handy during the validation and debugging process. It can help you find specific lines in a template file that a validation tool has returned a fix for. This is also helpful for other template or extension instructions given by author, which refer to a specific line of code that needs editing.

- **View syntax colors**: Any worth while HTML editor has this feature, which is usually set as a default. The good editors let you choose your own colors. It displays code and other markup in a variety of colors, making it easier to distinguish various types of syntax. Many editors also help you identify "broken" XHTML markup, CSS styles, or PHP code.

- **View non-printing characters**: OK, you might not want this feature on all the time. It makes it possible to see hard returns, spaces, tabs, and other special characters that you may or may not want in your markup and code.

- **Text wrapping**: This, of course, lets text within the window, so you won't have to scroll horizontally to edit a long line of code. It's best to learn what the key-command shortcut is for this feature in your editor and/or set up a key-command shortcut for it. You'll find it easier to scroll through unwrapped, nicely-indented markup to quickly get a general overview or find your last stopping point. Turn it on quickly so in order to see and focus attention on one long line of markup or code.

Open source HTML editors: I've also used Nvu (`http://www.net2.com/nvu/`) and Kompozer (`http://kompozer.net/`). They're both free, open source, and available for Mac, PC, and Linux platforms. Kompozer was made from the same source as Nvu and apparently fixes some issues that Nvu has. (I haven't run into any major issue with Nvu myself—both editors are a bit limited for my regular use, although I do like being able to format XHTML text quickly and drag-and-drop form objects onto a page.) Both editors have a **Source** view, but you must be careful while switching between the **Normal** and the **Source** view tabs! Nvu and Kompozer are a little too helpful, and will try to rewrite your hand-coded markup if you haven't set your preferences properly! Linux users of Ubuntu and Debian (and Mac users with Fink) might also be interested in checking out Bluefish editor. I haven't used it myself, but the site's writeup looks great: `http://bluefish.openoffice.nl`.

Graphic editor

The next important piece of software you'll need is a graphic editor. While you can find plenty of CSS-only Joomla! templates out there, chances are, you'll want to expand on your design a little more and add nice visual enhancements. These are best achieved by using a graphic editor such as GIMP, Photoshop, or Fireworks. Adobe owns both Photoshop and Fireworks and also offers a light and less-expensive version of Photoshop called Photoshop Elements, which will allow you to do everything discuss in this book (`http://www.adobe.com/products/`).

While I'm an advocate of open source and enjoy working with GIMP, in my line of work, the industry standard is Photoshop or Fireworks. I'll be using Adobe Photoshop in this title and assume that you have some familiarity with it, or GIMP, and with working with layers. Any graphic editor you prefer is fine. One that allows you to work with layers is very helpful, especially with the **design comping** (aka mockup) techniques suggest in *Chapter 2*.

Need a great graphic editor? **Try GIMP**. If you're on a budget and in need of a good image editor, I recommend you use GIMP. It is available for PC, Mac, and Linux. Get it from `http://gimp.org/`.

Prefer vector art? **Try Inkscape**. Inkscape is also available for PC, Mac, and Linux. Bitmap graphic editors are great in that they also let you enhance and edit photographs, but if you just want to create buttons or other interface elements and vector-based illustrations, Inkscape is great, has a low learning curve, and is worth trying out (`http://inkscape.org`).

Firefox

Last, you'll need a web browser. Here, I'm not so flexible. I strongly suggest you use the latest, stable version of the Firefox browser (`http://mozilla.com/firefox/`).

Why Firefox? I view this browser as a great tool for web developers. It's as essential as my HTML editor, graphics, and FTP programs. Firefox has great features that we'll be taking advantage of to help us streamline the design-creation and template-development process. In addition to those built-in features, such as the DOM Source Selection Viewer and adhering to CSS2 (and CSS3) standards as specified by the W3C, FireFox also has a host of extremely useful extensions such as the Web Developer Toolbar and Firebug, which I recommend to further enhance your work flow (I'll discuss these two extensions in detail in *Chapter 4*).

Get the extensions now: You can get the Web Developer Toolbar from `https://addons.mozilla.org/en-US/firefox/addon/60` and FireBug from `https://addons.mozilla.org/en-US/firefox/addon/1843`.

Be sure to visit the developers' sites to learn more about each of these extensions.

We'll be developing for Firefox first, then IE and other browsers

In addition to Firefox having all the helpful features and extensions, IE6 and even IE7 have a thing called **quirks mode**, which we will learn all about in *Chapter 4*. While Microsoft has attempted a lot of improvements and tried to become more W3C compliant with IE7 and now IE8, there are still *some* CSS rendering issues between this browser and others.

Your best bet will be to design for Firefox first, and then, if you notice things don't look so great in IE6, IE7, or IE8, there are plenty of standardized fixes and workarounds for these two browsers, because their "wonks" are just that—wonks and well documented.

As we'll learn in *Chapter 4*, if you design only looking at one version of IE, then find it a mess in Firefox, Opera, or Safari, or the new Google Chrome, you're going to have a much harder time fixing the CSS you made for IE in a more "standards-compliant" browser.

Firefox doesn't have to become your only browser. You can keep using IE or any other browser you prefer. I myself prefer Opera for light and speedy web surfing. As a designer who works with and for other creative Mac-based professionals, I regularly check my work in Safari. Nevertheless, Firefox is one of my key web development tools.

Summary

To get going on your Joomla! 1.5 template design, you'll want to understand how the Joomla! CMS works and have your head wrapped around the basics of the Joomla! project you're ready to embark on. If you'll be working with a more technical Joomla! administrator and/or PHP developer, make sure your development installation, or sandbox, will have the same Joomla! extensions the final site needs to have. You'll want to have any software tools that are recommended installed and ready to use as well as brush up on those web skills, especially XHTML and CSS. Get ready to embark on designing a great template for one of the most popular, open source, CMSs available for the Web today!

Up next in *Chapter 2*, we'll plan our template design and develop it using my own **rapid design comping** technique. You'll end up with a working XHTML/CSS mockup that can be easily modified into a fully functional Joomla! 1.5 template.

2
Template Design and Approach

In this chapter, we're going to take a look at the essential elements you need to consider when planning your Joomla! 1.5 template. We'll then move on to discuss the best tools and processes for making that design a reality. I'll let you all in on my own **rapid design comping** strategy and give you some tips and tricks to help you define your color scheme and graphic style, as well as go over some standard techniques for extracting images for your design.

By the end of this chapter, you'll have a working table-less XHTML 1.0 Transitional and CSS2 "comp" or mockup of your template, ready to be coded up and assembled into a fully functional Joomla! 1.5 template.

Things to consider

First of all, before we start, I'll acknowledge that you probably already have a design idea in mind and would like to just start producing it. Chances are, unless you're learning Joomla! template development solely for yourself, you probably have a client or maybe a web site partner who would like to have input on the design. If you have neither, congratulations! You're your own client. Whenever you see me reference "the client", just switch your perspective from "Template Designer" to "Client/Web site User".

At any rate, before you start working on that design idea, take a moment to start a checklist and really think about two things: What type of site the template is going to be applied to and what, if any, modules, components, or plugins might be used within the template.

Types of sites

Let's take a look at the following types of sites. These are not *genres*. Within these types of sites, just about any genre you can think of can be applied, that is, horseback riding, cooking, programming, various entertainment, and so on.

You may be designing a template for a specific site that has a targeted genre. You may want to make a generic template that anyone can download and use with his/her Joomla! 1.5 installation. Still, if you target your template to fit one of the types of sites that follow, you might get more downloads of it just because it's targeted to a specific type of site.

There's a reason why Joomlashack's *Weblogic* Joomla! 1.5 template is a popular template for news and magazine sites (`http://demotemplates.joomlashack.com/weblogic/`). People who want to start a news site or blog are aware that this template will work for their type of site. No need for them to look through dozens or even hundreds of generic templates wondering if they can modify them to accommodate their site.

Just read through the following site types and notice which one of these types your template fits into. Again, don't worry about genres or other details. Knowing what type of site you want to design for will help you determine how the content should be structured and how that might affect your template's design.

- **The Professional Expert Site**: This is an individual or a group whose site focuses on their area of expertise to increase their exposure and standing.

  The type of design that can be applied to this site is diverse, depending on the type of expertise and what people's expectations are of that genre. For example, lawyers may have more people that are just content searchers. The cleaner and more basic the design, the better. Designers need to give the user a great visual experience, in addition to the content. People in media might want to create a template design that lends itself to listening or viewing podcasts and media.

- **The Educational Site**: This is a site whose main focus is teaching and/or engaging the user in enrolling in the educational program.

  The type of design that is usually applied here is, naturally, focused on the content. Unfortunately, this often means that the design was not considered at all. Even though the experience should be "plain", you'll still want to pay a lot of attention to typography, use of colors, and page layout. You'll want users to be able to find the content they want to learn about and ensure they are able to easily learn from it by having it to be clean and clear with text and headers that are easily scanned.

- **The Corporate Site**: A company site designed to reach customers and encourage closer relationships, sales, and referrals.

  Here, the user is actually a content searcher, so you might think a site that's simpler and focuses on text would do better. They just need the specific information about products and services, and, maybe, would like the opportunity to post a comment to a relevant site post by the corporation. However, the corporation paying you to design the template is really hoping to further engage the user with a great site experience and immerse the user in their brand.

- **Online News Source/Magazine Site**: A site that provides content on a particular topic, usually funded by ads.

  A design for this kind of site depends on how traditional the news content is or "magazine-ish" the content is. People looking for news and the latest updates in a genre might prefer template designs that remind them of the experience of reading a news paper, while magazine readers — especially for fashion, travel, people, and "bleeding-edge" technology — tend to like the site for the design experience of it as well as the content. Just pick up a paper version of any current news source or magazine and you will quickly become aware of what design experience people in that genre are expecting.

- **The Campaign Site**: Not-for-profit sites run by charities or "causes".

  The information needs to be structured for clarity and winning people over to understanding and championing the cause or candidate. Most users will be content searchers and while appreciative of a nice clean content structure and design experience, depending on the campaign or cause, users may become critical if the site is too well designed: "This is nice, but is it where they spend the money I donate, instead of on the cause!?"

- **The Entertainment Site**: A site that provides entertainment, usually through images and other media, as well as with written content, usually funded by ads.

  Here, the design experience of the site is often part of the entertainment. The interface should be compelling and lend itself to the user being drawn to and able to focus on the content. Usually, very eye-catching icons are used to draw the user to click. Darker backgrounds lend colorful photographs and videos the illusion of "popping" off the page.

Keeping the mentioned site types in mind, you can now think about the design you have in mind and assess how appropriate it is for the type of site you want to create a template for the kind of experience you want to give users, as well as what you think the users' expectations are of what the content and experience should be.

Modules, components, and plugins

The second consideration you'll want to make is about modules, components, and plugins. All three items listed above are the types of extensions that you can manage in the Joomla! 1.5 Administrator panel. As mentioned in *Chapter 1*, I'm assuming you're familiar with the basics of administering a Joomla! 1.5 site, but here's a quick overview of those three types of extensions:

- Modules usually consist of menus and small bits of content, such as sidebars and footers, which you can place anywhere on your Joomla! 1.5 site. Modules are usually small and/or intended to complement components.

- Components are more prominent and, in many cases, essential to Joomla. They usually control different types of content and pages and, thus, sometimes need multiple administration panels to manage them. In fact, the most important component is the content component. While other installed components are listed under the **Administrator | Component** menu in the **Administrator** panel, the content component gets its very own menu item called **Content,** because it gets used the most and needs several administration panels to manage all its aspects.

The more you understand about the content component, the more you'll understand how to administer your site. For more information, I recommend you read *"Building Websites With Joomla! 1.5"*, *Hagen Graf, Packt Publishing. Chapter 8* of this book covers the content component menu in detail.

- Lastly, plugins handle and extend the functionality of your Joomla! site, such as adding additional WYSIWYG editors for content writers to choose from, setting user logins, generating pagination, cloaking emails, and so on. While most plugins work on the backend, aiding in administration functionality, don't forget about them! They can generate frontend links and, occasionally, affect the display of the content. You'll want to understand what plugins will be used and if you'll need to account for them in your design.

Modules, components, and plugins usually place requirements on a template: certain CSS ID's and classes may be generated and placed into the site for headers or special text areas. You'll need to find out what the output of any module or component you plan to use is, so that you may accommodate it when you code up your template.

What kinds of extensions are available? You can see all the types of extensions available on the `joomla.org` site by viewing this URL: `http://extensions.joomla.org/`.

This book will walk you through adding various components, modules, and plugins to your template in *Chapters 7, 8*, and *9*.

When you begin work on your design, you'll want to compare your sketches and design comp(s) against your modules and components checklist and make sure you're accommodating them.

Getting ready to design

Design Comp (an abbreviation used in design and print): A preliminary design or sketch is a "comp", comprehensive artwork, or composite. It is also known as comp, comprehensive, mockup, sample, or dummy.

You may already have a design process similar to the one I detail next; if so, just skim what I have to say and skip ahead to the next main heading. I have a feeling though, that many of you will find this design comping technique a bit "unorthodox", but bear with me, it really works.

Here's how this process came about, whether or not you design professionally for the client or for yourself, you can probably identify with parts of this experience:

We have a problem

Up until a couple of years ago, in order to mock up a site design, I loaded up Photoshop and began the rather time-consuming task of laying down the design's graphical elements and layout samples, which entailed managing what sometimes ended up being a *very large* amount of layers, most of which were just lots of text boxes filled with Lorem Ipsum sample text.

I'd show these mockups to the client, they'd make changes, which more often than not were just to the text in the mockup, not to the overall layout or graphical interface. As my "standard design procedure" was to have a client approve the mockup before production, I'd find myself painstakingly plodding through all my Photoshop text layers, applying the changes in order to show the mockup to the client again.

Sometimes, I would miss a small piece of text that should have been updated with other sets of text! This would confuse (or annoy) the client, and they'd request another change! I guess they figured that since I had to make the change anyway, they might as well request a few more tweaks to the design, which, again, were usually more textual than graphical and took a bit of focus to keep track of.

The process of getting a design approved became tedious and, at times, drove me nuts. At one point, I considered dropping my design services and just focusing on programming and markup so that I wouldn't have to deal with it anymore.

It gets worse

Upon, finally, getting an approval and starting to produce the design comp into XHTML and CSS for a Joomla! template, no matter how good I got at envisioning how the CSS would work while I was mocking up the layout in Photoshop, I inevitably would include something in the layout that turned out to be a bit harder than I'd thought it would be to reproduce with XHTML and CSS.

I was then saddled with two unappealing options: either go back to the client and get them to accept a more reasonable "reality" of the design or spend more time doing all sorts of tedious research and experimentation with the XHTML and CSS to achieve the desired layout, or other effect, across all browsers, including Internet Explorer.

The solution: Rapid design comping

I soon realized the problem was hanging onto a very antiquated design process of what the *mockup* was and what *production* was. Before late 2005, I never would have cracked open my HTML editor without a signed design approval from the client, but why? Who said that design mockups could only be graphical?

The Web was originally made for text. Thus, it has a very nice, robust markup system for categorizing that text (that is, HTML/XTHML). Now with browsers that all adhere (more or less) to CSS standards, the options for displaying those marked-up items are more robust, but there are still limitations.

Photoshop, on the other hand, has no display limitations. It was made to edit and enhance digital photographs and create amazing visual designs. It can handle anything you layout into it, be it realistic for CSS or not. It *was not* designed to help you effectively manage layers upon layers of text that would be best handled with global stylings!

This realization led me to this 10-step process I've termed "rapid design comping". The term is a bit of a play on the phrase "rapid prototyping", which had become very popular at the time this design process emerged for me, which is indeed inspired by and bears some similarities to rapid prototyping.

Here is the overview; we'll go over each step in detail afterwards:

1. **Sketch it**: Napkins are great! I usually use the other side of a recycled piece of photocopied paper—the more basic the better. No fine artistic skill required!

   Perk: Using this sketch, you can not only get your graphic interface ideas down, but also already start to think about how the user will interact with your template design and re-sketch any new ideas or changes accordingly.

2. **Start with the structure**: I create an ideal, un-styled semantic XHTML document structure and attach a bare bones CSS sheet to it.

3. **Add the text**: Lots of text, the more the better! A sample of actual content is best, but Lorem Ipsum is fine too.

4. **CSS typography**: Think of your typography (what font families you'd like to use and where you'd want text to be bolded, italicized, or otherwise decorated and varied) and assign your decisions to the stylesheet. Review! Don't like how the formatted text looks in-line? Being separated into columns with fancy background graphics won't make it any better. Get your text to look nice and read well now before moving on to layout.

5. **CSS layout**: Set up the layout—this is where you'll see upfront if your layout idea from your sketch will even work. Any problems here and you can re-think the design's layout into something more realistic (and usually more clean and elegant).

   Perk: Your client will never see, much less become attached to, a layout that would cause you problems down the road in CSS.

6. **CSS color scheme**: Assign your color scheme basics to the CSS. We're close to needing Photoshop anyway, so you might as well open it up. I sometimes find it useful to use Photoshop to help me come up with a color scheme and get the hex numbers for the stylesheet.

7. **Take a screenshot**: Time for your favorite image editor! Paste the screenshot of your basic layout into a Gimp or Photoshop file.

8. **Image editing**: Relax and have fun in Gimp, Inkscape, Photoshop, or Illustrator (I often use a combination of a vector editor and bitmap image editor) to create the graphical interface elements that will be applied to this layout over your screenshot.

9. **Send for approval**: Export a .jpg or .png of the layout and send to the client.

   Perk: If a client has text changes, just make them in your CSS (which will update your text globally—no layer hunting for all your headers or links and so on) and re-snap a screenshot to place back in the Photoshop file with the graphic elements. If they have a graphical interface change, that's what Photoshop does best! Make the changes and resend for approval.

10. **Production**: Here's the best part: you're more than halfway there! Slice and export the interface elements you created over (or under) your screenshot and apply them with the background image rules in your CSS.

    Because you worked directly over a screenshot of the layout, slicing the images to the correct size is easier, and you won't discover as much need to tweak the layout of the CSS to accommodate the graphic elements.

> If you start getting really good and speedy with this process, and/or, especially, if you have text overlaying complicated backgrounds, you can also just export your images to your CSS file right away and send the client a straight screenshot from the browser to approve. Play with this process and see what works best for you.

For the purposes of this title, there's actually an eleventh step of production, which is, of course, coding and separating up that produced mockup into your Joomla! 1.5 template. We'll get to that in *Chapter 3*.

Let's get started!

After taking all of the given items into consideration, I've decided the type of template I'd like to create, and the one we'll be working on throughout this book is going to be a **Campaign** type of site. Our site's content will be focused on Green Energy alternatives. Even though this type of site usually does very well by just focusing on content, I would like to give the users the design experience of a somewhat trendy, clean and fresh interface that's friendly to navigate. I'll also keep it basic, so you can clearly see how to apply the techniques in this book to any type of site you might create with a Joomla! template.

Think about it: Positions

Before we even start the first step, take your design idea and consider it from an important aspect of Joomla! sites: positions. While my goal for this chapter is to make you design free of having to think too much about any Joomla! 1.5 "constraints", such as Joomla's basic CSS styles (which are covered when you need them in *Chapters 3* and *6*); however, if you're sure your template is going to be used in a Joomla! site (as it's pretty obvious, you're reading this book after all), then thinking about your design in terms of Joomla! positions is the best way to start. Joomla! templates use `jdoc` tags as placeholders, called **positions**, to hold content in the template and display database information into it. This makes Joomla! and the templates designed for it very flexible. Joomla! site administrators can assign modules to different positions within the **Module Manager** and, thus, without touching any code, change their site's appearance and the way it is used or navigated. One administrator might have his/her `main_menu` module assigned to the `left` position and another administrator may choose to assign it to the `top` position.

What positions are available depends on what positions have been added to the `templateDetails.xml` file. These positions can be anything you want, which is good, since we're not going to worry about the `templateDetails.xml` file just yet (We'll cover it in full detail in *Chapter 5*).

Generally, people tend to name their `jdoc` positions similarly to what the default positions were called in Joomla! 1.0. This is good for two reasons:

- The original Joomla! 1.0 positions are named pretty clearly, defining the standard and common areas of a web page. Why fix what isn't broken?
- It's nice to name them the same, especially if you think your template may be installed and used by someone who is familiar with Joomla! 1.0 and has moved on to Joomla! 1.5. The position selection drop-downs in the **Module Manager** won't be confusing to them (or again, as they're named so well already, anyone else for that matter).

Here are the most common `jdoc` position names:

- `banner`
- `breadcrumbs`
- `debug`
- `footer`
- `hornav`
- `left`
- `right`
- `search`
- `syndicate`
- `top`
- `user1`
- `user2`
- `user3`
- `user4`
- `user5b`
- `user6`
- `user7`
- `user8`
- `user9`

To have an idea of how these work in your design layout, here is how a few of those positions are used in Joomla! 1.5's default template: `rhuk_milkyway`. The text inside the solid rectangles denotes the position names and the dashed outlines with light grey background denote the position's area.

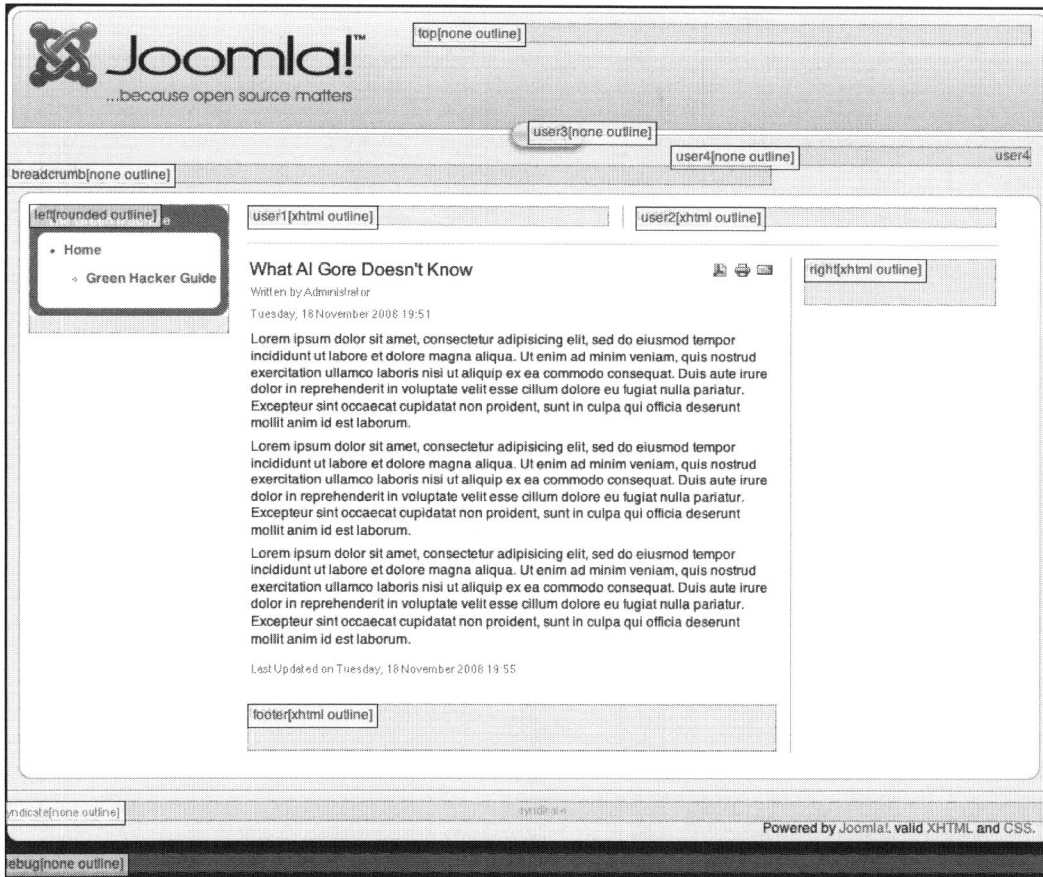

Sketch it

Now that you're thinking about positions, you can start sketching your design. The whole point of this step is to just get your layout down, along with figuring out your graphic element scheme. You don't have to be a great artist or technical illustrator; as you'll see next, I'm clearly no DaVinci! Just put the gist of your layout down on a sheet of paper, quickly.

The best place to start is to reference your checklist from the steps I provided, which considers how the site is going to be used. Focus on your desired layout: are you going to have columns? If so, how many? On the left or the right? How tall is your header? Will your footer be broken into columns? All of these things will determine the structure of your design. You can then move on to any graphic element schemes you might have in mind; that is, would you use rounded corners on box edges or a particular icon set? Where? How often?

In the following figure, I've sketched a basic three-column layout, which uses using Joomla! 1.5 to manage and feature "campaign-style" articles and information.

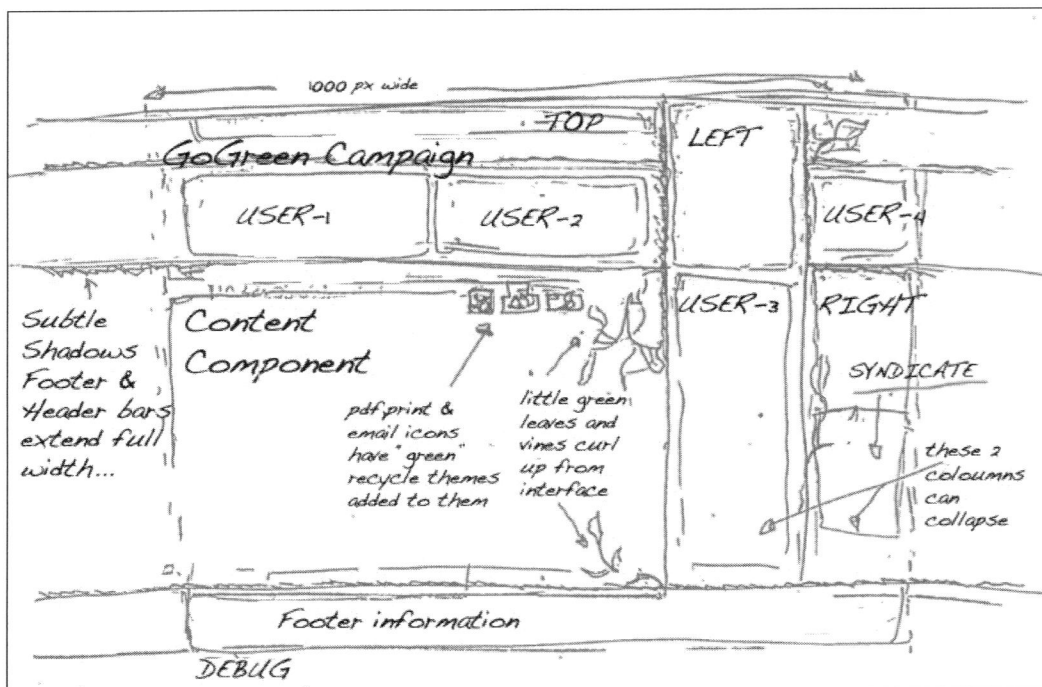

Because my site will focus on bringing people around to "going green" (in other words, being more aware of using earth-friendly energy resources, products, and controlling waste), the design experience I'd like to convey should be energetic and uplifting. The visual scheme for my graphic elements is going to focus on creating the illusion of green leaves and vines poking out through the interface and columned layouts.

Consider usability

Once you've created your sketch based on your considerations, look at it for usability. Imagine you are someone who has come to the site for the information it contains.

What do you think the users will actually do? What kinds of goals might they have for coming to your site? How hard or easy will it be for them to attain those goals? How hard or easy do you want it to be for them to attain those goals?

Are you adhering to standard web conventions? If not, have you let your users know what else to expect? Web standards and conventions are more than what's laid out in a lengthy W3C document. A lot of it conforms to what we as web users expect! For example: if text has underlines in it and/or is of a different color, we expect that text to be a link. If something looks like a button, we expect that clicking on it will do something, such as process the comment form we just filled out or adding an item to our cart.

It's perfectly OK to get creative and break away from the norm and not use all web conventions. But be sure to let your viewers know upfront what to expect, especially as most of us are simply expecting a web page to act like a web page.

Looking at your sketch, do any of the given scenarios make you realize any revisions that need to be made? If so, that's pretty easy to do. Make another sketch.

Start with the structure

The previously mentioned usability scenarios deal with someone who will be looking at your content through your fully CSS-styled template. What if someone views this content in a mobile browser? A text-only browser? Or a text-to-speech browser? Will the un-styled content still be understood? Or, will someone be scrolling or, worse, listening and trying to tab through 13 minutes of your sidebar "blog roll", Flickr image links, or other unrelated links before getting to the page's main content? To ensure such a scenario doesn't happen, we'll dive into our design comp by starting with the semantic XHTML structure. I like to make sure the raw, un-styled content appears in the most logical and useful order possible.

So, what's semantic? Overall, I use the word semantic in making sure the un-styled order and structure of my content makes sense. Concerning strictly HTML, semantic refers to the separation of style from content by avoiding the use of presentational markup in HTML files. It also requires using the available markup to differentiate the meanings of various content in the HTML document. For instance, naturally you're familiar with headers being wrapped in `<h1>`, `<h2>`, and so on, header tags, images wrapped in `<img.../>` tags, and sections of textual content wrapped in `<p>` paragraph tags.

You can also define the content even further by taking care to place email addresses inside `<address>` tags, acronyms inside `<acronym>` tags, quotes inside `<blockquotes>` tags, and citations inside `<cite>` tags (the list goes on). This lets anyone as well as different processors (from browsers to other kinds of software) understand the document's content more easily.

You can learn more about semantic HTML from Wikipedia: `http://en.wikipedia.org/wiki/Semantic_HTML`.

For a comprehensive list of XHTML tags you can define your content with, check out W3Schools: `http://w3schools.com/tags/default.asp`.

While the HTML editors I recommended in *Chapter 1* will drop these tags in for you, the more you understand about the XHTML tags and how to use them properly as well as how they should look directly in the code view, the more solid, compliant, and accessible your mark up will be.

Time for action: Starting to create your design

We're now ready to open up our HTML editor and start producing our design mockup.

Open up your HTML or text editor and create a new, fresh `index.html` page.

The DOCTYPE

XHTML has two common DOCTYPES: **Strict** and **Transitional**. There's also the newer 1.1 DOCTYPE for "modularized" XHTML. The Strict and 1.1 DOCTYPE is for the truly semantic. Its requirements suggest you have absolutely no presentational markup in your XHTML (though in Strict 1.0, any `strong`, `em`, `b`, `i`, or other presentation tags that slip in, will still technically validate on W3C's service; it's not just the recommendation for how to remain "Strict").

You can use what you'd like, especially if it's your own Joomla! 1.5 site. However, if the site will not remain completely under your control, you can't control everything that other content authors will add to the posts and pages. It's safest to use the 1.0 Transitional DOCTYPE, which will keep your template valid and have more flexibility for different kinds of users and the type of content they might place into the system. This DOCTYPE is also best, as third-party modules, components, and plugins rarely adhere to the Strict DOCTYPE. Generally, it's much easer to maintain and keep your XHTML and CSS valid.

Time for action: Adding the DOCTYPE

Let's add the first line of code to our mockup.

For my "Go Green Campaign" template, I'll go ahead and use the `1.0 Transitional` DOCTYPE:

```
<!DOCTYPE html PUBLIC "-//W3C//DTD XHTML 1.0 Transitional//EN"
    "http://www.w3.org/TR/xhtml1/DTD/xhtml1-transitional.dtd">
```

You should note, while being integral to a valid template, the DOCTYPE declaration itself is not a part of the XHTML document or an XHTML element. It does not use a closing tag, even though it does look a bit like an empty tag.

Check your editor's preferences

Some editors automatically place a `DOCTYPE` and the required `html`, `header`, `title`, and `body` tags into your document when you open up blank file. That's great, but please go into your editor's preferences and make sure your **Markup** and **DTD** preferences are set to: **XHTML** and **Transitional** (or **Strict**, if you prefer). Some editors that offer a "design" or WYSIWYG view will overwrite the `DOCTYPE` to whatever the preferences are set to when you switch between the **Design** and **Source** (that is, **Code**) views. DreamWeaver doesn't seem to have this problem, but you should set your DOCTYPE preferences there too, just to be safe.

The main body

Let's add the XHTML file requirements.

Time for action: Adding the XHTML file requirements

Our XHTML mockup, like all XHTML files, requires a few additional tags, which we'll now add in.

After our DOCTYPE, we can add in the other essential requirements of an XHTML file, which are as follows:

```
<html xmlns="http://www.w3.org/1999/xhtml" xml:lang="en" lang="en">
<head>
<title>My New Joomla! 1.5 Template Title</title>
</head>
<body> body parts go here </body>
</html>
```

Attach the basic stylesheet

At this time, since we have created our basic header tags, I go ahead and attach a bare bones stylesheet. This stylesheet has general items, matching div ids and placeholders that I use for most CSS styling. But it's just the "shell". There are no display parameters for any of the rules.

Time for action: **Attaching the CSS file**

Let's set up the link to a CSS file. (We'll get to creating that in a minute.)

1. In your index.html file, add your CSS import link within the header file. Note the empty javascript link tag. This is recommended by CSS Zen Garden to correct the unsightly "Flash of Unstyled Content". For more information check out: http://www.bluerobot.com/web/css/fouc.asp:

   ```
   <head>
   <title>My New Joomla! 1.5 Template Title</title>
   <script type="text/javascript" src=""></script>
   <style type="text/css" media="screen">
   @import url("css/template.css");
   </style>
   </head>
   ```

2. Next, create a template.css file and include the following basic shell:

   ```
   /*

       Enter Joomla! 1.5 Design & Creation Comments Here

   */


   /*////////// GENERAL //////////*/

   body {}

   #container {}

   #container2 {}
   ```

```
#container3 {}

/*////////// TYPEOGRAPHY //////////*/

h1 {}

h2 {}

h3 {}

h4 {}

p {}

a {}

a:hover {}

a:visited {}

/*////////// HEADERS //////////*/

#header {}

/*////////// CONTENT //////////*/

#content {}

/*////////// SIDEBARS //////////*/

#sidebarLT {}

#sidebarRT {}

/*////////// NAV //////////*/

/*////////// FORMS //////////*/

/*////////// FOOTER //////////*/

#footer {}

/*////////// IMAGES //////////*/

/*////// FUN CLASSES //////////*/

/*any little extra flares and fun design
elements you want to add can go here*/
```

Basic semantic XHTML structure

Referring back to our sketch and the conversation we had earlier about semantics, we'd like our template to have a standard header that stretches across three columns. I'd like to break away from the common Joomla! three-column structure, which has the main content in the middle. So, in my example, the far left column will house the main content, the middle column will hold additional navigation and side bar information, and the third column on the far right will hold tertiary information, such as links and/or advertisements. A footer will run across the bottom of all the three columns, naturally falling beneath the longest extending column, no matter which of the three it is.

Time for action: **Laying out the meaning and order**

We're now ready to work on in what order we want our content to be served up, so that it has better meaning to us as readers as well as search engine bots.

Let's start off with some very basic code within our body tag to get that going. I've included relevant `id` names on each `div` in order to keep track of them and later assist me with my CSS development.

```
...
<body>
<a name="top"></a><!--anchor for top-->
<div id="container"><!--container goes here-->
<div id="header">
<em>Header:</em> background image and text elements for header will go
inside this div.
</div><!--//header-->
<!-- Begin #container2 this holds the content and sidebars-->
<div id="container2">
<!-- Begin #container3 keeps the left col and body positioned-->
<div id="container3">
<!-- Begin #content -->
<div id="content">
<em>Main Content:</em> Joomla! content component will display here.
</div><!-- //content -->
<!-- #left sidebar -->
<div id="sidebarLT">
<em>Left Side Bar:</em> Will contain content related items/links
</div><!--//sidebarLT   -->
</div><!--//container3-->
<!-- #right sidebar -->
<div id="sidebarRT">
<em>Right Side Bar:</em> This will include additional ads, or non-
content relevant items/links.
```

```
</div><!--//sidebarRT -->
</div><!--//container2-->
<div id="top_navlist">
<em>Top Nav:</em> For reading through straight text, it's best to have
links at bottom (css will place it up top, for visual ease of use)
</div><!--//top_navlist-->
<div id="footer">
<em>Footer:</em> quick links for CSS design users who've had to scroll
to the bottom plus site information and copyright will go here

</div><!--//footer-->
</div><!--//container-->
</body>
...
```

My New Joomla 1.5 Template ... ⊗ Go Green Campaign - Adminis... ⊗

Header: background image and text elments for header will go inside this div.
Main Content: Joomla content component will display here.
Left Side Bar: Will contain content related items/links
Right Side Bar: This will include additional ads, or non-content relevant items/links.
Main Menu: For reading through straight text, it's best to have links at bottom (css will place it up top, for visual ease of use)
Footer: quick links for CSS design users who've had to scroll to the bottom plus site information and copyright will go here

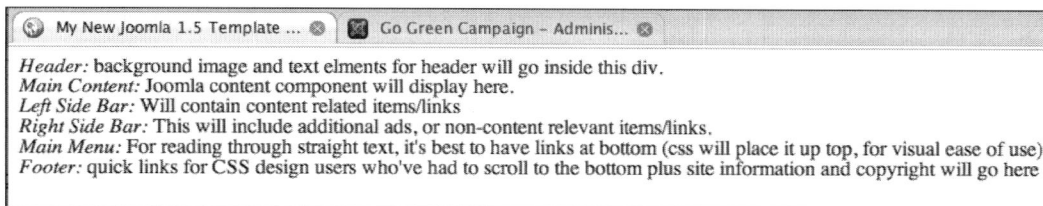

Not much to look at so far, but you can see our semantic goals at work. For instance, if a search engine bot or someone using a text-only browser or mobile device came and viewed our site, this is the order they'd see things in:

- **Header**—because it's good to know who's stuff you're looking at
- **Main content**—get right to the point of what we're looking for
- **Left column content**—under the main content, should have next most relevant and interesting links/items
- **Right column content**—secondary information, irrelevant information such as advertisements and non-content-related links/items
- **Main menu navigation**—even though in the design this will be on the top, it's best to have it at the bottom in text-only viewing
- **Footer information**—if this was a page of real content, it's nice to see whose site we're on again, especially if we've been scrolling or crawling down for some time

Moving navigation to the bottom: Some SEO experts believe that another reason to semantically push the navigation items as far as possible down the page after the body of content is that it encourages search engine bots to crawl and index more of the page's content before wandering off down the first link it comes to. The more content the bot can index at a time, the sooner you'll have it displayed on the search engine. Apparently, it can take months before a site is fully indexed depending on its size. I have no idea if this is actually true, but it's in-line with my semantic structure based on usability, so no harm done. You'll have to tell us at Packt Publishing if you think your content is getting better SE coverage based on this structure.

Adding text: Typography

We're now ready to make our typography considerations. Even if you're designing far into the "experience" side of the scale, text is the most common element of a site, so you should be prepared to put a fair amount of thought into it.

Start with the text

I like to add an amount of text that has a site name and description paragraph right on top in my header tags, the main body text up high in the content tags, secondary then tertiary text below that (some of which usually ends up in a side bar), and the navigation at the very bottom of the page in an unordered list. You know, it's basically that "perfect page" SEO experts go on and on about—a Google bot's delight, if you will.

Minimally, I include `<h1>`, `<h2>`, `<h3>`, and `<h4>` headers along with links, strong and emphasized text, as well as other markup such as `blockquote` tags and anything else the site might use. If I know for sure that the site will be using specific markup such as `<code>` or form elements such as `<textarea>` or `<input>`, I try to include examples of text wrapped in these tags as well. This will help me ensure that I create style rules for all the possible basic markup elements.

To help myself out visually, I do tweak the text a bit so that it fits the site's goals and is similar to what the Joomla! site might output. I put in a sample page or news item, along with example text of features I want the site to have, and a sample of what kind of links the Joomla! system will provide.

If I know that the text will be part of a Joomla! 1.5 position, which will need to be positioned by CSS later on, I go ahead and wrap that basic text in a `div` with an `id` tag, which I give the same name as the Joomla! position. (You don't have to do this, it just keeps things very simple and clear for me.)

Time for action: Adding `div` **tags to the** `header` `div`

To make sure our layout will come together, we'll need to add a few `div` tags to "hold" it.

For instance, in my sketch, within my `header`, I note I want the `user1` and `user2` positions to display side by side, so when I add that text, I'll just wrap them in `div` tags with an `id` like the following:

```
...
<div id="header">
<h1>Go Green Campaign</h1>
<h4>It's not easy being green... but worth it.</h4>

<div id="user1">
<h2>User1 Position</h2>
Quick site snippet... Lorem ipsum dolor sit amet, consectetur
adipisicing elit, sed do eiusmod tempor incididunt ut labore et dolore
<a href="#">magna aliqua.</a>
</div>

<div id="user2">
<h2>User2 Position</h2>
Quick site snippet... Lorem ipsum dolor sit amet, consectetur
adipisicing elit, sed do eiusmod tempor incididunt ut labore et <a
href="#">dolore magna</a> aliqua.
</div>

</div><!--//header-->
...
```

Later on, I'll have `div` `ids` to use in my CSS sheet, to help me position them accurately.

Actually, start with a lot of text

Here's my secret: I use a lot of sample text. A major issue I've always noticed about design comps and reality is this: we tend to create a nice mockup that's got clean, little two-word headers followed by trim and tight one- or two-sentence paragraphs (which are also easier to handle if you did the entire mockup in an image editor such as Photoshop or Gimp).

In this optimally minimalist sample, the design looks beautiful. However, the client then dumps all their content into the CMS, which includes long, boring, two-sentence headlines and reams and reams of unscannable text. Your beautiful template design now seems dumpy and suddenly the client isn't happy and want you to incorporate many suggestions in order to compensate for their text-heavy site.

Just design for lots of text upfront. If the site ends up having less text than what's in your comp, that's perfectly fine. Less text will always look better. Getting mounds of it to look good after the fact is what's hard.

Now our layout looks like this:

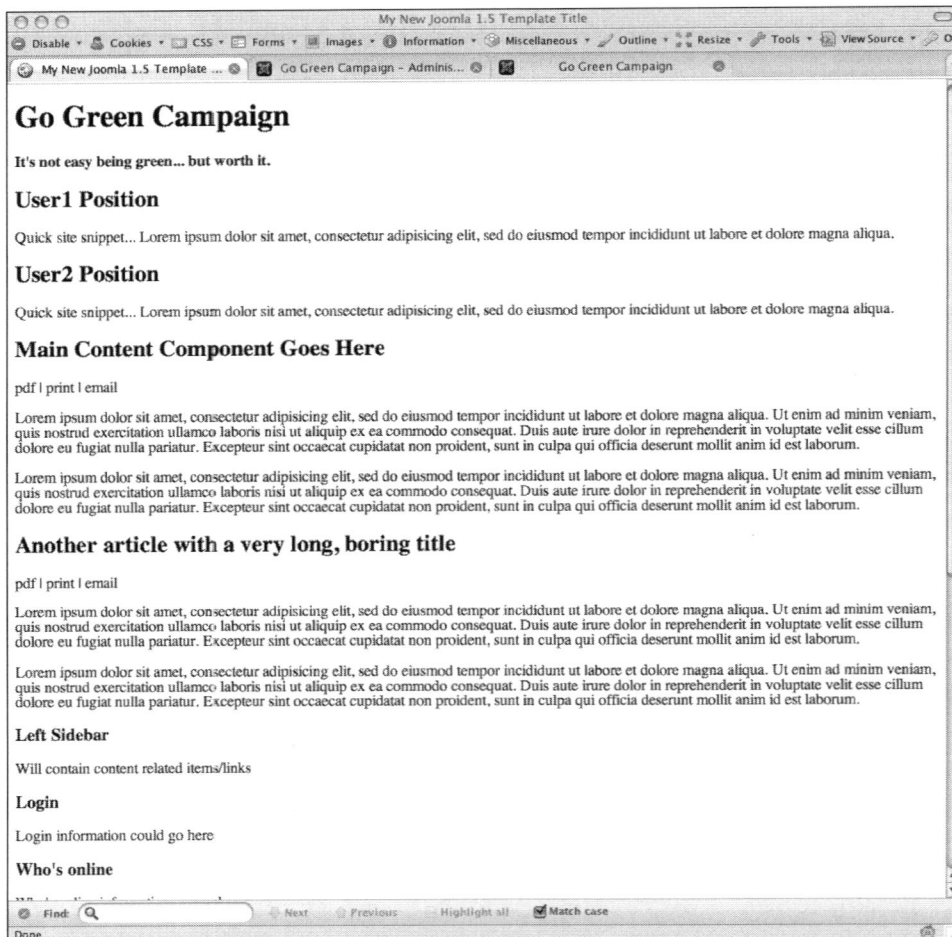

A quick note about starting to style with CSS

Some of you may already be wondering when Joomla! is going to come into play. We will discover that Joomla! 1.5 outputs lots of `class` and `id` names that can be leveraged and styled through CSS. Many Joomla! template developers recommend taking a rendered page of Joomla! content and "scraping" that into a local HTML page to use for generating CSS stylesheets. This is a good approach, but can sometimes make for a lot of unnecessary work. You'll notice that in the previous code examples I've placed dummy content in my container divs, using nothing but very basic XHTML markup tags, such as headers `<h1>`, `<h2>`, `<h3>`,`<p>` tags, `<div>` tags, `<a>` links, `<ul>` and `<ol>` lists, and so on.

I find that approaching template design from the ground up makes for a much more solid, yet flexible template. By making sure that all your basic XHTML object tags are styled well, from headers and paragraph tags to link tags, list items, blockquotes, and all those other semantic tags we've previously discussed, you can combine those styles with strong layout techniques applied to your original containing `div`s. Using this method, you'll find that you don't really need a lot of complicated CSS stylesheets, or to address every single little `class` and `id` name that Joomla! spits out.

You'll end up with a great looking template that can handle administrators choosing to do odd things with it, things that we designers would never think someone would do, or understand why they'd want to do it (until they do it and make our nice template design look odd or broken). Instead of smacking your head when the administrator decides to, say, place the `main menu` module in the `user9` position, you'll be able to smile wryly, because in spite of that, your design holds together well and looks coherent, as your CSS layout wasn't completely dependent on Joomla!-specific `id` and `class` names and/or combinations of those styles.

Once you've coded up your template enough to apply it to Joomla! and start seeing it with dynamic content, you'll be able to use Joomla's `classes` and `ids` to your advantage and assign CSS styles to only those you've carefully chosen, which give your template those nice, extra details that really polish it off.

Font choices

When it comes to fonts on the Web, we're limited. You should generally design for the most common fonts that are widely available across operating systems. That doesn't mean you shouldn't spend time really considering what your options are.

I think about the type of information the site provides and what's "expected" along with what's "in vogue" right now. I then consider my fonts and mix them carefully. I usually think in terms of headers, secondary fonts, blockquotes, specialty text (such as depicting code), and paragraph page text.

Ultimately, you can use any fonts you want as long as you think there's a really good chance your site viewers will have the same font on their computers. The following is a list of the basic fonts I mix and match from and the reasons why:

- **San-serif fonts**: These fonts don't contain "serifs" (hence san-serif). Serifs are the little "feet" you see on the appendages of type faces. San-serif fonts are generally considered more modern.

- **Verdana**: This font is common on every platform and was specifically designed for web reading at smaller web sizes. When you really want to use a san-serif font for your body text, this is your best bet. (Side note for the "font freaks" out there: there was a great article in the *The New Yorker* in 2005 about the designer of this font, Matthew Carter).

- **Arial and Helvetica**: Common on every platform. A little tame. Great for clean headlines, but a bit hard to read at smaller font sizes.

- **Trebuchet**: Fairly common now-a-days, and a pretty popular font on "Web 2.0" styled sites. Clean like Arial with a lot more character. It reads a little better at smaller sizes than Arial. This was originally a Microsoft font, so sometimes it doesn't appear in older Mac or Linux OSs. (Verdana is a MS font too, originally released with IE 3, but its design for screen readability got it opted quickly by other OSs.)

- **Century Gothic**: Fairly common. Clean and round, a nice break from the norm. Reads terrible at small sizes though, use for headings only.

- **Comic Sans Serif**: Another MS font, but common on all platforms. Fun and friendly. Based on traditional comic book hand lettering. I've never been able to use it in a design (I do try from time to time and feel it's "hokey"), but I always admire when it's used well in site design.

- **Serif fonts**: These fonts are considered more traditional, or "book-ish", as serif fonts were designed specifically to read well in print. The serifs (those "little feet") on the appendages of the letters form subtle lines for your eyes to follow.

- **Times New Roman and Times**: Very common on all platforms; one of the most common serif fonts. Comes off very traditional, professional, and/or serious.

- **Georgia**: Pretty common, again predominately a Microsoft font. I feel it has a lot of character, nice Serifs, and big and fat body. Like Verdana, Georgia was specifically designed for on-screen reading for any size. Comes off as professional, but not quite as serious as Times New Roman.

- **Century Schoolbook**: Pretty common. Similar to Georgia, just not as "fat".

- **Courier New**: This is a mono-spaced font, based on the old typewriters and often what your HTML and text editor prefers to display (the point of mono-type is that the characters don't merge together, so it's easier to see your syntax). As a result of that association, I usually reserve this font for presenting code snippets or technical definitions within my designs.

Get daring: Font stacks

Today, more and more people are on newer computers with more fonts available to them. Starting off with the basic "web-safe" font choices I discussed, you're free to branch out if you know that a very large portion of your site's users probably has a specific font that you're interested in using. For instance, many users on a new Window's Vista machine will have the "Cambria" font, or you might feel that a lot of your viewers, being fellow designers, will have the "Book Antiqua" or "Baskerville" fonts.

While many site users will not have special fonts installed, if the users you'd like to focus on probably do, go ahead and design the site for them. You can then (as we'll see next) easily assign backup font choices (that is, "stacks") for all the other viewers out there. For a comprehensive article about taking full advantage of this technique, along with eight great font stacks to get started with, check out Michael Tuck's article on *SitePoint*: `http://www.sitepoint.com/article/eight-definitive-font-stacks/`.

sIFR

There is another accessible font replacement technique that takes advantage of the Flash player called **sIFR (Scalable Inman Flash Replacement)**. I only recommend this technique for main display and/or heading text in your site. We'll look at this technique in detail in *Chapter 7*, when we examine ways of using the Flash player in our Joomla! 1.5 site.

Cascading fonts

When assigning font families to your CSS rules, you can set up backup font choices. This means that if someone doesn't happen to have Century Schoolbook, then he/she probably has Georgia, and if he/she doesn't have Georgia either, then he/she definitely has Times New Roman... and if he/she doesn't have that? Well, at the very least you can rely on his/her browser's built-in "generic" assigned font. Just specify: `serif`, `sans-serif`, or `mono-space`.

Time for action: Setting up font families

Let's take a look at setting up the tone of our site with CSS font families.

Because I want the style of my site's text to convey a "friendly" and modern tone, I'm going to have my headers to be a mix of Georgia and Trebuchet, while the body content of text will be only Trebuchet. My font families will look something like the following:

For body text:

```
...
#container {
    font-family: "Trebuchet MS", Arial, Helvetica, sans-serif;
}
...
```

For h1 and h4 headers:

```
...
h1, h4 {
    font-family: "Trebuchet MS", Verdana, Arial, Helvetica, sans-serif;
}
...
```

For h2 and h3 headers:

```
...
h2, h3{
font-family: Georgia, Times, serif;
}
...
```

Font sizing

Thankfully, we seem to be out of the trend where intsy-teensy type is all the rage. I tend to stick with common sense: is the body text readable? Do my eyes flow easily from header to header? Can I scan through the body text landing on emphasized or bold keywords, links, and sub-headers? If so, I move on to the next step.

I can't help you is determining how to size your fonts. The W3C recommends using em sizing for fonts on web pages. I, who normally treat anything the W3C recommends as "scripture", actually use (gasp!) pixels to size my fonts.

Why? Because it's simpler and quicker for me to work with. This might not be the case for you, and that's fine. Yes, I've read the evidence and understand the logic behind em sizing, but I usually design my sites for FireFox, IE6 and IE7, Opera9, and Safari3 (in about that order of importance). These browsers all seem to resize pixel-sized fonts and line-heights just fine. I also tend to design my sites with locked widths, assuming vertical expansion. Hence, resizing fonts up or down from within any of these browsers may not look wonderful, but it does not "break" any of my designs—it just gives you bigger text to read and a little more scrolling to do.

You may not agree with using pixels to size, and if you intend for your template's layouts to be flexible and resizable, as we'll look into in *Chapter 9*, then you'll definitely want to go with em sizing (for a lot of elements, not just your fonts). Whatever you chose, em or px, your best bet for consistency is to pick one method and stick with it in your stylesheet to avoid unexpected results.

Time for action: **Setting font sizes**

You can set your font sizes to anything you'd like. Let's take a look at the container and heading rules. I've set my container and heading rules to the following:

```
...
#container {
  font-family: "Trebuchet MS", Verdana, Arial, Helvetica, sans-serif;
  font-size: 12px;
}
...


...
h1 {
  font-size: 32px;
}

h2 {
  font-size: 22px;
}

h3 {
  font-size: 16px;
}

h4 {
  font-size: 14px;
}
...
```

Want more info on the pros and cons of em and pixel sizing? *A List apart* has several great articles on the subject. The two most relevant are *How to Size Text in CSS* (http://www.alistapart.com/articles/howtosizetextincss) and *Setting Type on the Web to a Baseline Grid* (http://www.alistapart.com/articles/settingtypeontheweb).

Really interested in web typography? Be sure to check out http://webtypography.net/.

Paragraphs, blockquotes, and other text markup

No matter what sizing method you decide on, px or em, be sure to give yourself space. With just the right amount of space between the lines, the eye can follow the text much more easily, but not too much! By setting your line-heights to a few more pixels (or em percentages) than the "auto" line-height for the font size, you'll find the text much easier to scan online. Also, add a little extra margin-bottom spacing to your paragraph rule. This will automatically add a natural definition to each paragraph without the need for adding in hard return breaks (<br/>). You'll need to experiment with this on your own, as each font family will work with different line-height settings and font sizes.

Time for action: **Setting the main text and blockquote display**

The majority of our text will inherit the container and paragraph rule's parameters.

I've set my container rule to have a line-height of 16px and my paragraph rule to allow a bottom margin of 18px. I've also added in a rule for block-quotes so that they can be made prominent:

```
...
#container {
  font-family: "Trebuchet MS", Verdana, Arial, Helvetica, sans-serif;
  font-size: 12px;
  line-height:16px;
}
...


...
p {
  margin-bottom: 18px;
}
...


...
blockquote{
  font-size: 18px;
  margin-bottom: 24px;
}
...
```

Default links

Many of the links in our template are going to be custom designed, based on the div id they are located in. Still, I've gone ahead and decided to adjust my basic link or a href setting. I like my links to be bold and stand out, but not have what I find to be a distracting underline. However, I do feel the underline is an essential part of what people expect a link to have, so if they do decide to move the mouse over to any of the bold text, an underline will appear and they'll immediately know it's a link.

Time for action: **Setting the default link parameters**

Let's set up our basic links to my preference as mentioned.

I've set the bold and underline for my links as follows:

```
...
a {
   text-decoration: none;
   font-weight: bold;
}
a:hover {
   text-decoration: underline;
}
...
```

Let's now take a look at our typography.

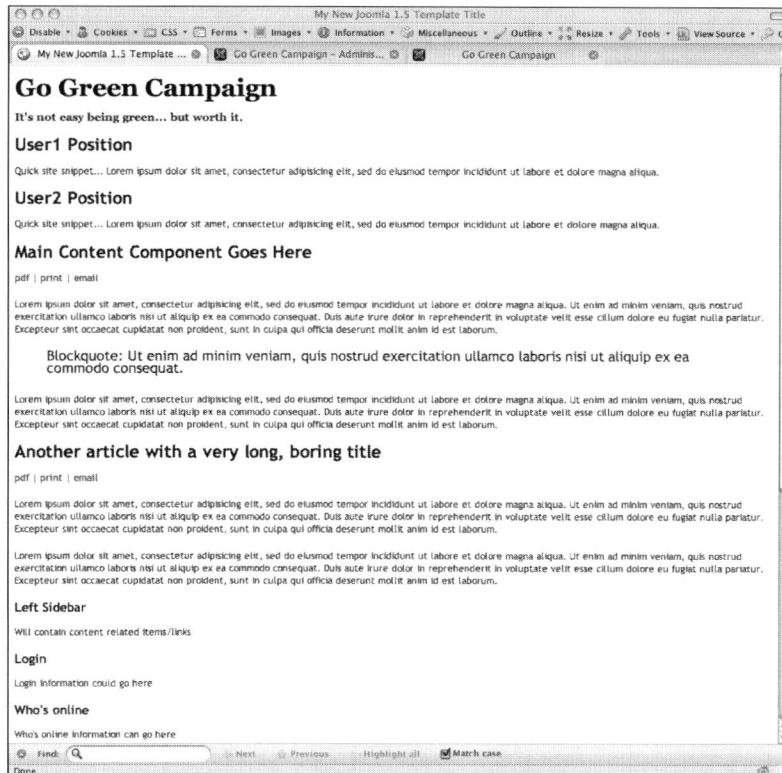

> **Remember**
>
> If you don't like how your text looks here, a bunch of graphics, columns, and layout adjustments really won't help. Take your time now to get the text to look nice and read well. You'll have less edits and tweaks to make after the fact.

Form elements

I didn't include it in my sample text, but Joomla! 1.5 can output several types of forms that mostly consist of various `<input.../>` and `<textarea>` tags.

Time for action: Styling basic form elements

I like a "flat" look for form elements, with nice border color. Let's create those styles now. I'll prepare form elements by including the following CSS under the /* //FORMS// */ place holder in the stylesheet:

```
...
form {
   font-size: 10px;
}
input {
   background-color: #FFFFFF;
   color: #000000;
   border: 1px solid #999999;
   font-size: 11px;
   padding: 3px;
}
textarea{
   background-color: #FFFFFF;
   color: #000000;
   border: 1px solid #999999;
   font-size: 11px;
   padding: 3px;
   width: 300px;
   height: 150px;
}
.button{/*this class allows me to treat an input element like a
                                                  button*/
   border: 1px solid #FFF0CC;
   background-color: #999999;
   color: #F0E0C2;
   font-size: 10px;
```

```
    font-family: Verdana, Arial, Helvetica, sans-serif;
    font-weight: bold;
    width: 150px;
    height: 22px;
    cursor: pointer;
}
...
```

The layout

At last, let's start to get this stuff looking like our sketch!

You'll notice in our XHTML markup, each of our `divs` has an `id` name and the `divs` that are going to be our three columns are wrapped inside an outer `div` called `container2`. The main and left columns are wrapped in a `div` called `container3`, the entire set of `divs` including the `header` and `footer` are wrapped in a main `div` called `container`.

This structure is what's going to hold our content together and lets Joomla! 1.5 display semantically with the main content first, yet with the style allowing the left column to show up on the left. This structure also insures that the footer stays at the bottom of the longest column, no matter which one it is.

How wide to make your site?

How wide to make your site is entirely up to you. It does help to have an understanding of your site's key demographic. Some groups of people may not have upgraded their monitors in a while, while most 25 to 45 year old users will probably be on 13" to 17" laptop screens. Of course, there are media specialists and "super gamers' who'll have extra large monitors with very high resolutions. Generally, you do want to accommodate the "lowest common denominator", but I'm happy to report I no longer consider this to be 800 pixels wide.

The minimum monitor resolution I currently consider is 1024. I like fixed-width sites that have scaling backgrounds. This makes it easer to create a great layout that holds well, but doesn't look so stark and empty on a really large monitor. While I do take a look at the site's demographic, as possible, I find that a good rule of thumb for a Joomla! site, which is usually a content-heavy site, is to match what other content-heavy sites are doing. *The NYTimes* site is a good example to follow (`www.nytimes.com`). At the time I'm writing this, their site is 950 pixels wide, which looks good on most laptop screens and browsers with a monitor resolution of 1024 and up. Based on that, I've decided that a width of 900 is plenty small enough for my design.

Time for action: Setting up layout positions

In the stylesheet, I've set up my basic CSS positioning as follows:

```
. . .
body {
 margin: 0px;
}

#container {
  margin: 0 auto;
  width: 900px;
  border: 1px solid #666666;
  font-family: "Trebuchet MS", Verdana, Arial, Helvetica, sans-serif;
  font-size: 12px;
  line-height:16px;
}

#container2 {
  border: 1px solid #0000ff;
}

#container3 {
  width: 670px;
  float:left;
  border: 1px solid #ff0000;
}
. . .

. . .
#header {
  border: 1px solid #00ff00;
  width: 930px;
  height: 300px;
}

#user1{
  border: 1px solid #ff6600;
  width: 250px;
  float: left;
}

#user2{
  border: 1px solid #ff6600;
  width: 250px;
  float: right;
}
#user3{
```

```css
  border: 1px solid #ff6600;
  margin-top: 100px;
}

#user4{
  border: 1px solid #ff6600;
}

.leftWidth{/*class allows for quickly ensuring anything on the left
                                              side can be set*/
  width: 520px;
}

.quickMargin{/*adds 10px of margin to anything*/
  margin: 10px;
}
...


...
#content {
  margin:0 10px;
  width: 420px;
  float:left;
  border: 1px solid #333333;
}
#pushbottom{
  clear:both;
}
...


...
#sidebarLT {
  margin:0 5px;
  width:200px;
  border: 1px solid #ff9900;
  float:right;
}
#sidebarRT {
  margin:0 10px;
  width: 200px;
  float: right;
  border: 1px solid #0000ff;
}
...
```

```
...
#top_navlist {
  position: absolute;
  top: 170px;
  width: 900px;
  text-align:right;
  border: 1px solid #003333;
}
...


...
#footer {
  border: 1px solid #000033;
  height: 85px;
  width: 930px;
}
...
```

Adding the previous code to my stylesheet gives me a layout that looks like this:

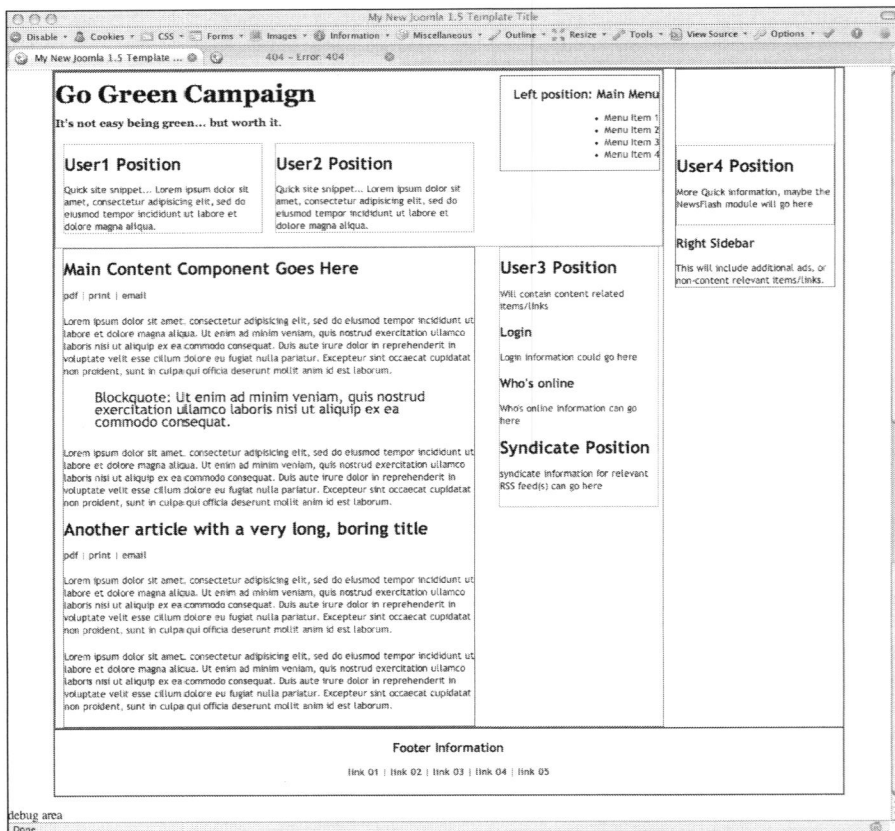

> **Quick CSS layout tip**
>
> You may not be able to tell from the screenshot above but, I like to initially place bright-colored borders in my CSS rules, so that I can quickly glance to check if my widths (or heights) and positioning for each of my `divs` is on target. I tweak from there. As I continue to bring all the details into each CSS rule, I remove these border elements or change them to their intended color. You can also use the Web Developer Toolbar to quickly see the border area of `divs` as you drag your mouse over them.

CSS tables versus floating divs

IE8 finally offers full support of CSS tables (which are actually a CSS2 standard and not a CSS3 standard). There's no doubt that CSS tables relieve a lot of frustration in dealing with column layouts in design. In this design, however, you'll note a more traditional floating/cleared `div` structure. My main reason for sticking with that is for easy viewing in IE6 and IE7. Plus, transitioning to CSS tables means losing control over your semantic "source order" of content. Whatever is on the far left needs to come first, then the middle, and last the right. While that would work well for this layout, if I ever decide to place the main content in the middle, I would then have less important content above my main content when viewed by an SEO bot, text browser, or mobile browser.

Despite what Rachel Andrew and Kevin Yank have to say in their book *"Everything You Know about CSS is Wrong"*, *SitePoint*, I'm not as sure as they are, that source order isn't very important for SEO and accessibility. So, I'm not ready to give up control of it. I can't vouch for how source order truly affects SEO. However, as someone who uses her Palm Centro's browser to Google items on the go, and is then frustrated at having to scroll through piles of "junk" before getting to the page's content, and as someone who has sat in a room with a blind person using the JAWS text-to-speech web browser to test content for accessibility, I can definitely see the usability and accessibility difference when it comes to a site where the content's source order is not semantic.

Finding what I searched for right up top under a few lines of header information, versus buried underneath a heap of navs and blog roll links, is gratifying yet rare in my mobile surfing. Also, I can't begin to tell you how horrible it is to have to sit through and listen to a, 508 compliance tester's browser read off 12 minutes or more of unrelated links and call out all table structures (that were being used to control layout and not relevant to the content) before getting to any real content.

You're more than welcome to not support IE6 and IE7 and go headlong into using CSS tables. I myself am going to hold off on that technique for a bit. If you'd like more information on using CSS tables, Rachel and Kevin's book is a wonderful source. You can also check out *A List apart's* article "*Practicle CSS Layout Tips, Tricks & Ideas*": `http://www.alistapart.com/stories/practicalcss/`.

Navigation

Joomla! modules allow you to specify how menu links are outputted. This allows us to generat menu items with list `<li>` tags wrapping each link item. Even though by default all lists are rendered vertical with bullets, using CSS you have a wide range of options for styling lists. You can turn them into horizontal menus, and even multi-level drop-down menus. (I'll show you how to create drop downs and more beginning in *Chapter 7*.)

> **Awesome CSS list techniques**: *Listamatic* and *Listamatic2* from *maxdesign* (`http://css.maxdesign.com.au/index.htm`) are wonderful resources for referencing and learning different techniques to creatively turn list items into robust navigation devices.
>
> Although I won't be using the functionality right away, I want my main menu navigation in the left position to be flexible enough to handle drop-down menus down the road. So, I'll use the basics from *HTML Dog*'s *Son of Suckerfish* to style my main menu. Again, we'll go over drop-down menus in detail, but you can take a sneak peak at Patrick and Dann's code for now: `http://htmldog.com/articles/suckerfish/dropdowns/`.

Time for action: **Creating the main navigation styles**

I tweaked the XHTML code from the Son of Suckerfish CSS in a few ways:

1. I added `class="menu"` to my `ul` inside my `top_navlist` div.

```
...
<div id="top_navlist">
   <h3>Left position: Main Menu</h3>
   <ul class="menu">
   <li><a href="#">Menu Item 1</a></li>
   <li><a href="#">Menu Item 2</a></li>
   <li><a href="#">Menu Item 3</a></li>
   <li><a href="#">Menu Item 4</a></li>
   </ul>
</div><!--//top_navlist-->
...
```

2. I also hid my `h3` headers for the main navigation and footers that I would like people reading my site in-line and un-styled to see, but which would be unnecessary for people viewing the styled site:

```
...
#top_navlist h3{
   display: none;
}
...


...
#footer h3{
   display: none;
}
...
```

3. I massaged the height and width padding on my main nav `li a` to be about the height and width I imagine my graphical interface images to be.

4. The final CSS code looks like the following:

```
...
#top_navlist {
   position: absolute;
   top: 6px;
   margin-left: 550px;
   border: 1px solid #ffff00;/*to help see positioning*/
}
#top_navlist h3{
   display: none;
}
.menu, .menu ul { /* all lists */
   padding: 0;
   margin: 0;
   list-style: none;
   float : left;
   width: 220px;
   font-family: "Trebuchet MS", Verdana, Arial, Helvetica, sans-
                                                          serif;
   font-size: 14px;
   font-variant: small-caps;
}
.menu li { /* all list items */
   position : relative;
   float : left;
   line-height : 1.25em;
   margin-bottom : -1px;
}
.menu li a {
```

```
    width: 190px;
    line-height: 30px;
    display : block;
    color : #453110;
    font-weight : bold;
    text-decoration : none;
    text-align: right;
    border-bottom : 1px solid #666;
    padding-right: 30px;
}
...
```

More navigation: Joomla! 1.5 specific styles

Again, Joomla! 1.5 does output many predefined CSS `id` and `class` styles for modules and content. The `main_menu` module outputs several. The main output we're going to be taking advantage of is the `current` id tag.

Multiple class styles assigned to the same XHTML object tag?

Yep, as you can see in the DOM Source of Selection graphic above, you can have as many classes as you want assigned to an XHTML object tag. Simply separate the class names with a blank space and they'll affect your XHTML object in the order that you assign them. Keep in mind, the rules of "cascading" apply, so if your second CSS rule has properties in it that match the first, the first rule's properties will be overwritten by the second. There are more suggestions for this trick in *Chapter 9*.

Time for action: Making sure the main navigation will work with Joomla!

Again, a goal of mine in this chapter was not to bog you down in Joomla! CSS styles, but knowing about this helps us out a lot.

This is great as it means we can take advantage of our Suckerfish CSS id `#current` within an `a: href` item. This will let us see which menu item has been selected:

```
...
#.menu #current a{
    color: #3d7d89;
    text-decoration: underline;
}
...
```

We now have a page layout with main navigation that looks like the following:

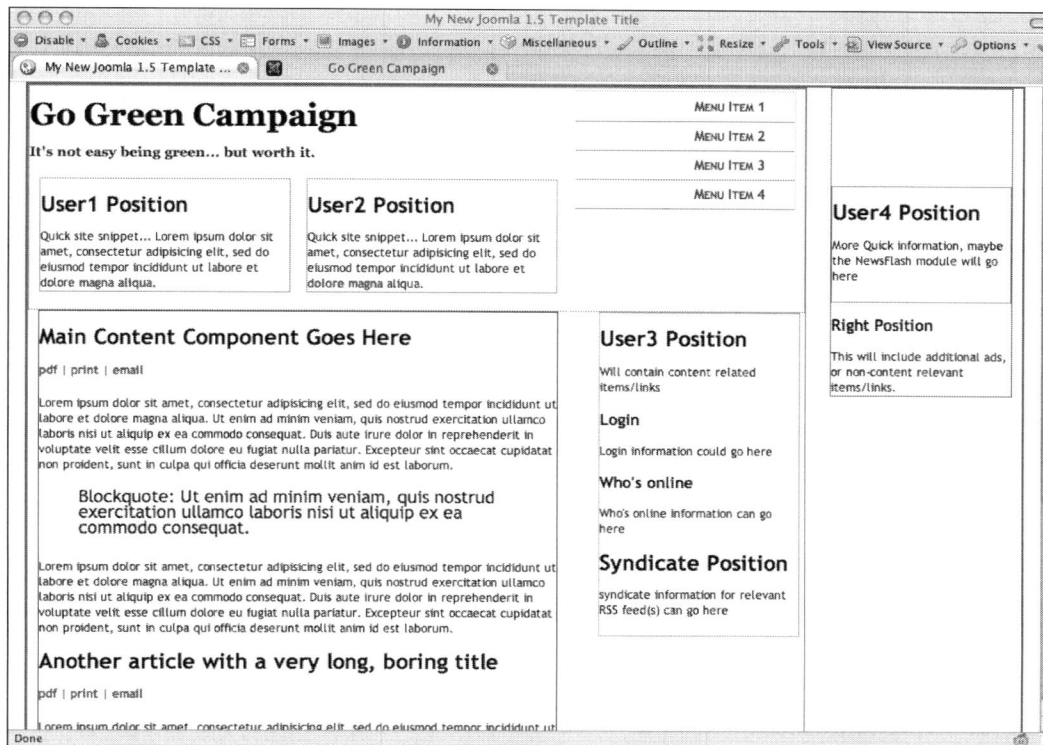

Color schemes

Now that the general layout is hammered down, we're ready to move on to more exciting design elements.

You'll want a predefined palette of three to ten colors arranged in a hierarchy from most prominent to least. I like to create a simple text file that lists the color's hex values and then add my own comments for each color and how I plan to use it in the template. This makes it easy for me to add colors to my CSS file and then later to my layered image editor files as I create graphic interface elements.

How many colors should you use?

I've seen designers do well with a scheme of only three colors; however, six to ten colors is probably more realistic for your design. Keep in mind, Joomla! 1.5 will automatically generate several types of links you'll need to deal with, which will probably push your color scheme out.

You might have noticed, color schemes are the hardest thing to start pulling together. Designers who have years of color theory under their belt still dread coming up with eye-catching color palettes. But the fact is, color is the first thing people will notice about your site, and the first thing that will help them not notice that it is just another Joomla! site (especially if you're taking the *Simplicity* route and modifying an existing template).

Two-minute color schemes

When it comes to color schemes, I say, don't sweat it. Mother nature, or at the very least, someone else, already created some of the best color schemes for us. Sure, you can just look at another site, or the site you like, and see how it handled its color scheme, but it's hard to look at someone else's design and not be influenced by more than just its color scheme.

For those intent on an original design, here's my color scheme trick: if your site will be displaying a prominent, permanent graphic or picture (most likely in the header image), start with that. If not, go through your digital photos or peruse a stock photography site and just look for pictures which appeal to you most.

Look through the photos quickly. The smaller the thumbnails the better; content is irrelevant! Just let the photo's color "hit" you. Notice what you like and don't like (or what your client will like, or what suits the project best, and so on) strictly in terms of color.

Color schemes with Gimp or Photoshop

Pick one or two images that strike you and drop them into Photoshop. A thumbnail is fine in a pinch, but you'll probably want an image a bit bigger than the thumbnail. Don't use photos with a watermark, as the water mark will affect the palette output.

Lose the watermark: Most stock sites have a watermark and there's nothing you can do about that. You can create a free login on *gettyimages'* *photodisc*: `http://Photodisc.com`. Once logged in, the water mark is removed from the comp images preview, which is about 510 pixels by 330 pixels at 72dpi, perfect for sampling a color palette.

The watermark free image is for reference and mockups only. We won't be using the actual images, just sampling our color palettes from them.

If you do end up wanting to use one of these images in your site design or for any project, you must purchase the royalty-free rights (royalty-free means: once you buy them, you can use them over and over wherever you want), or purchase and follow the licensing terms provided by GettyImages LTD for rights-managed images. (Rights-managed images usually have restrictions for where you can use the image, how long it can be on a web site, and/or how many prints you can make of the image).

Once you have an image with colors you like opened up in Photoshop, go to **Filter | Pixelate | Moziac** and use the filter to render the image into huge pixels. The larger the cell size, the fewer colors you have to deal with but, unfortunately, the more muted the colors become.

I find that a cell size of 30 to 100 for a 72 dpi web image is sufficient (you might need a much larger cell size if your photo is high-resolution). It will give you a nice, deep color range and, yet, few enough swatches to easily pick five to ten for your site's color scheme. The best part: if you liked the image in the first place, then any of these color swatches will go together and look great—instant color scheme.

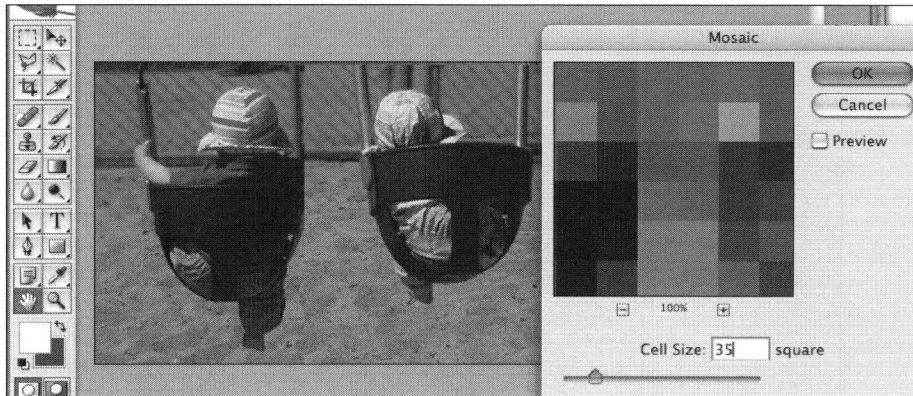

Once the image has been treated with the mosaic filter, just pick up the eye dropper to select your favorite colors. Double-clicking the foreground palette in the tool bar will open up a dialog box where you'll be able to copy-and-paste the hex number from into your text file.

Keep track of this text file! Again, it will come in handy when you're ready to paste items into your `style.css` sheet and create graphic interface elements in your image editor.

My site's color scheme isn't going to be that complex, and I want the colors to be pretty primary—a few bright shades of green with some deep offset blues and the occasional use of orange and yellow for highlighting. Rather than using a photo to start with, I used the swatch pallet in Photoshop to pick the colors I knew I wanted. Using the color picker from the swatch pallet in Photoshop, I copied out the following hex numbers into my list:

```
⊙ ◯ ◯  📄 joomla1.5gogreenScheme.txt

#45B20A — bright green (dark)
#2BCB02 — bright green (lighter)
#9FD780 — light green
#0059B2 — bright blue (dark)
#0066CC — bright blue (lighter)

#FF6600 — bright orange
#FFCC33 — bright yellow

#393939 — darkish grey
#565656 — mid grey
#CCCCCC — light grey
```

Adding color to your CSS

After some thought, I've gone through my CSS sheet and added some color to the existing `class` and `id` rules. I used the `color:` property to change the color of fonts, and even though I'll probably be adding background images to enhance my design, I've gone ahead and also used the `background-color:` property to add color to the backgrounds of `div`s in my layout that are similar to the base color of the background image I'll probably be designing.

The benefits of using the `background-color` property (even though you intend to create images for your design) are as follows:

- In the event your images happen to load slowly (due to server performance, not because they're too big), people will see CSS color that is close to the image and the layout won't seem empty or broken.

- If you can't finish designing images for every detail, sometimes the background color is enough to take the site live and still have it look pretty good. You can always go back in and improve it later.

Let's take a look at the layout with its basic color scheme placed in.

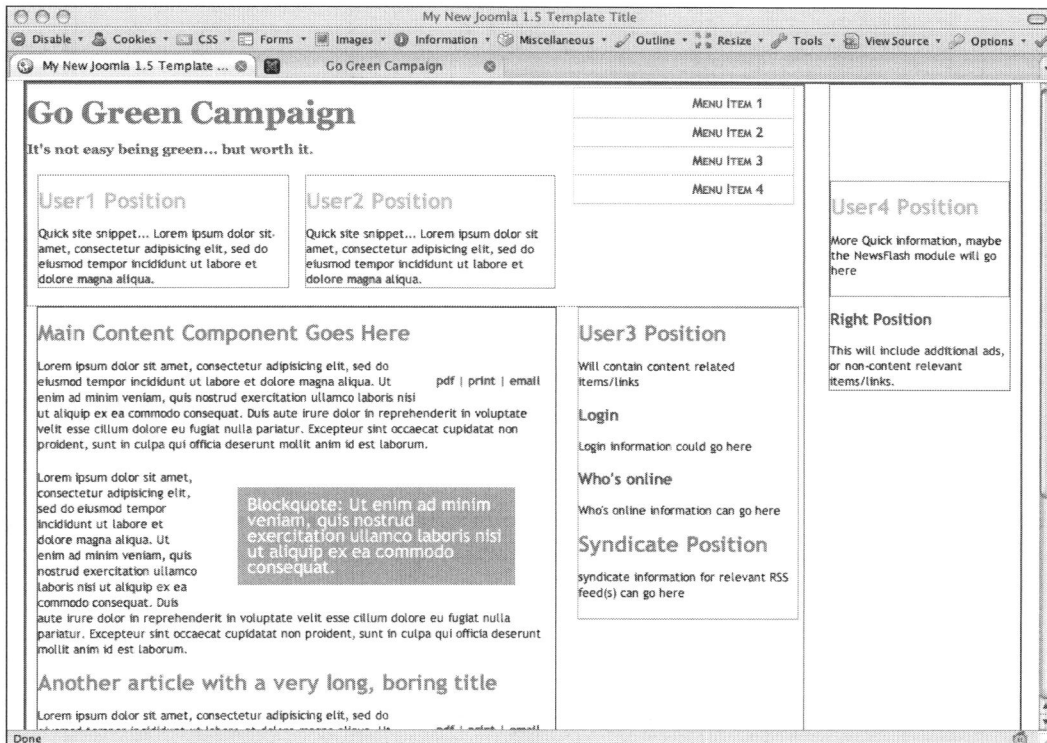

Create the graphical elements

Now, except for those multi-colored borders I've put around each of my containing `divs` (which will be removed shortly), I have an XHTML and CSS design that's not half-bad. Let's polish it off!

Graphic styles

You'll find Joomla! 1.5 to be a helpfully icon-oriented CMS from the Administrator panel to the frontend content options for PDF, Print, and Email. Skeeping this in selecting icons, or deciding how you want to handle Joomla's standard features upfront, will smooth the rest of the design process as well.

I have three suggestions on this front:

- Invest in a good-quality royalty-free icon set that includes modifying authoring files as you wish (preferably, in a vector format). I like `iconbuffet.com` and `stockicons.com`, and I often generate custom icons by working from a font set I bought years ago, called "ClickBits". A quick Google search will turn up many more icon sites. (Be sure you read the royalty-free agreement and have proper usage rights to modify the icon set you purchase.)

- Find your icons at `http://openclipart.org`. *Open Clip Art* offers illustrations in a native vector SVG format. They're easy to edit into your own creations with a vector or image editor (especially an SVG vector editor such as InkScape).

- Don't worry about icons! The default icons that come with 1.5 have a clean look that goes with just about anything. Plus, if you'll be in control of the site, you can go even more minimalist and turn off the icon display in favor of text links.

The icons you choose, and the way you decide to treat them, can be used as a guide for how to handle the rest of your template's elements.

Are your icons cartoon-y with bold lines? You'll then want to repeat that effect in other site elements, such as making sure navigation buttons or header backgrounds have their edges outlined. Are they somewhat photo realistic with drop shadows or reflections? Again, you'll want to think of ways to subtly repeat those elements throughout your site. This is a simple detail, yet little things like this bring a template design together, making it look sharp and highly professional.

Again, I'm going to recommend that you make a list and take notes on this process (I know, me and these lists!). If you apply a style to an icon and reuse it somewhere in your design, note it down so that you can reference it for future elements. That is, "All background header images, while being different colors for different uses, get the 'iMac' highlight applied to them as used in the main icon set. Another example would be, "All side elements have a bottom border with a color that fades up with a 90 degree gradient path".

No matter how well you plan the layout in your mockup phase, you may find later on (especially while coding it up with dynamic content) that there's an element you need to go back and design for. Having a style list for your elements will become an invaluable time saver. You'll have something to reference and won't waste time figuring out how the module element should be styled in relation to other similar elements or how you created a particular style effect.

I've decided to use that ClickBits font set I mentioned earlier as the base for my PDF, print, and email icons. But as this is a site about "being green", I want to add a "leaf" to the electronic, paper-friendly options, and a "recycle" sign to the print icon, to remind users to recycle the paper they print on.

Time for action: Start working in your image editor

Snap a screenshot (*Ctrl+Prt Scr* on PC, or use Grab, the free capture program on Mac) of your layout and paste it into a blank document in your image editor. I'm a fan of both GIMP and PhotoShop. For this example, I'll be using Photoshop.

Now, this is where (after realizing that blocking out layout directly in CSS isn't so bad) I've had web designers argue with me about this "rapid design comping" process. All your text is now an uneditable graphic and trapped on one opaque layer. Any graphics you place on top of it will obscure the text underneath it and any graphics you place underneath it, well, can't be seen at all!

So? We're in Photoshop, that program that edits graphic images so well? Keeping in mind that images in your template design will need to be added using CSS `background-image` techniques, it will probably be best to have your interface graphics set up behind your text layer.

Simply use the **Select | Color Range** tool to select and delete, knock out the blocks of colors you want replaced with background images in your CSS. A **tolerance** setting of **32** is more than enough to grab all the blocks of colors. Sure, there are probably places where you plan to replace the text entirely with a graphic, in which case you can apply the graphic over that area.

Here is what my screenshot looks like with the white background knocked out in Photoshop.

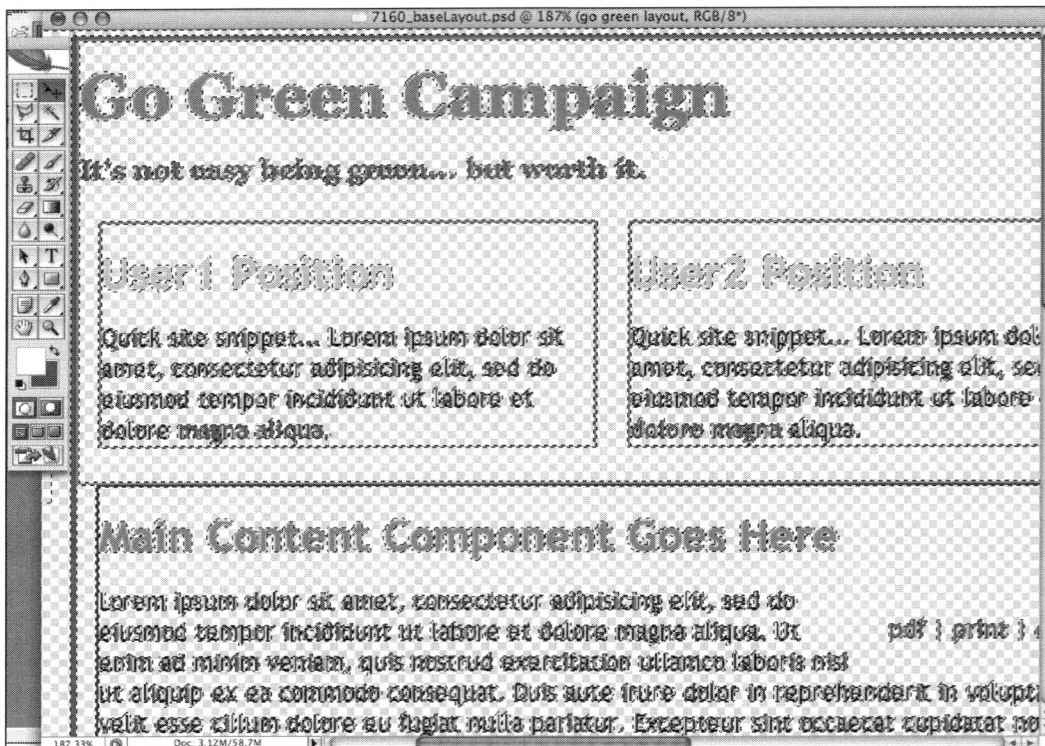

Handling edits and changes

But what if your client or you decides to make a change to the text stylings? Easy. Make the requested change to your CSS file and take another screenshot of the updated `index.html` page in your browser and place it back inside your image editor file. Yes, you'll have to re-knock out some of the blocks of colors so that your graphic interface elements can be seen again. Does making two mouse selections to do that take more time than finding all the layers of relevant text and making the style change?

At best, it might be close. But, don't forget the real perk: your design comp is more than half way ready for production (that is, turning into a working Joomla! 1.5 template). If the whole mockup was done in an image editor such as Photoshop, you'd still have all the XHTML and CSS creation to go through and then hope you can recreate what's in your image-only design comp across browsers.

What about designing in a vector program?

If you really love Illustrator or Inkscape, you can do one of the two things: just design over your screenshot layer and, if you really must show a comp to a client, add a little text back over the areas obscured by your graphic. Or, you can open the image into Photoshop or GIMP and just as I have suggested, use Select | Color Range to knock out the main blocks of background colors that will be replaced with graphics. Then, save the image as a transparent GIF or PNG, and import it into your vector editor and proceed, as I have suggested above, on layers underneath the screenshot.

Relax and have fun designing!

Now that I have my layout set up in Photoshop with the white background knocked out, I can proceed with designing my graphic interface elements in the layers underneath.

As you work in your graphic editor, you may come across items that need to be updated in the CSS to accommodate the interface elements you're designing. I usually deal with these in two ways:

- If the CSS properties I'm dealing with need to change in size, say for instance, I wanted the `top_navigation` tabs to be taller, or decided the padding around the Joomla! 1.5 items inside the `sidebarLT` div should be taller or wider to accommodate a graphic, then, as described, I would make the change in my CSS stylesheet and take another screenshot to work with.

- If the CSS property is just being removed or handled in a way that doesn't change the size, such as borders and display text, I don't take another screenshot. I just edit it out of the PSD layout and make a mental note or production to-do list item to remove the CSS property. Properties that need removing or that are set to `display: none` are pretty obvious and easy to take care of while you insert your graphic element images into the CSS as `background-image` properties.

The border properties I've set up for my main layout elements will help me lay out my graphic elements, and as the elements become finalized, I just take the eraser tool, or use **Select | Color Range** again, to remove them. (Good thing I made each `div` border property a different color!)

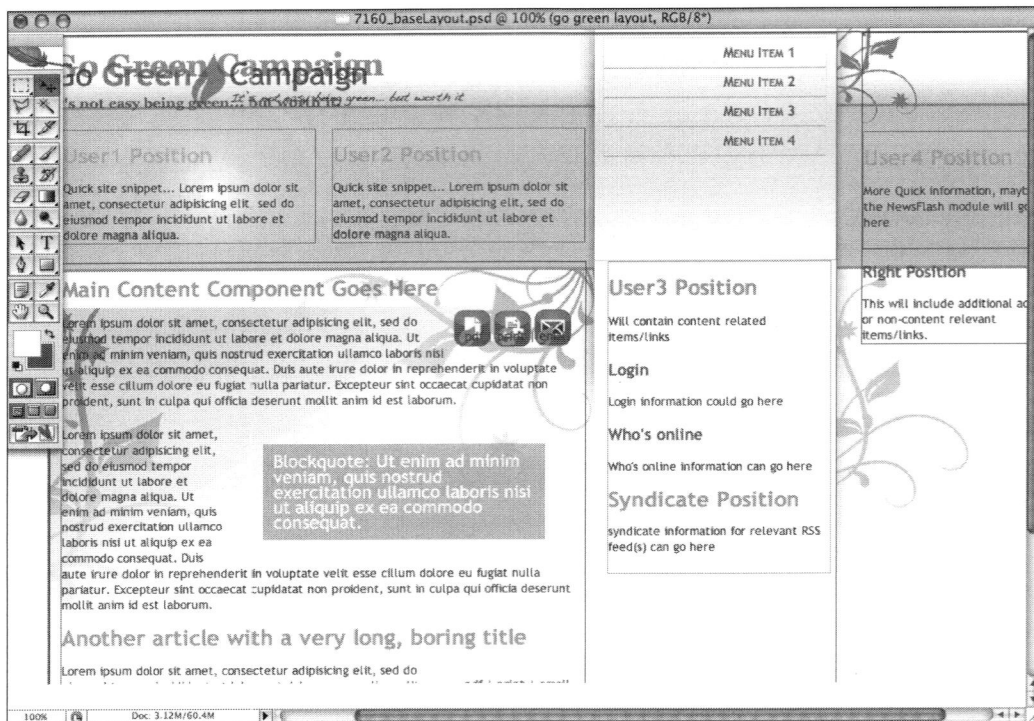

You can see the base result, which will be similar to when we set the lines and text that will be set to `display:none` or `text-aliged` out of the way:

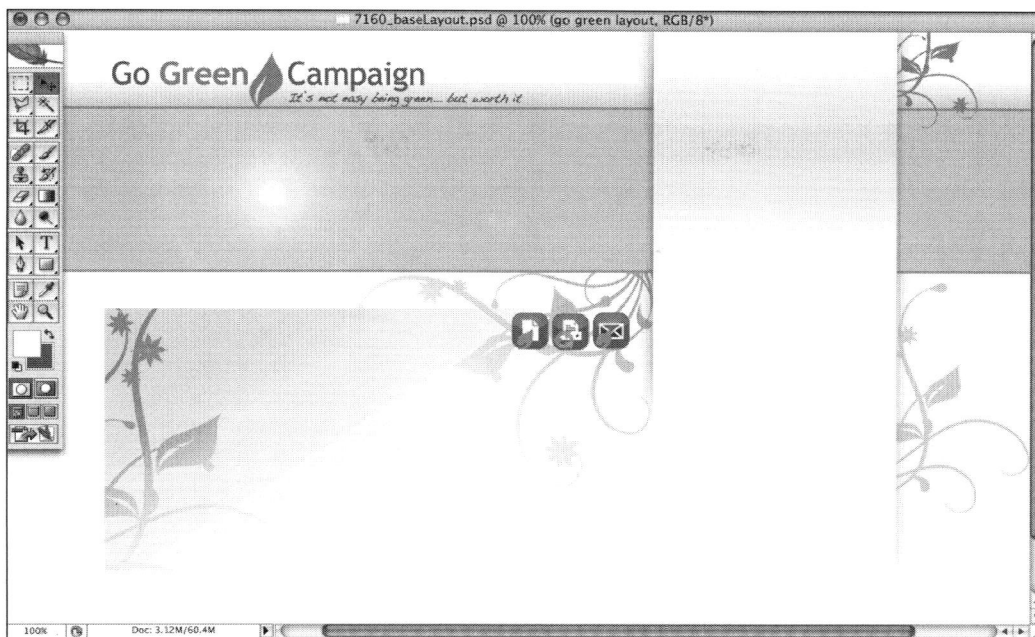

Slice and export

When getting ready to slice your images for export, keep in mind that through the background properties in CSS, you can control the top, bottom, left or right placement, x and y repetition, as well as make the image non-repeating. You can also set the background image to "fixed", and it will not move with the rest of your page if it scrolls.

You'll need to look at your design and start thinking in terms of what will be exported as a complete image, and what will be used as a repeating background image. You'll probably find that your header image is the only thing that will be sliced whole. Many of your background images should be sliced so that their size is optimized for use as a repeated image.

If you notice that an image can repeat horizontally to get the same effect, then you'll only need to slice a small vertical area of the image. Same goes for noticing images that can repeat vertically. You'll only need to slice a small horizontal area of the image and set the CSS repeat rule to repeat-x or repeat-y to load in the image.

Take a look at how I intend to slice and export the images from my design:

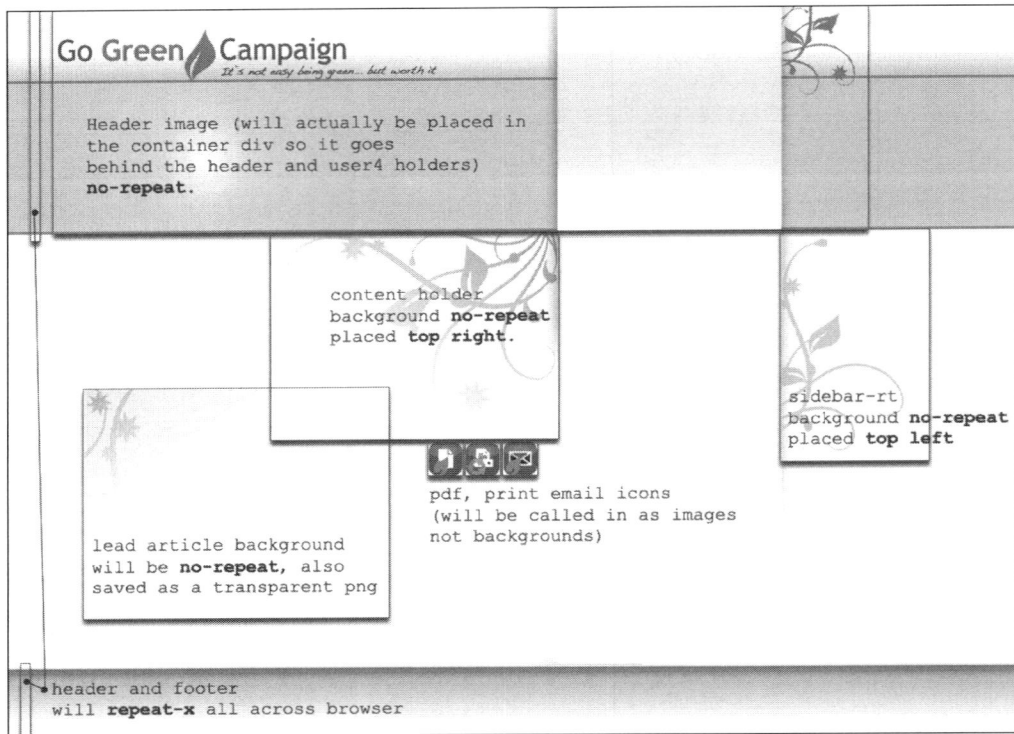

If you'd like more information on how to slice and work with background images, repeating and non-repeating for use with CSS, check out this article from Adobe's site:

`http://www.adobe.com/devnet/dreamweaver/articles/`
`CSS_bgimages.html`

Now that you've placed the slices for each of your template image elements, export them using the smallest compression options available. Once you have each image, aside from the PDF, print, and email icons(which are automatically imported into Joomla! if named correctly, as we'll learn in *Chapter 3*), you can import them into your XHTML/CSS mockup using the `background-image`, `background-repeat`, `background-attachment`,and `background-position` CSS properties.

Naming the PDF, print, and email icons: As long as you save these images in the PNG format and name them correctly (watch out for uppercase and lowercase you Windows users!), just including them in your template's image folder and `templateDetails.xml` file will include them into your template design. Here are the names: `pdf_button.png`, `printButton.png`, and `emailButton.png`.

These are the same naming conventions used in Joomla! 1.0, and as someone who finds naming conventions important, I'm a bit "irked" that the `pdf_button.png` doesn't follow the same camel case convention of the print and email buttons, but, hey, I guess you can't have it all.

Using CSS "shorthand" you can handle all of the properties I just mentioned, including the `background-color` property, via the asic `background` property. For example:

```
background: #fff url(img.gif) no-repeat fixed 10px 50%;
```

Only three letters in a hex color? You'll note in my background property shorthand that I've denoted the color "white" with just three characters, `#fff`, instead of six, `#ffffff`. I don't want to go too off topic, but to understand this, a hair better we'll need to meander a bit:

Hex colors use numbers in what's known as **base 16**. We normally view numbers in **base 10**, hence in most of our everyday lives, numbers simply run from 0 to 9 and then start incrementing in sets: 10's, 20's, and so on. We also place decimal points at the "tenth" positions. Binary numbers are in **base 2**, making you work with either 0 or 1 before building out sets. To be in base 16, you need more "numbers" than we're used to. Hence, each "slot" of a hex number can have 0 through 9, and then run from the letters A to F to give the number set the last six "digits" that total up to 16. That explains why there're letters in hex numbers. Now, to shorten a hex number down, just note that the first two "slots" of a hex number represent the "R" or red value of the hex color, the second two slots represent the "G" or green value of the color, and the last two slots represent the "B" or blue value of the color. You can visualize it this way: #RRGGBB. Web colors are essentially in RGB format, so they display on monitors well. In a hex color, if your R digits, G digits, and B digits are the same—for example, `#ffffff`—you don't have to notate both sets, just one. Browsers that can read CSS2 and above will assume that a three-digit hex number is shorthand for a doubled-up set; so, `#fff` will render as white, `#000` will render as black ,and `#999` as grey. Keep in mind that this works for colors too! As long as each RGB set is the same, `#f60` will render as `#ff6600` orange and `#036` as `#003366` greenish-blue.

After including my header image to the `container` div, I need to remove the text-header information from the `header` div. Rather than just delete it from the XHTML page, I set the display for `h1`, `h4` properties to `none`. That way, people who view the content un-styled will still see appropriate header information. Once that information is no longer displaying, I also added some padding up top in the `header` div to make sure the `user1 div` and `user2 divs` were still in the correct place over the header graphic.

Here're our `body`, `#header`, and a few new `id` rules, which handle our images:

```
...
body {
  margin: 0px;
  background: url("../images/bg_top_across.png") repeat-x top left;
}
...


...
#container {
  margin: 0 auto;
  width: 1000px;
  /*border: 1px solid #666666;*/
  font-family: "Trebuchet MS", Verdana, Arial, Helvetica, sans-
                                                        serif;
  font-size: 12px;
  line-height:16px;
  background: url("../images/gogreen_header.jpg") no-repeat top
                                                          left;
}
...


...
#acrossBottom {/*allows full width image behind footer*/
  width: 100%;
  background: url("../images/bg_footer_across.png") repeat-x 0 -4px;
}
...


...
/*////////// HEADERS //////////*/
#header {
  /*border: 1px solid #00ff00;*/
  height: 156px;
  padding-top: 90px;
}
#header h1, #header h4/**/ {
  display: none;
}
...
```

I also went through my entire template CSS sheet and made sure to null out all `border` properties that I was using to aid in layout positioning.

> You can delete the border properties if you want, and eventually all properties not used in the final template should be deleted before your template goes live. While in development, I like to keep the border properties nulled out, so that I can easily "un-null" them if I need help in debugging what's going on with that particular `div`.

To see this final table-less XHTML/CSS mockup's `template.css` and `index.html` files, please download this title's code packets from `http://www.packtpub.com/files/code/7160_Code.zip`.

The final template mockup looks like the following in the Firefox browser:

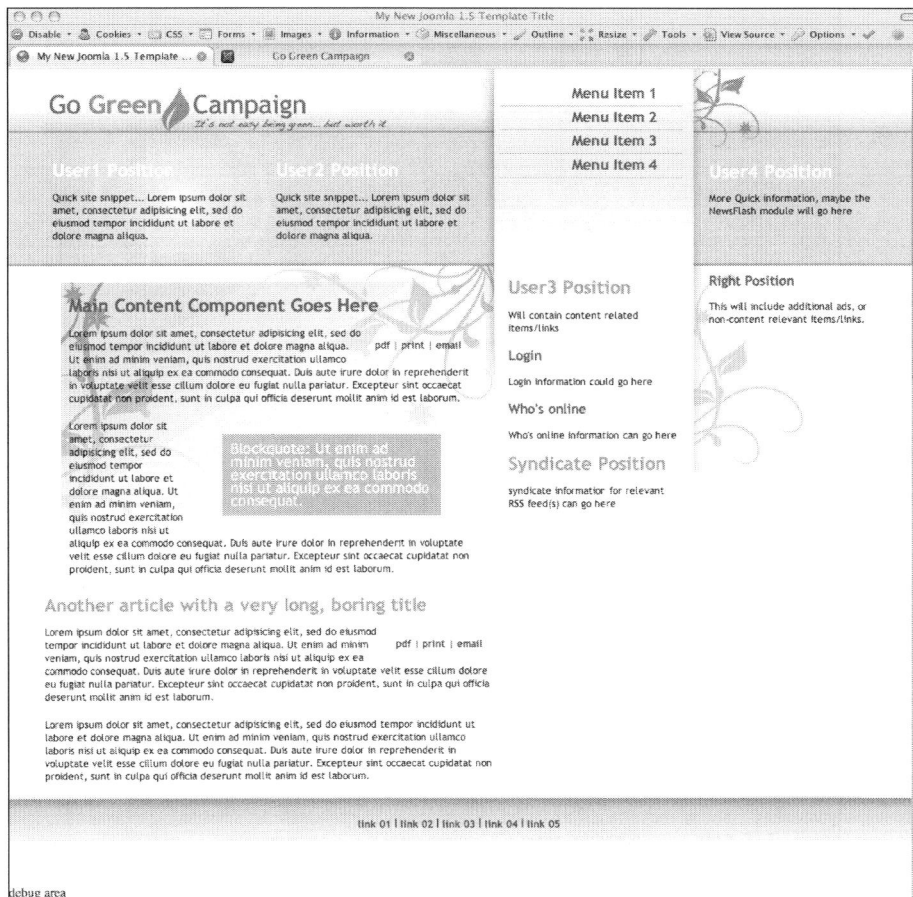

Yes, the final XHTML/CSS mockup is very similar to the Photoshop mockup. It should be almost perfect! You may still notice some slight differences. As I was working with the top navigation, I discovered that the links needed to be a bit larger, so I set the `font-size` property in my `.menu li a` rule to `18px`.

Don't forget your favicon!

One of the biggest giveaways that a site uses Joomla! is the favicon, and while it's cool to promote you use Joomla to power your site, many designers view it as an indication that the site's designers didn't go that extra mile.

Favicons are those little 16x16 icons that appear next to the URL in the address bar of a web browser. They also show up on the tabs (if you're using a tabbed browser) in your bookmarks, as well as on shortcuts on your desktop or other folders in Windows XP and Vista.

The easiest (and quickest) way to create a favicon is to take your site's logo, or key graphic (in this case, the little leaf that separates my logo text), and size it down to 16x16 pixles, then save it as a `.gif` or `.png` file.

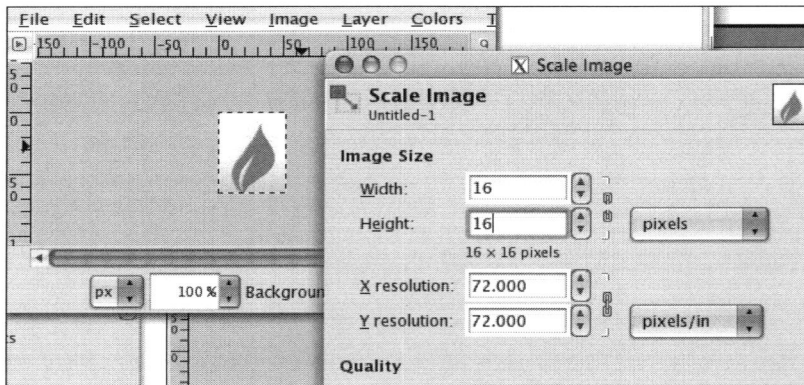

Place this file in the root of your site, and include it with the following tag placed in the header of your `index.html` file. (In *Chapter 3*, we'll discuss the details of making it a part of the template):

```
<link rel="icon" href="favicon.png" type="image/png">
```

This works great in all browsers except IE, and that includes IE7 and IE8 (to my disbelief). To ensure your favicon works in all browsers, you must save it in the official Windows Icon `.ico` format.

If you're using Photoshop, you can install a plugin provided by *telegraphics*, ICO Format, that will allow you to save out in the Windows Icon format: `http://www.telegraphics.com.au/sw/` (available for Windows and Mac). Installing this plugin will allow you to save in the Windows Icon format when you select **Save As** from your **File** options.

If you're using GIMP, well, then it's even easier. Although I do most of my design work in Photoshop when it comes to generating favicons, I gladly just switch over to GIMP. Simply choose to **Save As** in the **Microsoft Windows icon (*.ico)** format instead of PNG or GIF.

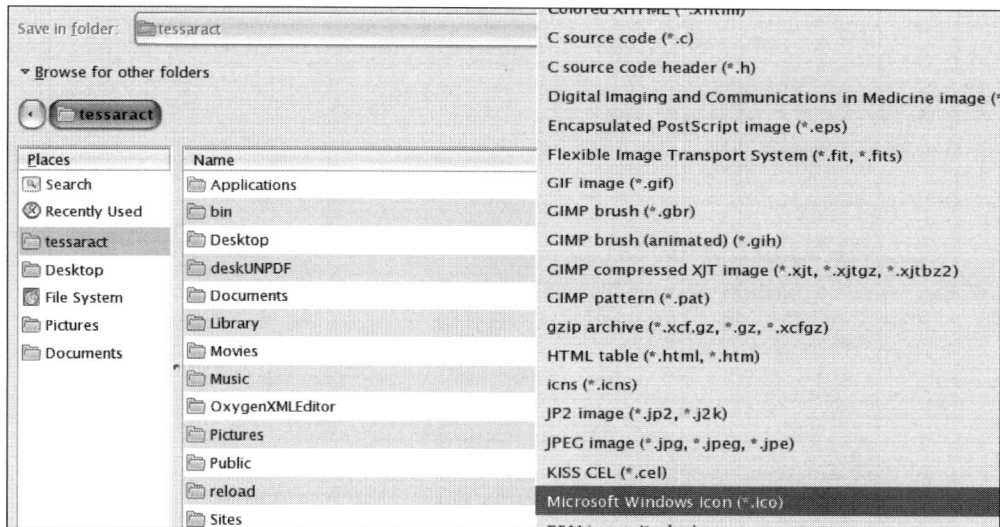

Once you have your `favicon.ico`, place the file in the root of your site's directory and place this code in the header tags:

```
<link rel="icon" href="/favicon.ico" type="image/x-icon">
```

Make sure to name your file `favicon.ico`. For some reason, even though you call the file by name in the link tag within your header tags, it just won't work if it's not named "favicon".

Also, you may find you need to clear your cache and reload several times before you see your new favicon. Make sure to actually clear your cache through your browser's preference panel. The keyboard shortcut *Shift+F2* (Refresh) sometimes only clears the web page cache. Some browsers' cache favicons in a separate directory.

Make your favicon high resolution

A little known fact about the `.ico` format is that it can contain multiple versions of itself at different color depths and resolutions. This is how your operating system is able to display those "smooth icons" that seem to be the right resolution no matter how large or small they're displayed. You may have noticed that some favicons if saved as shortcuts to your desktop look great and others look jaggy and terrible. The ones that look great take advantage of this feature.

The three main sizes that Windows will display a favicon are 16x16, 32x32, and 48x48. I've seen favicons that go all the way up to 128x128. It's up to you; just remember, the more resolutions, color depths, and transparencies you add, the larger your favicon file is and longer it will take to load.

You'd basically use the same steps listed above to create your favicon, just starting with 48x48 pixels, then **Save As** (as to not overwrite your original file) down to 32x32 and last 16x16. I save each icon res, initially in PNG format, especially if I want the background to be transparent.

Again, if you're using Photoshop, *telegraphics* makes an additional plugin that will bundle all your favicon resolutions into one `.ico` file. It's called the IcoBundle Utility, and it can be found at the same URL as the ICO Format plugin.

If you don't want to use Photoshop, GIMP can again easily handle this task for you. Simply open up your largest icon file and then copy-paste each additional resolution into a **New Layer** within that file. Then follow GIMP's **Save As** options to save it as a **Windows Icon *.ico** file. I've found Dave's article on *egressive's* site a wonderful reference for putting a multi-resolution and transparent favicon together using GIMP:

```
http://egressive.com/creating-a-multi-resolution-favicon-microsoft-
windows-icon-file-including-transparency-with-the-gimp
```

Summary

You now have learned key template design considerations to make when planning a Joomla! 1.5 template. We've also created a great XHTML/CSS functional mockup. Let's dive right in to coding it up into a fully-working Joomla! 1.5 template!

3
Coding It Up

We're now going to take our XHTML/CSS mockup and start turning it into our Joomla! 1.5 template. We'll take a look at how to incorporate Joomla! 1.5 `jdoc` tags into the mockup to get it working. Once our basic template is functional, we'll take a look at how to use **template overrides** to further enhance its accessibility.

Got Joomla?

First thing's first! If by some chance you don't have one yet, you'll need an installation of Joomla! 1.5 to work with. As I explained in *Chapter 1*, I assume you're familiar with Joomla! 1.5 and its Administration panel basics, and have a development sandbox installation to work with.

Sandbox?

I recommend you use the same Joomla! 1.5 version, modules, components, and plugins the main project will be using, but don't use the "live site" installation of Joomla. Using a development installation (also called "the sandbox") allows you to experiment and play with your template creation freely while the main project is free to get started using a built-in default template to display content. You then also don't have to worry about displaying anything "broken" or "ugly" on the live site while you're testing your template design.

Many hosting providers offer Joomla! 1.5 as an easy "one-click-install". Be sure to check with them about setting up an installation of Joomla! 1.5 on your domain.

New to Joomla?

If you require help getting your Joomla! 1.5 installation up and running, or need an overview of how to use the Joomla! 1.5 Administration panel, I highly recommend you read *"Building Websites With Joomla! 1.5"*, *Hagen Graf, Packt Publishing*.

Want to work locally?

I spend a lot of time on my laptop, often without a WiFi "hot spot" in sight. Having a local install of Joomla! 1.5 comes in very handy for template development. You can install local running versions of PHP5, Apache, and MySQL on to your machine, and, afterward, install the latest stable version of Joomla! 1.5.

PC users: WAMP Sever2 is a great way to go. Download it from `http://www.wampserver.com/en/`.

Mac users: You can install MAMP for Mac OSX. Download MAMP here `http://www.mamp.info/en/`.

How to: Compass Designs, a leader in developing Joomla! templates since the CMSs' inception, has a great article on installing Joomla! 1.5 on WAMP and MAMP: `http://www.compassdesigns.net/tutorials/17-joomla-tutorials/120-how-to-install-joomla-15.html`.

Understanding the Joomla! 1.5 template

Let's get familiar with the parts of a template that our XHTML/CSS mockup will be separated into. Keep in mind, we're now going to be talking about specific files, rather than the module positions we discussed in *Chapter 2*.

Basic, core template files

Within a template, you'll find several individual files. They mainly consist of an XML file and, at least, one CSS file inside a directory called css, as well as XHTML and PHP code in `index.php` file and `template_thumbnail.png` file. These files are required to structure your site, its content and functionality.

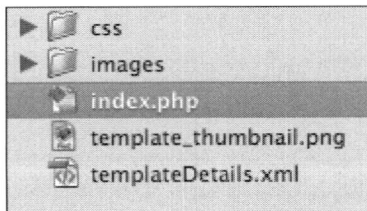

Watch your spelling

I can't mention this enough, about the differences between Windows servers and Linux. Windows will ignore differences in capitalization of file requests compared to the actual capitalization of file. Linux is not near as lenient as Windows and requires file requests to be exactly the same as file name. Even so, you must be ever more watchful when it comes to these particular template files and their structure. Joomla! 1.5 requires their spelling, capitalization, underscoring, directory names, and file location to be exact in order to work properly, regardless of your installation being on a Windows server (WAMP), Mac server (MAMP), or a Linux server (LAMP).

Let's go over each directory and file in detail:

- `css` directory: It must contain at least one CSS file, usually named `template.css`, though you can also call it `default.css`.

- `images` directory: This directory contains the images your template will need. I simply drop in the `images` directory that was used when creating my XHTML/CSS mockup.

- `index.php`: This file will have the core `jdoc` and PHP code placed in it, which will define your module positions, Content component, and other Joomla! functionality, along with the structural XHTML your template requires placed in it.

- `template_thumbnail.png`: This is the thumbnail view of your final template that administrators can preview before assigning it.

- `templateDetails.xml`: This file is overall the most essential to your template. It contains a listing of all the files your template requires to look and work right. It's essentially an installation file, and it ensures your template installs correctly into other installations of Joomla. We'll go over this file in great detail in *Chapter 5*.

Advanced template files

Now, if you've cracked open someone else's Joomla! template, or even just the default templates that come with your Joomla! 1.5 installation, you've probably noticed a few, or quite a few, other files, such as the `param.ini`, and possibly the `component.php` files, or maybe even the whole `html` directory with loads of directories that start with `mod_` or `com_` and have many files within them as well. What the heck are these things?

You can relax, those are simply files that can be used to enhance functionality and/or override Joomla's core XHTML output (that is, those template override files mentioned a few times so far). We'll get to those in some time within this chapter. We'll also cover param.ini files in detail in *Chapter 9*. *Chapter 6, Joomla 1.5 Template Reference*, will have a full listing of what mod_ and com_ template override files are available and how to name your own custom overwrite files.

Your Joomla! 1.5 work flow

Your work flow will pretty much look like this:

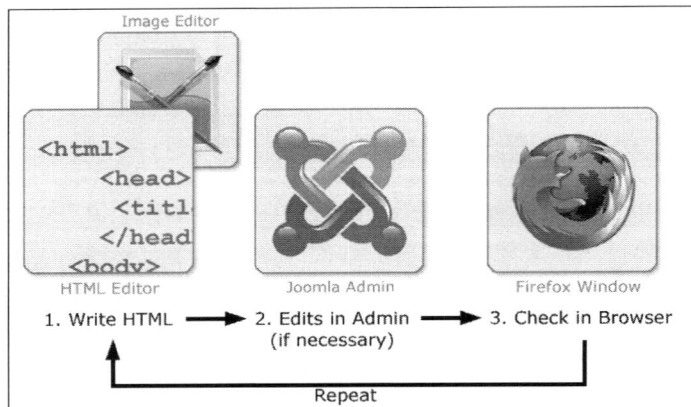

You'll be editing your CSS and XHTML mockup code in your HTML editor, removing static text display items and placing in Joomla! and PHP code so that your template will start to work with Joomla's content. After each edit, you'll hit **Save**, then use *Alt+Tab* or task bar to move over to your browser window. You'll then hit "Refresh" and check the results. (I'll usually direct you via *Alt+Tab*, but whichever way you get to the directed window is fine.) Depending on where you are in this process, you might also have two browser windows or tabs open—one with your Joomla! 1.5 template view and the other with your Joomla! 1.5 Administration panel. It's handy to have the Administration panel open so that you can add content on-the-fly or adjust module positions to see how they work with your template's layout as you code it up.

Whether you're using Dreamweaver or a decent text editor, such as TextWrangler, TextMate or Coda on a Mac, or HTML-kit on a PC, all of these editors let you FTP directly via a site panel and/or set up a working directory panel (if you're working locally on your own server). *Be sure to use this built in FTP/local file feature.* The following image shows the **Local/Remote** (FTP) files in the panel on the left within Coda.

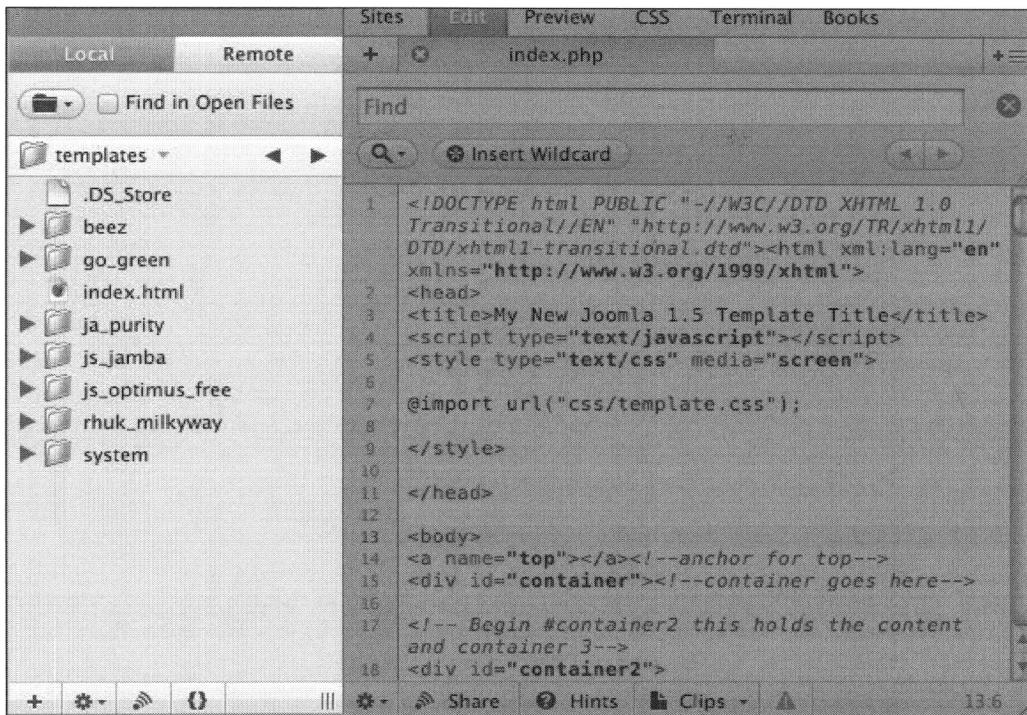

This feature will let you edit and save to the actual template files and stylesheet without having to stop and copy to your working directory or upload your file with a stand alone FTP client or stop and copy-and-paste everything into Joomla Administration panel's **Edit CSS** view, which can be found by navigating to **Template Manager | Default Template | Edit CSS** view. All of those approaches will work, but they are time consuming in comparison to directly editing and saving locally or remotely.

You'll then be able to use *Alt+Tab* to shift to a browser and view your results instantly after hitting **Save**. Again, this is one of the reasons you're working on a development/sandbox installation of Joomla. You can save directly to the currently selected template's files and do not have to worry about temporarily having something ugly or broken appear on the live site.

Be sure to save regularly and make backups

Backups are sometimes more important than saving. They enable you to roll back to a previously stable version of your template design should you find yourself in a position where your XHTML and CSS have stopped playing nice. Rather than continuing to futz with your code wondering where you broke it, it's sometimes much more cost effective to roll back to your last good stopping point and try again. You can set your preferences in some editors, such as HTML-kit, to auto-save backups for you in a directory of your choice. However, only you know when you're at a "Hey, this is great!" spot. When you get to these points, get into the habit of using the **Save a Copy** feature to make backups. Your future-futzing-self will love you for it.

Let's build our template!

Have your HTML editor open and set up to display an FTP or local working directory panel where you have access to your Joomla! 1.5 installation files. Also, have a couple of browser windows open with your Joomla! 1.5 home page loaded into them as well as the Joomla! 1.5 Administration panel.

Tabs

Use tabs. They're one of those neat built-in FireFox features I was talking about (OK, OK. Every decent browser has them now). Keep all your Joomla! 1.5 development and admin views in one window. Each tab within a FireFox window is accessible via *Ctrl* (or *Cmnd* on Mac) *+1*, *Ctrl* (*Cmnd*) *+2*, and similar keystrokes. It makes for a much cleaner work space, especially as we'll already be in constant *Alt+Tab* flip mode. Flipping to the wrong browser windows gets annoying and slows you down. You'll quickly get into the habit of using "*Alt+Tab, Ctrl+1*" (or *Ctrl+2, Ctrl+3*, and so on) to jump right to your Joomla! 1.5 template view or administration page, or even your original html mockup, and so on.

Tabula rasa

What's with the Latin? It means "blank slate". Sometimes you may just want to slightly modify a Joomla! template to fit your site's branding and needs (we discussed this *Simplicity* approach in *Chapter 1*), but generally, it is often much harder to try to map your custom design to an existing Joomla! template. We'll be starting with a blank slate, using the bare minimum files listed above, and will build our Joomla! template from there.

When you're trying to put your template together, initially this can be quite overwhelming. My approach to coding up your template entails the following five steps:

1. Create an empty directory in the `templates` directory in your installation files.

2. Upload your `images` directory, `index.html` directory, and `css` directory with your `template.css` file inside it into the new directory, and rename your `index.html` file to `index.php`. Also place in a copy of the `templateDetails.xml` file from one of the default templates that came with your Joomla! installation.

3. Piece by piece, starting with the Content component and working your way around to all your module positions, add essential Joomla! 1.5 PHP code and `jdoc` tags to your design so that Joomla! CMS content shows up.

4. Update your `templateDetails.xml` `<position>` tags to reflect the position `jdoc` tags you just added to your template, so that you can assign modules to them and test them out.

5. Once your template's Joomla! 1.5 content is loading in and if your XHTML and CSS still work and look correct, you can easily finalize any remaining display issues using the CSS classes and IDs that the Joomla! 1.5 system outputs.

One advantage to this approach is if any part of your template starts to break, you can narrow it down to the specific `jdoc` tags or PHP code you last worked with that weren't copied into the template file correctly.

Time for action: **Creating an empty theme directory**

To get started, we'll create that empty theme directory. I'm using a development installation of Joomla! 1.5 on my local machine within MAMP. If you're working remotely, you can follow my instructions using an FTP client, instead of desktop "copy" and "paste" commands.

1. Inside your Joomla! 1.5 installation, in the `templates` directory, create a new directory that has a completely unique name that best suites your project.

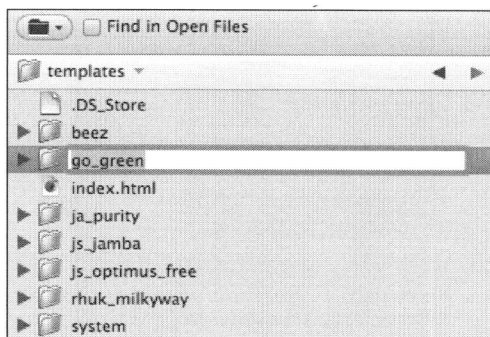

2. Copy your XHTML and CSS mockup's `images` folder, `css` folder with `template.css` in it, and `index.html` sheet (renaming your `index.html` file to `index.php`) into the directory.

3. Grab the `templateDetails.xml` file from one of the other default templates and place a copy of it into your new theme directory. We'll go over the `templateDetails.xml` file in exact detail in *Chapter 5*, but just to get our development started, go ahead and update the following:

   ° The name of your directory needs to go inside the `<name>...</name>` tags exactly as you named it in your directory, that is, `<name>go_green</name>`.

   ° Go ahead and place in any other obvious information you'd like to at this time. Again, we'll go over all this in *Chapter 5*, but much of the beginning tags are obvious, and you can fill them out now: the `creationDate`, `author`, `authorEmail`, `authorUrl`, or `description`. Make sure you only edit between the tags and don't accidentally delete any carrots or backslashes in the tags. The following image shows my `templateDetails.xml` file's initial information

Naming your new template

As I mentioned, your template has to be unique. If you name it something that already exists, Joomla! will not display it for selection in the Admin panel. The odds that someone would install your template into a system that happens to have another template with the exact same name are slim, but to be sure, I like to include a number in my template and/or have two words separated by an underscore. Although I didn't do so for this template, sometimes I also attempt to name my template so it is closer to the top of the list. That way it becomes very easy for administrators to find it and assign it after installing it.

4. In your Joomla! 1.5 Administration panel, go to **Extensions | Template Manager**. There, you'll be able to select the new template you just created.

5. Click on the left radio button to select it, and chose **Default** from the top-right. The following screenshot shows the new go_green template and the **Default** selector highlighted.

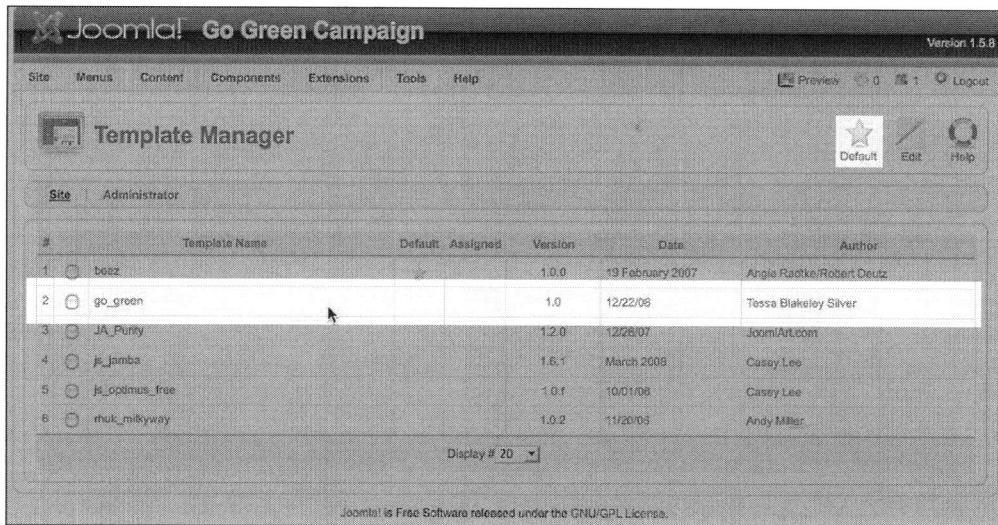

Use the Admin panel's navigation. Not your browser's.

You've probably run across this issue; if not, you're likely to when working with other team members on a Joomla! project. Always use Joomla's interface to navigate the Administration panel and navigate away to other Joomla! options and screens by hitting **Cancel** or **Save**.

Hitting the "**Back**" button in your browser has the potential for getting files locked in the Joomla! database, as Joomla! believes your user account still has the file(s) open. On the whole, this is a good thing. It keeps data and files from being touched by multiple people and lost or corrupted, but when you're off on vacation with no cell reception or email connectivity and someone else needs to edit a template file (or article, or module, and so on) that you didn't properly save and close, it's really irritating. If you find that you don't have access to a template file, piece of content, or extension because it was not checked back in properly, you must locate the person with "Super Admin" capabilities who can do a global check in of all checked out items. The other option (especially when it's the Super Admin who's on vacation) is to find someone who has FTP and MySQL access and is comfortable enough with MySQL to go into the content or extension's table and manually set its "checked out" field to "checked in". In both cases, it's a lot better if you and the team get used to using Joomla's navigation menu to avoid these problems in the first place.

Including Joomla! 1.5 content

When you point your browser to your Joomla! 1.5 Installation, you should see your mockup's un-styled XHTML. Not too inspiring, but a good start, as it means that Joomla! is reading your new index.php page that you just renamed from index.html. If by some chance, you don't see your un-styled mockup, you can try clearing your cache and refreshing. If that doesn't work, you'll need to again repeat the steps listed in the previous section to ensure you're pointing to your new template directory. The following image shows our un-styled XHTML mockup loading in via our Joomla!.

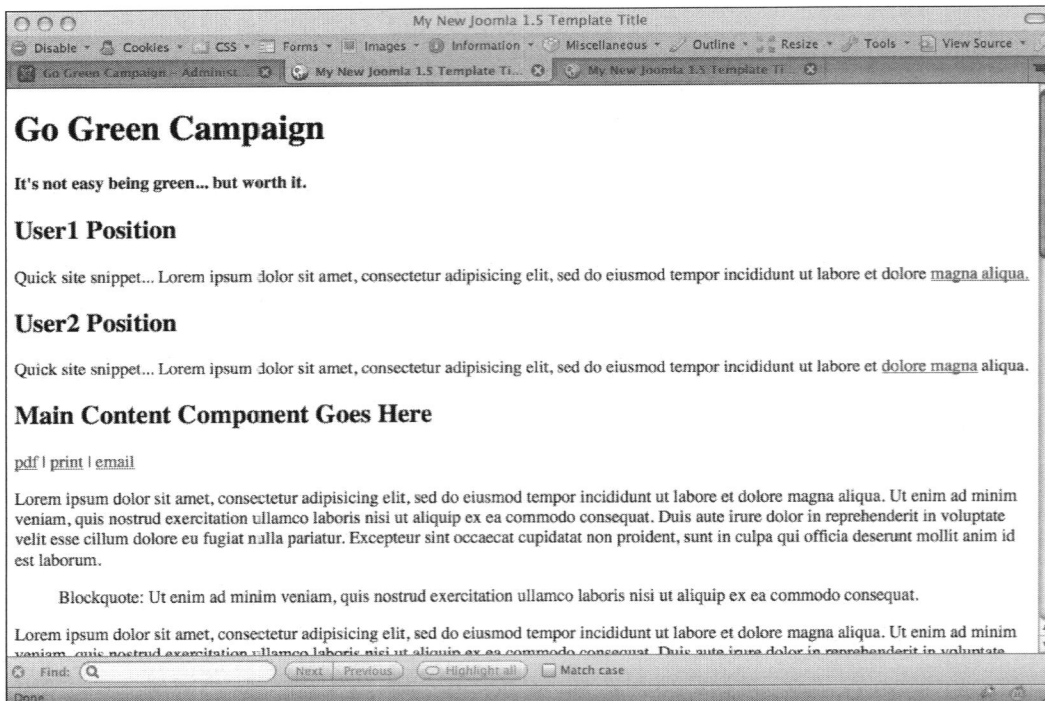

Time for action: Getting your CSS to appear

Our next objective is to get our template.css stylesheet properly linked back to our index.php file.

1. To get your index.php page to read your template.css file, you must first tweak the header of your template with a bit of PHP (I know, I know. I've been promising you didn't need much PHP, and you don't—this will be painless).

To start, place this bit of PHP syntax on the very first line of your `index.php` file, starting with the less-than carrot `<`:

```php
<?php
defined('_JEXEC') or die('Restricted access');
?>
```

Note the highlighted syntax. All PHP code must be wrapped in those `<` `>` carrot brackets with `?` question marks. The first bracket, after the question mark is always denoted with `php`. This tells the web server to call PHP to action and start parsing through the code.

This bit of code is important in that it ensures that no one can navigate or "hack" directly to your template's `index.php` page. If the file isn't loaded normally, via the main Joomla! index page, it will "die" and not display any of your template's markup.

2. First up, let's make sure that anyone who uses your template can load the languages they prefer into it. Replace this code (which is now on line **5** in your editor):

```
<html xml:lang="en" xmlns="http://www.w3.org/1999/xhtml">
```

With the following code (and again, note the highlighted PHP syntax):

```
<html xmlns="http://www.w3.org/1999/xhtml" xml:lang="<?php echo
    $this->language; ?>" lang="<?php echo $this->language; ?>">
```

3. Next, we're now ready for our first `jdoc` tag! Right inside your `<head>` tag, on line **7**, replace your `<title>...</title>` tags with this `jdoc` tag:

```
<jdoc:include type="head" />
```

This tag will replace your title tag with a dynamically created title tag that will contain the Site Name entered into the Joomla! Administration panel when you set up your installation. It will also automatically generate several meta tags that work with Joomla's CMS for you. One of those meta tags is quite important, as it defines the standard Joomla! character set (as well as a good character set to use for any web site):

```
<meta http-equiv="content-type" content="text/html; charset=UTF-8"
    />
```

Now, if you Refresh your site, you'll now see that the title bar of your template page reflects the Joomla! name of our site rather than **My New Joomla! 1.5 Temlate**.

4. Last, we'll use one more bit of PHP code and connect to our `template.css` stylesheet.

On line **11**, replace:

```
<style type="text/css" media="screen">
@import url("css/template.css");
</style>
```

With this markup (please note the PHP syntax in bold):

```
<link rel="stylesheet" href="<?php echo $this->baseurl; ?>
/templates/<?php echo $this->template; ?>/css/template.css"
type="text/css" />
```

You should note that adding the second bit of PHP code ensures Joomla's selecting from the current template, but some do view this as a bit redundant and extra characters the PHP processor has to slug through. If you know your template name is never going to change, you're welcome to just link directly to your template like so (replace `go_green` with your template's directory name):

```
<link rel="stylesheet" href="<?php echo $this->baseurl; ?>/
    templates/go_green/css/template.css" type="text/css" />
```

Congratulations!

That's your first bit of Joomla! 1.5 code! You should now see your CSS-styled mockup when you point your browser at your Joomla! 1.5 installation.

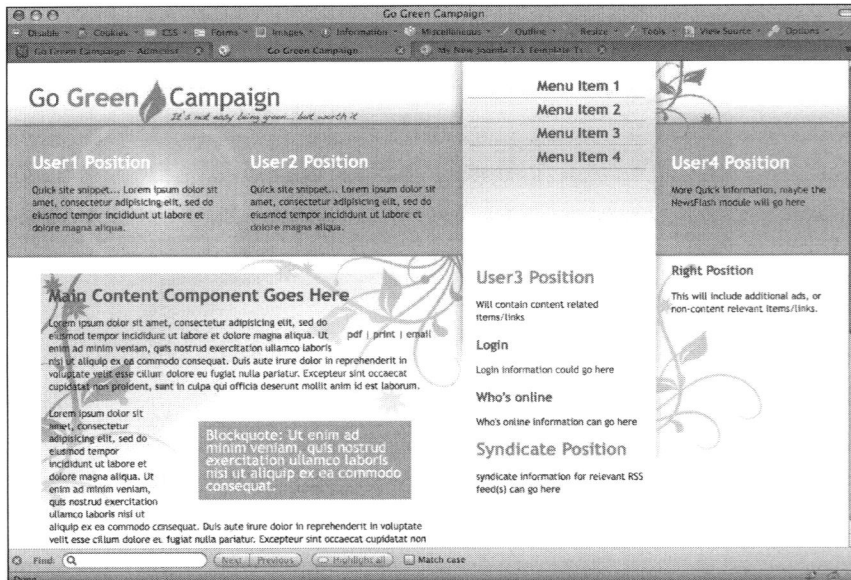

If you're going to be using any additional stylesheets, or other `includes` such as JavaScript toolkits, you can place them inside your template's folder, linking to them in the header using the same ...`<?php echo $this->baseurl; ?>`... technique.

General Joomla! stylesheets

One thing I do recommend is to also include these system stylesheets above your stylesheet. By placing them above your stylesheet, if you happen to create a rule for any Joomla! classes or XHTML objects that have a rule, your rules will overwrite Joomla's system CSS rules (return to the line with your stylesheet `include` and paste these in above that around line **10**):

```
<link rel="stylesheet" href="<?php echo $this->baseurl ?>
    /templates/system/css/system.css" type="text/css" />

<link rel="stylesheet" href="<?php echo $this->baseurl ?>
    /templates/system/css/general.css" type="text/css" />
```

These general system stylesheets will style various debugging/error messages and other system responses that Joomla! may render in addition to your CMS content that you probably didn't think to style for. I find having these two system stylesheets available takes care of a lot of little mundane details, which are easily overwritten if they show up and clash with my design.

The content component

The next (and I'd say, the most important) bit of Joomla! 1.5 code that I like to tuck into my mock up file is the component `jdoc` tag. It's an essential part of your Joomla! 1.5 template. It displays your main content as well as any other components installed and activated.

Time for action: **Adding the jdoc tag to the mockup file**

It's pretty simple. In my mockup, I'll remove everything that is inside the `content div` and replace it with this:

```
...
<div id="content">
<!--//start Joomla! component-->
<jdoc:include type="component" />
<!--//end Joomla! component-->
</div><!--//content-->
...
```

Upon reloading my page, I discover it works just fine and two sample articles that are assigned to the home page are indeed now showing up. Be aware, they're not as pretty as my mockup! Nevertheless, they are appearing as they should. Let's continue on for now and return to this layout issue later.

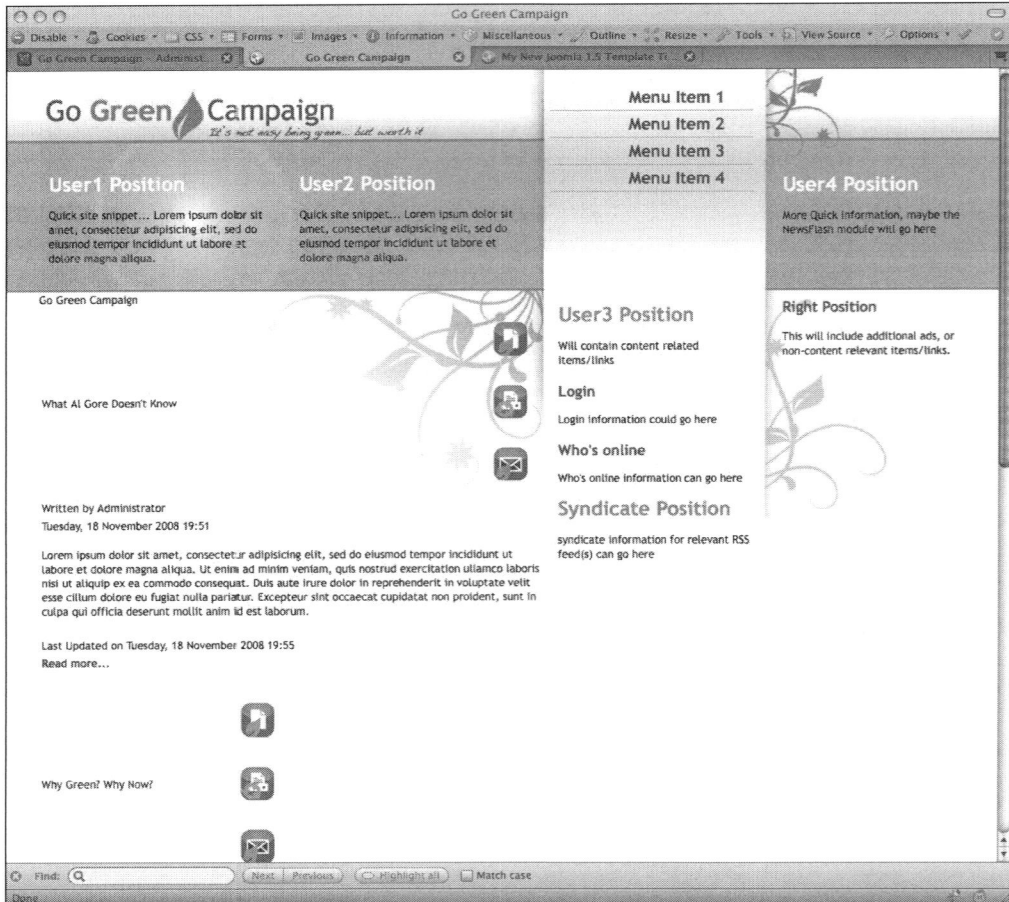

Module positions

I'm now ready to start inserting module position `jdoc` tags. Module position tags are what will hold the modules I've set up in Joomla. You can assign multiple modules to a single position and arrange their hierarchy in the Joomla's Admin panel. Be aware of this in your design! I attempted to make my layout flexible so that if an administrator decides to place multiple modules into a position, it will work. However, there are still positions in this template design, such as the `left`, `user1`, `user2`, and `user4` positions that really can't take multiple modules within them.

Jdoc tag overview

Before we get started, here's an overview of how the jdoc tag works for module positions:

The jdoc tag looks like this:

```
<jdoc:include type="module" name="user1" style="xhtml" />
```

- The type attribute we've seen before, when it was called head and component. This is where you tell Joomla! what type of item to place—head, component, module, as well as installation and message are the five types allowed in a jdoc tag. As a frontend template developer, you won' be using installation or message much if at all, but it is considered a good practice to incldue the `<jdoc:include:message />` after the `<body>` tag in your template. This ensures system information and/or error messages get the user's attention if there's a problem during site development. (I usually remove this tag when the site goes live so it doesn't distract the end user.)

- The name attribute can be named whatever you want, but again I highly recommend you use the relevant traditional module position names we discussed in *Chapter 2*.

- The style attribute works only with the module type attribute. This is your first step for controlling Joomla's **module chrome**. There are six built-in system module chrome outputs that you can chose from. (In *Chapter 9*, we will cover making your own module chrome, and you'll then be able to select its parameter via this attribute as well.)

    ○ tables—the module content loads in an XHTML table object with the .moduletable class applied to it.

    ○ horiz—the module content is again loaded into a table, but the second row displays horizontally.

    ○ rounded—this parameter is useful if you intend to apply traditional CSS2 rounded corners to a module. The title, if enabled, is wrapped in `<h3>`tags and four layers of divs. .module is applied to the outer div.

    ○ outline—it is good for debugging. It lets you label items to the left of the module output using an extra div with the .mod-preview-info class. .mod-preview class is applied to the outside div and .mod-preview-wrapper is applied to the inside div. The list's `<ul>` object has the .menu class applied.

- xhtml—this is the most optimal output and what I use and recommend. This wraps items in a div tag with .moduletable_ menu class and titles in <h3>headers and .menu class assigned to <ul> objects.

- none or raw—these are essentially the same, and they spit out the raw textual content of the module (in list format if applicable) and does not display the module's title. While very clean, the lack of being able to display the title is a drawback for most template developers.

Need a reference?

Chapter 6 will have a handy reference guide for the given module chrome styles and all the class styles they output. Be sure to also check out these two illuminating guides on Joomla's documentation site: *jdoc statements* (http://docs.joomla.org/Jdoc_statements) and *What is module chrome?* (http://docs.joomla.org/What_is_module_ chrome%3F). *Don't cut off that %3F! It's important to the URL.*

Now all of that might have seemed like a lot, but I can simplify it for you. If you're new to designing for Joomla! 1.5, your best bet is to stay away from the module chrome that generates tables and simply use the xhtml style. That chrome style will allow you to easily style the module in a variety of ways while allowing the Joomla! administrator to chose whether to display the module's title or not. If you're not going to be handing your template off to the public, and want more precise control over your modules, you can experiment with using rounded and none/raw.

Coffee break: Developer's tip

Create a code arsenal: Let's take a break. While reflecting all you've accomplished so far, sipping your coffee or beverage of choice, note that we've already come across some PHP code and several ways to use the jdoc tag. I don't know about you, but I'm terrible at remembering syntax for code, markup, and CSS. I often know what I need, but can never quite recall exactly how it's supposed to be typed. I used to spend hours going through various stylesheets, markup, and code from previous projects to copy into my current project as well as googling (and "re-googling") web pages that had samples of the syntax I needed (heaven help me if no connectivity was available).

If you're going to be developing a lot of Joomla! 1.5 templates (or doing a lot of web development or programming in general), you may want to invest in setting yourself up with a personal "code arsenal" using the **Snippets** or **Clip** features that are usually available in good HTML/Code editors. You simply type or paste the `jdoc` tags, PHP code, key CSS rules, or any syntax, whatever you find you need to use the most, into the **Snippets** or **Clips** panel available in your editor, and the application saves it for you for future use. Good editors such as Dreamweaver, HTML-Kit, and Coda usually have the ability to organize and keep them logically grouped and handy. Some editors will even let you assign custom "key shortcuts" and/or drag-and-drop your clips right into your working file. How easy is that?

Free your code arsenal from your code editor: Once you discover how handy this is, you might want to have your arsenal available to other programs you work with, especially if you switch between multiple editors and authoring environments. I suggest you invest in a multi-paste/clip board application that lets you save and organize your code snippets. When I was on PC, I used a great little app called Yankee Clipper 3 (which is free: `http://www.intelexual.com/products/YC3/`), and now on Mac, I use iPaste (which has a modest price: `http://www.iggsoftware.com/ipaste/`). In addition to having your arsenal handy from any application, being able to go back through the last 10 or so items you copied to the clip board is a real time saver when you're working on a project.

Take it with you: Lastly, as a freelancer, I occasionally work at client sites, on their computers, away from my laptop. I've been a Palm user for, well, over 10 years (I've been through many Palm devices—upgraded to a Palm Centro recently). Quite a while back, I started keeping a set of essential code snippets in my desktop notes that sync with my Palm memos within a category called "code". Memo/note apps on most devices sort by the first line of text of the note, so I simply name the first line of the memo with the type of code, such as `jdoc`, `xhtml`, `css`, `php`, `javascript`, `as2`, `as3` (for Flash), and so on, along with two or three words on what the snippet does. For example:

```
xhtml: trans 1.0 doctype
<!DOCTYPE html PUBLIC "-//W3C//DTD XHTML 1.0
Transitional//EN"
"http://www.w3.org/TR/xhtml1/DTD/xhtml1-transitional.
dtd">
```

Even away from my laptop, it's very easy for me to scroll through the code category or just use the **Find** feature to look up the syntax for, say, a bit of CSS shorthand, the exact parameters of that darn PHP function I constantly forget, or that really cool JavaScript trick I discovered two projects ago. Although I can't just copy-and-paste it from my Palm device, it's still useful to be able to see exactly what the syntax is supposed to look like.

Whether you use a Palm, Blackberry, Windows CE device, or other hand-held/smart phone, as long as it offers a notes or memos app, you can easily set up a system like this for an "on-the-go" arsenal (yes, even you "un-sync-able note" iPhone users can do this. Check out http://notespark.com).

OK, break's over. Get back to work!

Updating the templateDetails.xml file

Using my original sketch for reference, I'll want to paste in the `jdoc` tags for module positions into my `index.php` file. However, before I do that, I'll need to take a quick look at my `templateDetails.xml` file and make sure it accommodates the positions I plan to place into my `index.php` file.

Time for action: **Updating the templateDetails.xml file**

1. Open up your `templateDetails.xml` file. Mine was originally pulled from the `rhuk_milkyway` template, so down at about line **63**, where the `<position>` tags start. The `rhuk_milkyway` author also used many of the standard Joomla! position names, so all of my positions are already there. All I need to do is delete the position lines for `breadcrumb` and `syndicate`. The position breadcrumb is usually used for listing a trail of where you are in the site and syndicate position contains syndication information such as RSS feeds. In this book's case study, which is a custom template for a specific site, I didn't use the breadcrumb position, as the site will have very basic navigation and it's fine if syndication information is placed inside one of the other position tags. I can, technically, leave these positions there, even if I don't add the `jdoc` module position tags to my template, but it's bad form and will allow someone to try to assign something to a position that doesn't actually exist in the template.

2. I've deleted lines **63** and **73**, leaving me with just the positions I've intended to place into my template:

```
...
<positions>
 <position>left</position>
 <position>right</position>
 <position>top</position>
 <position>user1</position>
 <position>user2</position>
 <position>user3</position>
 <position>user4</position>
 <position>footer</position>
 <position>debug</position>
</positions>
...
```

Now that we have our positions in place, when we go to **Extensions | Module Manager** in our Administrator panel, for each Module, if we'd like, we can now assign it to one of the positions we set up in our templateDetails.xml file. The following image shows the **Position** drop-down menu from the **Details** panel in the **Module Manager**.

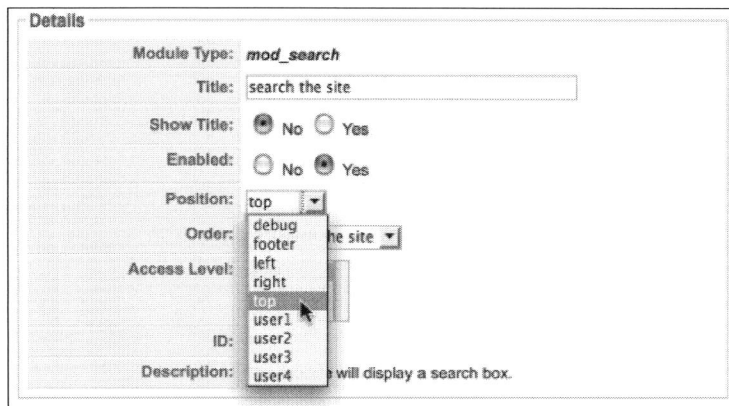

Placing module positions in the index.php file

Now that I'm sure the `templateDetails.xml` file will accommodate my module positions, I can begin adding them as follows:

1. `top`: This is where I'd like to place Joomla's search bar. In the `index.php` file around line **28** within the `#header div`, I add this `jdoc` tag:

```
...
<div id="head">
<!--//start top mod-->
<jdoc:include type="modules" name="top" style="xhtml" />
<!--//end top mod-->
...
```

2. `user1` and `user2`: These positions go within the header area, inside the layout `divs` I created, and will contain "top link" items or maybe a small article clip. At about line **37**, I delete my fake module text and add the `jdoc` tag:

```
...
<div id="user1">
<!--//start user1 mod-->
<jdoc:include type="modules" name="user1" style="xhtml" />
<!--//end user1 mod-->
</div><!--//user1-->
...
```

`user2`'s placement starts at around line **46**:

```
...
<div id="user2">
<!--//start user2 mod-->
<jdoc:include type="modules" name="user2" style="xhtml" />
<!--//end user2 mod-->
</div><!--//user2-->
...
```

So far, my three modules look like this:

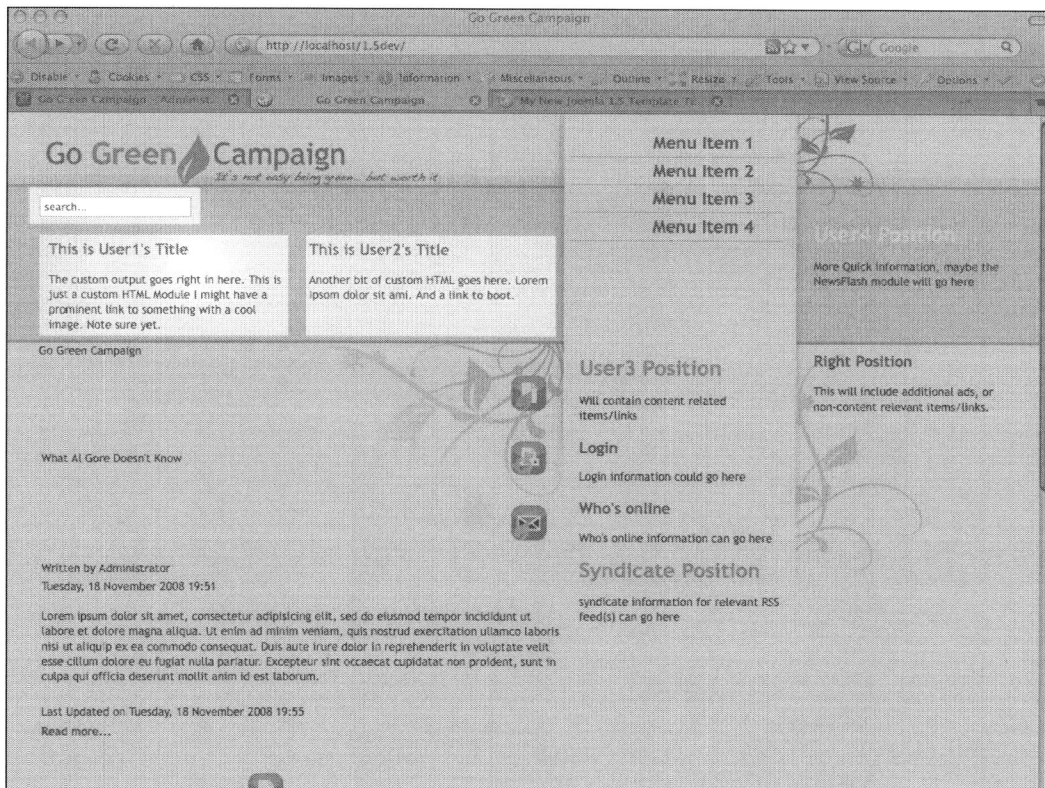

Again, it's not perfect, in comparison to my mockup, but the visual issues just require some CSS touching up. We'll get back to that. Let's just finish placing in the rest of the module positions.

3. `user3`: It will contain additional relevant info, syndication, top stories, login, who's online, and so on. This area starts around line **71** and, you guessed it, looks very similar to the `user1` and `user2` jdoc tags. Just replace the dummy text with the `jdoc` tag (and any XHTML comments you'd like to add). I think you get my "pattern" for placing in `jdoc` module position tags, so I'll save a few sheets of paper and just have you note each tag yourself.

   ```
   ...<jdoc:include type="modules" name="user3" style="xhtml" />...
   ```

4. `user4`: Another quick article snippet starts around line **85**.

   ```
   ...<jdoc:include type="modules" name="user4" style="xhtml" />...
   ```

5. `right`: This position is for non-relevant content, I'm thinking links to other sites, and people as well as advertisements. This starts around line **93**.

```
...<jdoc:include type="modules" name="right" style="xhtml" />...
```

6. `left`: My main page navigation will go in this position. It starts around line **107**. Now don't get confused! This is one instance where I didn't name the layout `div` similarly to the module position it holds.

   Most of the time, the `mod_mainmenu` is automatically associated to the `left` module position, so I'm going to place that position `jdoc` tag inside my `#top_navlist` div. That way, the main menu will display there, positioned absolutely. I chose to handle this module this way because many Joomla! users will have their main menu assigned to this position and the template will work upon install. The drawback is any other modules added to this position will overlap into the `user3` position below it, because it is absolutely positioned. While we'll cover what you need to know to get this module to output and be styled as the menu in our mockup, the `mod_mainmenu` module is probably one of the more important modules you'll deal with in Joomla (as important as the content component). You'll want to make sure that you fully understand how to administrate this module and add pages and links to it, as it will be the core of your site's navigation. Hagen Graf's *"Building Websites With Joomla! 1.5"*, *Hagen Graf, Packt Publishing*, covers this module in *Chapter 7*.

```
...
<div id="tcp_navlist">
<!--//start left mod-->
<jdoc:include type="modules" name="left" style="xhtml" />
<!--//end left mod-->
</div><!--//top_navlist-->
...
```

7. `footer`: This will contain some main navigation items and key info and copyright on the site. This `div` starts around line **121**.

```
...<jdoc:include type="modules" name="footer" style="xhtml" />..
```

8. `debug`: This is a good "catch all" position to have. You can quickly tuck modules into it to just test them out (below the fold so that if you're quick, most people won't notice). Also, there are third-party extensions that don't display anything but need to be on the page to work, such as analytics modules and the like. This is a good place to tuck those things into. This is the last `div` in the `index.php` file before the closing `</body>` tag.

```
...<jdoc:include type="modules" name="debug" style="xhtml" />...
```

XHTML comments

You'll also note that I'm placing most of my Joomla! 1.5 jdoc tags between `<!--//-->` XHTML comment tags. I do this so that scanning the "View Source" markup with Joomla! CMS content is easier for me and any other template developer who comes across it. You don't have to do this, but it's a nice template feature for those of you who are looking forward to creating commercial templates to make a little money. The more clear your markup, the less time you'll spend helping purchasers troubleshoot your template. I also like to indicate where positioning XHTML `div` tags end, as well as what kind of content I intend that part of the layout to hold. This proves useful, time and again, to me, if no one else!

Assign modules to your positions

Believe it or not, that's pretty much it! After including each `jdoc` module position, you'll want to log into your Administration panel and go to **Extensions | Module Manager** to ensure that each module is assigned to a position (preferably the position you want it to be assigned to). If you want, you can create and assign new modules. Just use the **New** button in the top-right of the **Module Manager** and follow the Administration panel's instructions to do that. For more information on creating modules in the **Module Manager**, be sure to check out Hagen Graf's *"Building Websites With Joomla! 1.5"*, *Hagen Graf, Packt Publishing*—*Chapter 10* covers the **Extensions Menu** and the **Module Manager** in detail. The following image shows the **Module Manager** with modules assigned to positions in our template and the **New** button highlighted:

Joomla! offers twenty great built-in modules to choose from. There's a whole world of third-party modules and other extensions out there (We'll cover what extensions — modules, components, and plugins — are exactly in *Chapters 8* and *9*). You simply assign modules to the appropriate position in that specific module's top-left **Details** panel. Let's take a look at how our template is coming along with Joomla's CMS module and content loading into it:

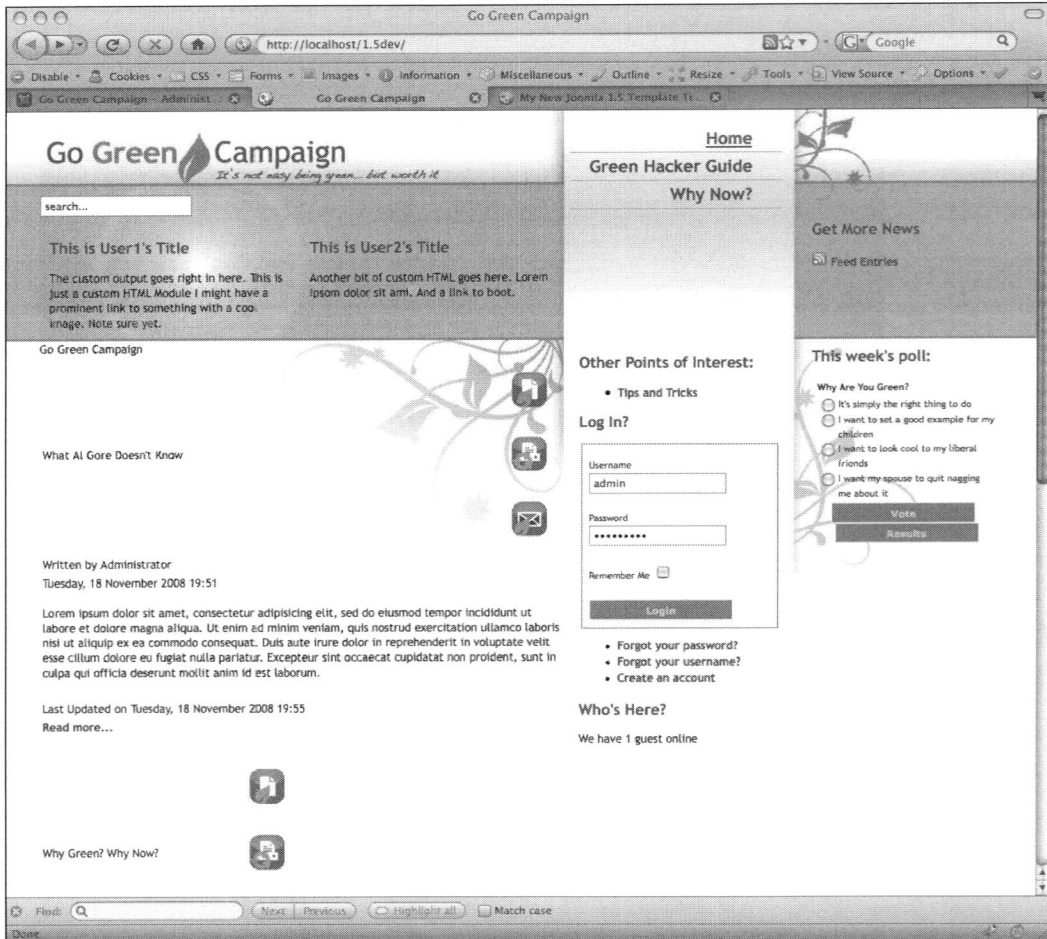

Our design is now implemented into Joomla! 1.5 and calling in our Joomla! CMS content. We can now use our Web Developer Toolbar to help us finalize any remaining CSS stylings and tweaks, but I don't think we're quite ready to do that yet.

Hello? Content is wrapped in tables. Gross!

Yes. You can see in the previous image that our articles come into the content component un-styled and strange. There are no header tags, and items seem to be "stacking".

While you can control the output of most modules, especially menu items as lists, Joomla's native core output for the content component and some modules (such as polls, which are components at their core) is still tables. If we use the **Outline Tables | Table Cells** feature in our Web Developer Toolbar, we'll see how many table cells there are. As you can see in the following image, it's a bit shocking!

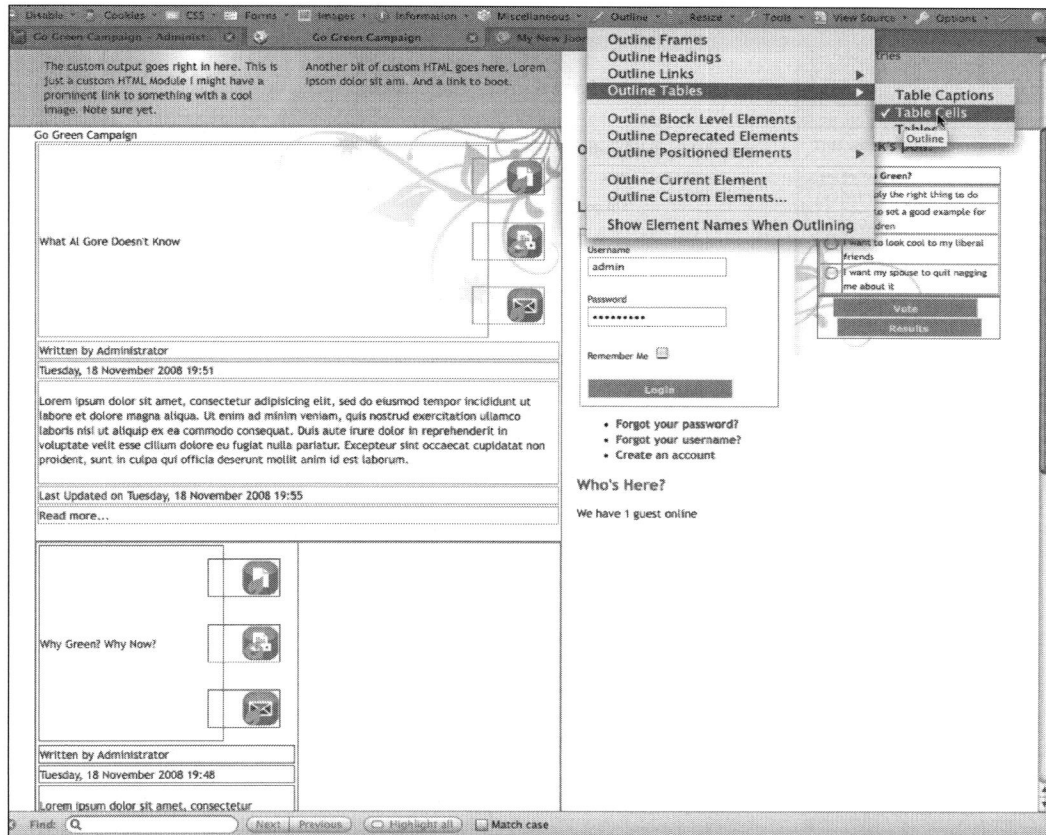

However, Joomla! did make huge strides with 1.5 by introducing that template override feature I've mentioned a few times. If you're new to Joomla! 1.5, I'll give you this bit of background so you can truly appreciate how wondrous this feature is.

Back in the "dark ages" of Joomla! 1.0, if you really wanted to remove all the tables from the core's output, you had to first really understand the installation files of Joomla!; secondly, be a bit of a "PHP wiz" to poke through Joomla's core files until you found the various `.content...` files your site used the most (don't ask); and then "hack" the tables out of them (hoping you didn't hack or break any essential PHP along the way).

This was an option used by many professional sites at the time to achieve impressive and flexible designs while taking advantage of the power of Joomla CMS.

The drawback of course is that the hack had nothing at all to do with your template. After spending hours (probably even days) doing all that "de-tabling" work, you couldn't then just hand it off for another Joomla! administrator to easily take advantage of. Plus, once you finished the hack, upgrading your Joomla! 1.0 installation just became a serious pain-in-the-rear. You either lost all your table-less markup with an upgrade and started over, or you painstakingly pulled it out, upgraded Joomla!, and then pieced your hacked files back in, having to double check each line of them to ensure you didn't overwrite some piece of the core's PHP that had been recently upgraded for one reason or another.

Extremely tedious, and not for the faint-of-heart!

Everything is better with Beez

Beez is a great template that comes with your Joomla! 1.5 installation. You've probably noticed it. It was created by Angie Radtke and Robert Deutz expressly for the purpose of producing an accessible, truly table-less template. The template takes advantage of Joomla's new template override feature.

Those additional files inside the `html` directory (as we mentioned at the beginning of this chapter) are structured and specifically named in such a way that the Joomla! 1.5 system checks for their existence in the applied template (or templates), and if an html directory is detected, and any of those `mod_` or `com_` directories and files are found, Joomla! will use the XHTML and PHP code from within those files rather than Joomla's system core output.

Using template overrides

Creating a template override file from scratch is still not for the faint-of-heart. If you're not a PHP developer who also understands a little of how Joomla's core works under the hood, I flat-out don't recommend it, which is another reason to be so grateful to the creators of the Beez template. They've done all the hard work of creating a complete component and module override set that has the tables removed. The Beez template override set doesn't cover everything, plus the kitchen sink, but they've done a solid job of creating overrides for the most common components and modules, at least the ones 90% of us use, which is more than adequate to get us going. The great thing about using template overrides is that when Joomla's system core or other components go through updates, the template overrides should not be affected (unlike hacking the old system as I have mentioned).

Today, Joomla! 1.5 developers who want to create a truly table-less design, need merely to copy the `html` directory from the Beez template and place it inside their root template directory.

> **Not satisfied with copying and pasting?**
>
> While there's a bit of PHP to it, stay tuned. In *Chapter 9*, we'll go over the basics for creating a template override. *Chapter 6* will of course have a reference of all the overrides you can make and what their naming conventions are.

Time for action: Placing the Beez template overrides into your template

Now, let's take a look at moving the Beez template overrides into our template directory.

1. Copy the `html` directory from the Beez template into your template's root directory.

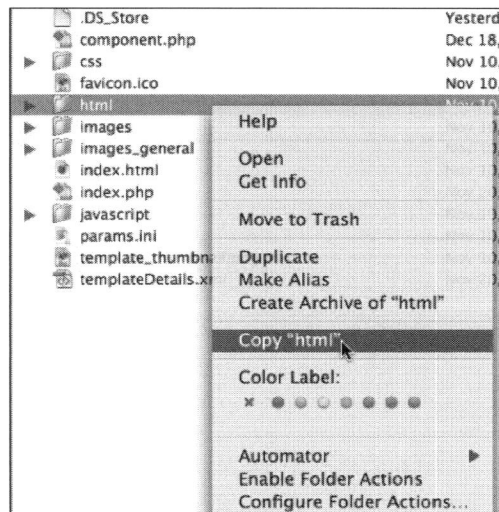

2. Refresh your Joomla! screen and check it out.

Layout looks better. And the tables are gone now. Sweet!

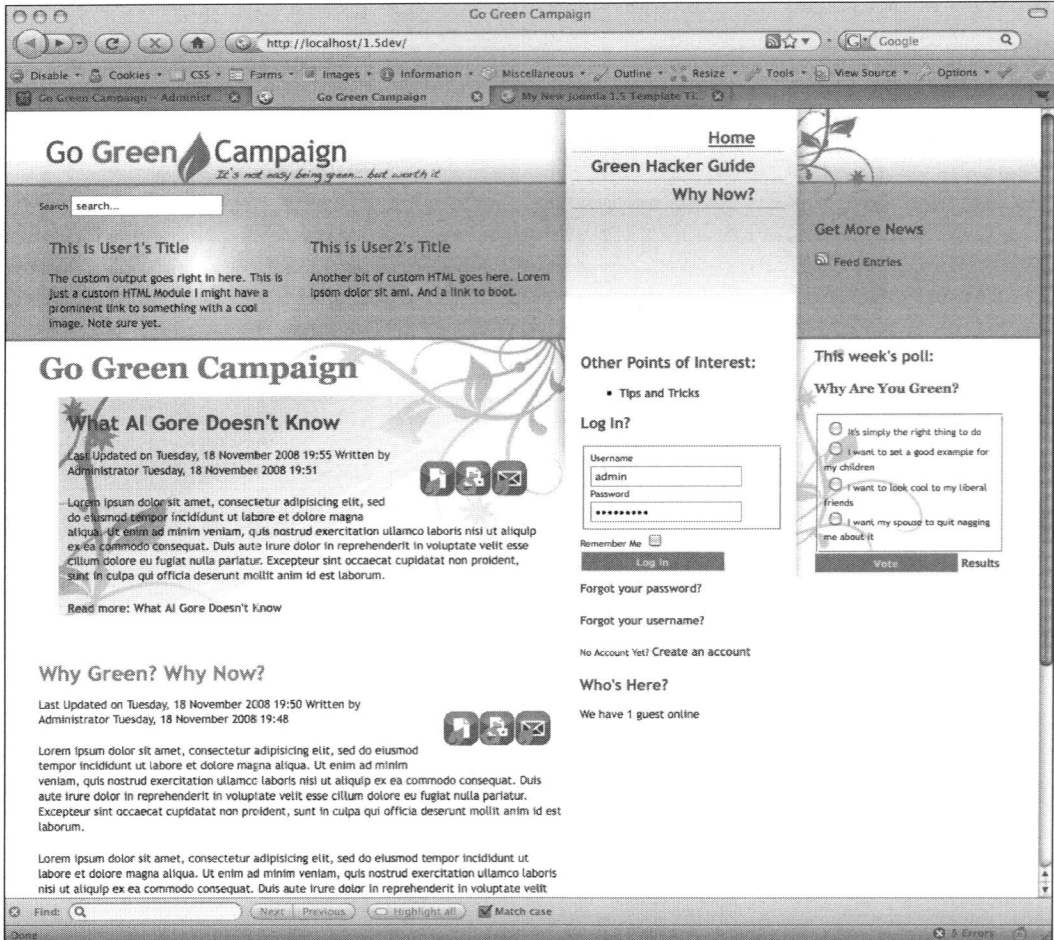

Learn about the Beez

No embarrassing birds involved. To find out more about this template and its creators (along with some ideas for making your own template overrides), be sure to check out http://www.joomla-beez.com.

Included the component.php **file?** You may recall, we noticed this file outside the html directory in another package earlier. It's also in the Beez template. I've searched high and low on the Web for a clear explanation of what the component.php file does, and at the time of this writing, have not had any luck. Poking through the file, I can see it recreates a basic layout that only displays the jdoc component tag along with a jdoc message type tag above that. I figure it must be useful for some instances of the component display, so I usually include it. But as far as I can tell, I have not ever had a template "break" for not having it included in the template's directory. If you do include this file, be sure to replicate everything inside your index.php file's <head></head> tags so that this file calls your template's stylesheets and any other included files that your template uses.

Final CSS tweaks and fixes

Now that our Joomla! template is truly table-less, we can start taking a look at its finer points to find any final touches and tweaks that can be done. On the whole, because we took the time and care in *Chapter 2* to create an XHTML/CSS mockup whose overall styling relied mostly on very basic XHTML objects, in contrast to specific classes and id's, we're already in pretty good shape. Of course, there's always a room for improvement!

Take your time and walk through the various pages and views you've set up on your Joomla! site. If you see anything you'd like to spruce up, I recommend you do the following:

1. Highlight it, and right-click (or *Ctrl*+click) on it to select **View Selection Source**.

2. The FireFox **Dom Source of Selection** window will appear and show you the markup and classes and ids of the code you've selected:

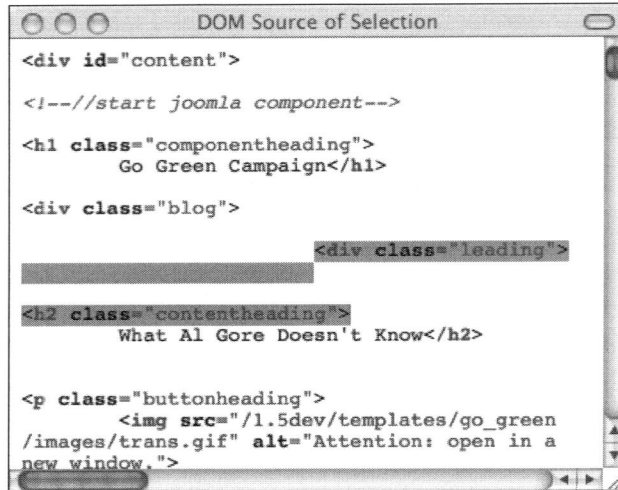

```
DOM Source of Selection

<div id="content">

<!--//start joomla component-->

<h1 class="componentheading">
        Go Green Campaign</h1>

<div class="blog">

                                    <div class="leading">

<h2 class="contentheading">
        What Al Gore Doesn't Know</h2>


<p class="buttonheading">
        <img src="/1.5dev/templates/go_green
/images/trans.gif" alt="Attention: open in a
new window.">
```

You can then see what classes Joomla's content is producing. With this information, along with the knowledge of your template's XHTML markup, you can create additional CSS rules to style the remaining details.

In my original mockup, I had created a box for a "lead" story with a transparent PNG background. I have a style rule set up for an id called #lead. To see what the creators of Beez have decided to wrap the lead story in, I selected the story and right-clicked and selected **View Source Selection** (the result is the previous screenshot).

It appears to be a class called .leading. I'll just change my template.css styles from #lead to .leading and Refresh.

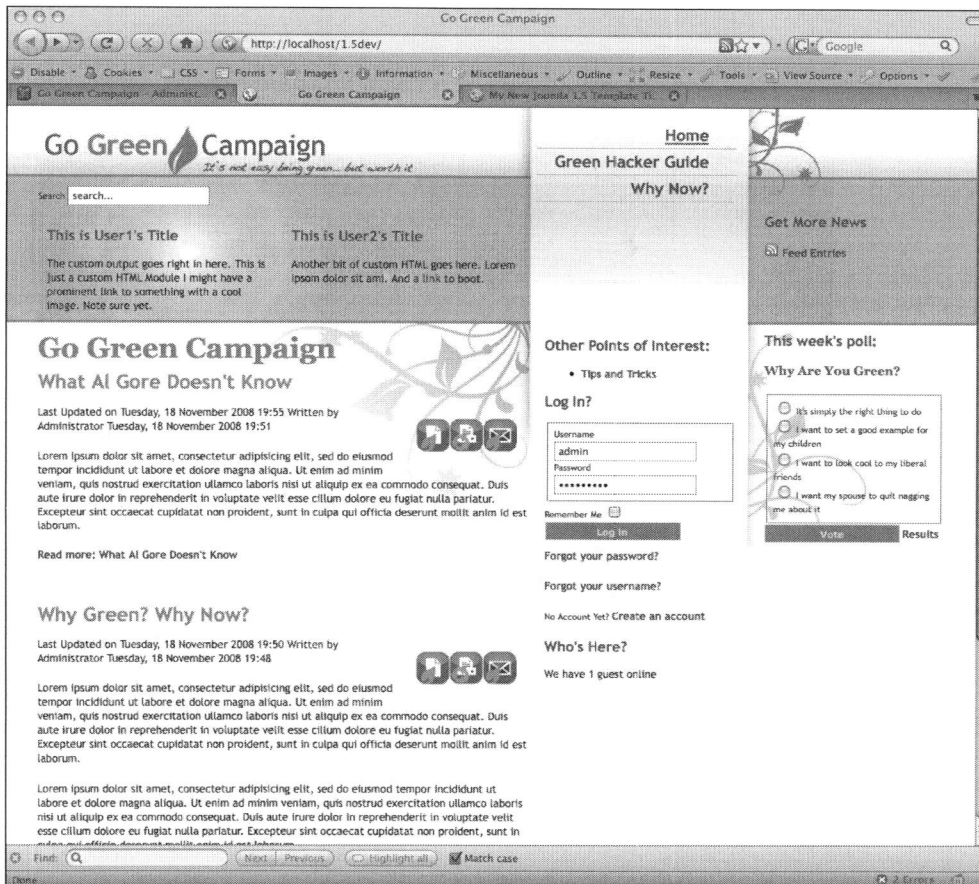

View Selection Source is going to become your best friend. If you need to see where the code is in the bigger picture of things, you can simply right-click (or *Ctrl*+click on Mac) and **View Page Source**, or use your Web Developer Toolbar and just select **View Source** right from it. Once that window displays with all of your template's markup and Joomla! content markup, you can use *Cmnd+F* (or *Ctrl+F* on PC) to envoke the **Find** feature and find the specific part of the page you want to inspect its markup.

For instance, in my XHTML and CSS mockup, I didn't think about stylings for form objects, such as radio buttons and input objects. Now that my content is appearing, I have a poll module displaying in the right column. While the poll is displaying OK, and is certainly functional, its buttons sure are ugly! (That's because I have a generic `.button` class in my stylesheet to remind me to style buttons.) Let's just take some time to spruce the poll and the `.button` class up a bit.

Time for action: **Styling the buttons**

Let's take a look at styling our poll's buttons.

1. Highlight the poll content in your browser and right-click and select **View Selection Source**. In the **Dom Source of Selection** panel, note the Joomla! classes as well as XHTML form objects associated with the poll.

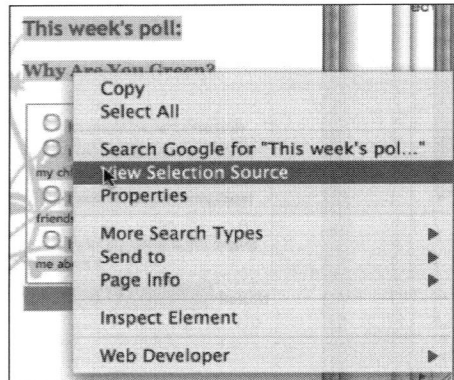

2. I can see I've got a standard class of .moduletable and another class on the form object called .poll, as well as input radio buttons and another input object used as a button with a .button class assigned to that. The questions are wrapped in XHTML <label> object tags. Plenty of options to work with here.

   My goal will be to tighten up the layout and get the questions to not wrap so awkwardly under the radio button elements (one of the advantages of tables, but we'll be fine with <div> and <label> objects).

3. In my template.css stylesheet, I'll add the following rules to my styles under the Forms section.

```
/*////////// FORMS //////////*/
...
.poll{
  border: none;
  margin: 0;
}
.poll label{
  display:block;
  width: 160px;
```

```
    padding-left: 25px;
    color: #4C341C;
}

.poll fieldset input{
  float: left;
  margin: 0;
  margin-top: 8px;
}

#right .moduletable h3{
  margin-top: 15px 0 0 0;
  padding-left: 10px;
  font-size: 14px;
  font-variant: small-caps;
}

#right .moduletable h4{
  margin: 5px 0 0 0;
  padding-left: 10px;
}

.poll .button{
  margin: 0px;
  margin-left: 30px;
  width: 60px;
}
...
```

4. Once I save and hit "Refresh" or *Cmnd+R* (or *Ctrl+R*) in my Joomla! window, I now see what my poll styles look like:

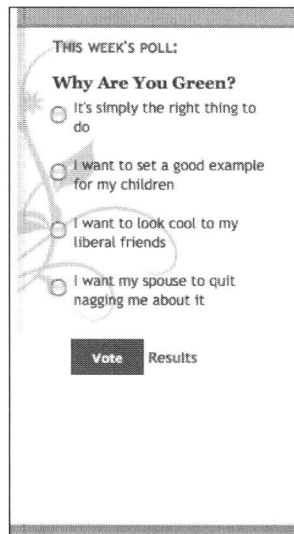

Now, once I'm done with the poll, there are several other items that need some sprucing up. To name a few:

- My search bar needs positioning.
- My mockup assumed that `<h2>` tags would load into the modules, but Joomla! actually displays `<h3>` tags. This is just what the default Joomla! core outputs for headers in modules.
- I'm now feeling as though some of the headers are a little too bright-green, so want to tone down that color.

As you can see, lots of things can be touched up. I'll be using the exact same technique to "hunt down" any unique classes, ids, or XHTML objects Joomla! outputs and then just make sure that I accommodate them in my CSS file and style to my preference.

However, at this point, we're no longer really talking about Joomla! 1.5 and only creating style rules using basic CSS2 techniques that render in all major browsers. Rather than bore you with each tedious little CSS tweak from here on out, I'll trust that after fixing up and styling the poll module, you understand my "Joomla! CSS sleuthing" method, and understand enough about CSS to achieve the final design and effects you desire for your own template.

This is the part of the cooking show where the chef says "Mix until even, place in the pan and bake for 45 minutes at 350 degrees" and then magically pulls a finished cake out from under the counter (which is not only baked, but appears to have another two hours of frosting and design embellishments added to it).

The final **Go Green Campaign** template looks like the following:

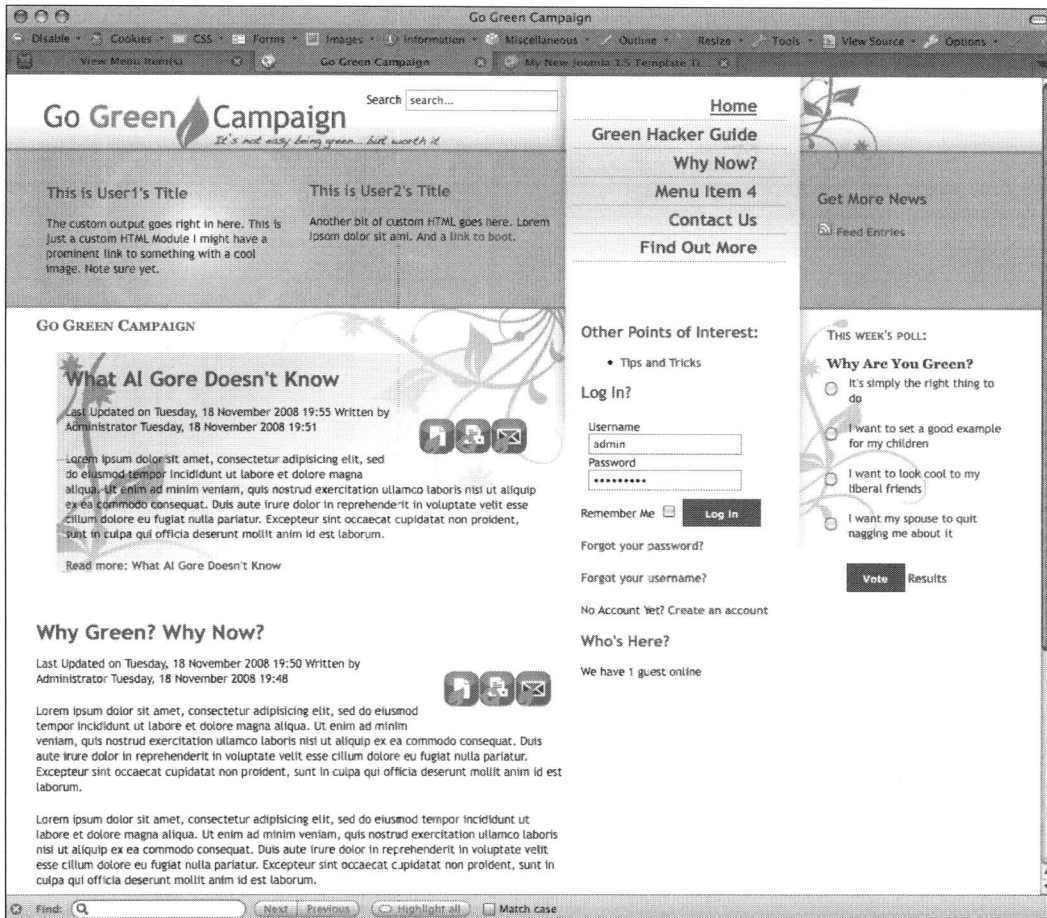

Even so, there is tons more we could do to this template (and we will in *Chapters 7, 8, and 9*). For instance, just adding eye-catching images and icons to the articles and user positions will really refine this site. But, we'll leave that up to the site's administrator and content authors.

For now, for just focusing on the template itself, its layout, CSS, and bare bones Joomla! `jdoc` tags, this is a great start. For those of you who are interested in all the CSS details, you can download this chapter's code packet, which contains the final Go Green Campaign template zip, and you can compare its `template.css` to what you've created working with me, and/or to *Chapter 2's* code packet, which contains our XHTML/CSS mockup files. Comparing those `template.css` files will show you exactly what CSS rules have been added to accommodate Joomla! 1.5 content. I'll let you know now that it's much less than you'd think! Download the code packets for this book from `http://packtpub.com/files/code/7160_Code.zip`.

Getting a heads up?

OK, I hear you. Right-clicking and poking through every little bit of Joomla! content can become quite tedious. On a big project with many different layouts, you may find yourself wondering, "wait, is that my layout's class? Or a Joomla! class?" It would at least help to know what you're looking for ahead of time. Never fear, *Chapter 6* has a complete-as-possible listing of all known Joomla! id and class names that I could research and find as of the time of this writing. Be sure to check that out. Also, stay tuned for *Chapter 7*, where we'll take a look at making this layout more flexible and dynamic.

Summary

We've now completed our basic Joomla! 1.5 template. Great job!

It's probably clear that you can take advantage of all sorts of Joomla! 1.5's HTML output and tweak your template endlessly.

How much customization your template requires depends entirely on what you want to use it for. If you know exactly how it's going to be used and you'll be the administrator controlling it, then you can save time by covering the most obvious component and module displays the site will need to get it rolling and occasionally create a few new styles, as the needs arise.

If you intend to release the template to the public, then the more flexible your layout is with module positions, as well as CSS that can handle as many of the most popular modules and components out there, the better. You never know how someone will want to use your template within his/her site.

You've now learned how to set up your development environment and an HTML editor for a smooth work flow. You now have a template design that uses semantic, SEO-friendly XHTML and CSS, and has been amended with PHP, jdoc tags, and Joomla! 1.5 override templates to display table-less Joomla! CMS content. Believe it or not, we're not quite done!

In the next chapter, we'll continue working with our all XHTML and CSS layout, learning tips and tricks for getting it to display properly in all browsers, debugging IE quirks, and running it through a thorough validation process. After that, we'll learn how to properly package it up with the templateDetails.xml file in *Chapter 5*.

4
Debugging and Validation

For simplicity's sake, I've made this process a separate chapter. However, as you work on and develop your own Joomla 1.5 template, you will no doubt discover that life will go much smoother if you debug and validate at each step of your template development process. The full process will go pretty much like this:

1. Add some code.
2. Check to see if the page looks good in FireFox.
3. Validate and fix errors.
4. Check it in IE and any other browsers you and your site's audience use.
5. Validate and fix errors again, if necessary.
6. Add the next bit of code.
7. Repeat as necessary until your template is complete.

In this chapter, I'm going to cover the basic techniques of debugging and validation that you should be employing throughout your template's development. We'll dive into the W3C's XHTML and CSS validation services, and I'll walk you through using FireFox's JavaScript/Error console for robust debugging, as well as introduce you to the FireBug extension and the Web Developer Toolbar. I'll also give you a little troubleshooting insight into some of the most common reasons "good code goes bad", especially in IE, and the various ways to remedy the problems.

Don't forget about those other browsers and platforms!

I'll mostly be talking about working in Firefox and then "fixing" for IE. This is perhaps unfair, assuming you're working on Windows or Mac and that the source of all your design woes will (of course) be Microsoft IE's fault. But as I mentioned in *Chapter 1*, this book is not about using only Firefox. You must check your template in all the browsers and, if possible, other platforms, especially the ones you know your audience uses the most.

I surf with Opera a lot and find that sometimes JavaScripts can "hang" or slow that browser down, so I debug and double-check scripts for that browser. (We'll discuss more about JavaScripts in *Chapter 8*.) I'm a freelance designer and find that a lot of people who are also in the design field use Mac (like me) and visit my sites using Safari, so I occasionally take advantage of this and write CSS that caters to the Safari browser. (Safari interprets some neat CSS 3 properties that other browsers currently do not.)

Generally, if you write valid markup and code that looks good in Firefox, it will look good in all other browsers (including IE). The markup and code that goes "awry" in IE is usually easy to fix with a workaround.

Firefox is a tool, nothing more. That's the only reason this book tends to focus on Firefox. Firefox contains features and modules that we'll be taking advantage of to help us streamline the template development process and aid the validation and debugging of our template. Use it just like you use your HTML/code editor or image editor. When you're not developing, you can use whichever browser you prefer.

Introduction to debugging

To refresh your memory, here's our initial work-flow chart from *Chapter 3*?

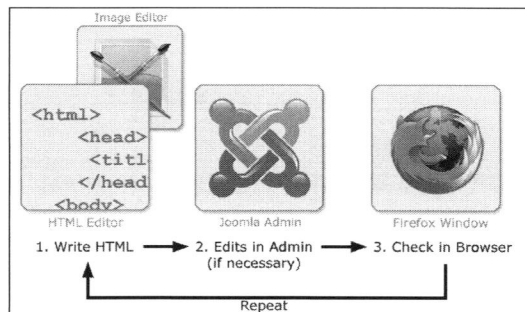

I was insistent that your work flow should pretty much be the following: *edit -> check it -> then go back and edit some more.* The main purpose of visually checking your template in FireFox after adding each piece of markup or code is, of course, to see if it looks OK. If it doesn't, then immediately debug that piece of code. Running a validation check as you work doubly ensures you're on the right track.

So, your work flow really ends up looking something more like the following:

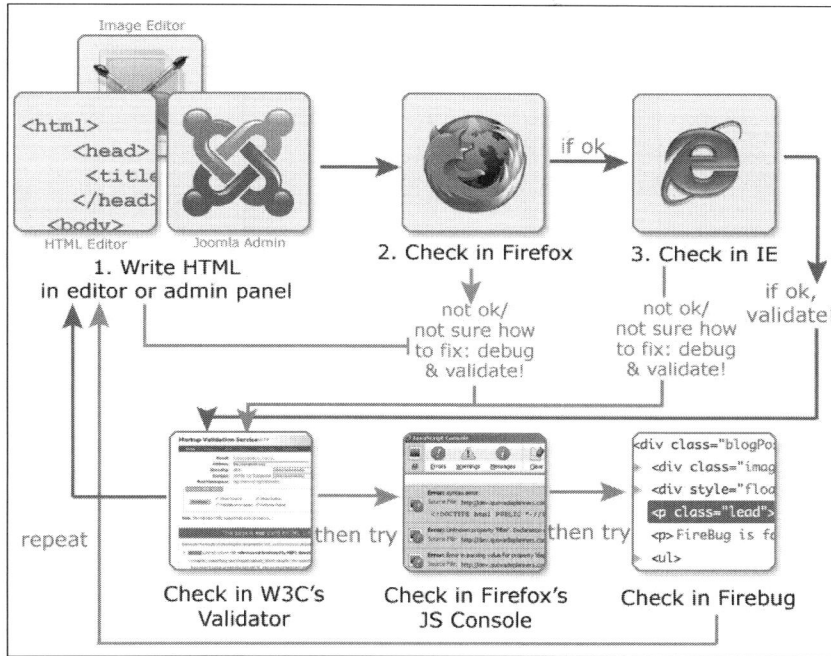

You want to work with nice, small pieces or "chunks" of markup and code. I tend to define a chunk in XHTML markup as no more than one `div` section and the internal markup and any Joomla 1.5 `jdoc` tags it contains. When working with CSS, I try to only work with one XHTML `object`, `id`, or `class` rule at a time. Sometimes, while working with CSS, I'll break this down even further and test after every property I add to a rule, until the rule looks as I intend it to look and validates.

As soon as you see something that doesn't look right in your browser, you can check for validation and then fix it. The advantage of this work flow is you know exactly what needs to be fixed and what XHTML markup or PHP code is to blame. You can ignore all the code that were looking fine and validating before. The recently-added markup and code is also the freshest in your mind, so you're more likely to realize the solution needed to fix the problem.

If you add too many chunks of XHTML markup or several CSS rules before checking it in your browser, then discover something has gone awry, you'll have twice as much sleuthing to do in order to discover which bit, or bits, of markup and code are to blame. Again, your fail-safe is your template's backup.

You should be regularly saving backups of your template at good stable stopping points. If you do discover that you just can't figure out where the issue is, rolling back to your last stable stopping point and starting over might be your best bet to getting back on track.

As mentioned in *Chapter 2*, you'll primarily design for FireFox and then apply any required fixes, hacks, and workarounds to IE. You can do that for each piece of code you add to your template. As you can see in the previous figure, first check your template in Firefox, and if there's a problem, fix it for Firefox first. Then, check it in IE and make any adjustments for that browser.

At this point, you guessed it, more than half of the debugging process will depend directly on your own eyeballs and aesthetics. If it looks the way you intended it to look and works the way you intended it to work, check that the code validates and move on. When one of those three things doesn't happen (it doesn't look right, work right, or validate), you have to stop and figure out the reason.

Troubleshooting basics

Suffice to say, it will usually be obvious when something is wrong with your Joomla 1.5 template. The most common reasons for things being "off" are:

- Mis-named, mis-targeted, or inappropriately-sized images
- Markup text or PHP code that affects or breaks the **Document Object Model (DOM)** due to being inappropriately placed or having syntax errors
- Joomla 1.5 PHP code copied over incorrectly, producing PHP error displays in your template, rather than content
- CSS rules that use incorrect syntax or conflict with later CSS rules

The first point is pretty obvious when it happens. You see no images, or worse, you might get those little ugly "x'd" boxes in IE if they're called directly from the Joomla 1.5 posts or pages. Fortunately, the solution is also obvious: you have to go in and make sure your images are named correctly if you're overwriting standard icons or images from another template. You also might need to go through your CSS file and make sure the relative paths to the images are correct.

For images that are not appearing correctly because they were mis-sized, you can go back to your image editor, fix them, and then re-export them, or you might be able to make adjustments in your CSS file to display a height and/or width that is more appropriate to the image you designed.

Don't forget about casing

If by some chance you happen to be developing your template with an installation of Joomla 1.5 on a local Windows machine, do be careful with the upper and lower casing in your links and image paths. Chances are, the Joomla 1.5 installation that your template is going to be installed into is more likely to be a UNIX or Linux web server. For some darn reason, Windows (even if you're running Apache, not IIS) will let you reference and call files with only the correct spelling required. Linux, in addition to spelling, requires the upper and lower casing to be correct. You must be careful to duplicate exact casing when naming images that are going to be replaced and/or when referencing your own image names via CSS. Otherwise, although it will look fine in your local testing environment, you'll end up with a pretty ugly template when you upload it into your client's installation of Joomla 1.5 for the first time (which is just plain embarrassing).

For the latter two points, one of the best ways to debug syntax errors that cause visual "wonks" is not to have syntax errors in the first place (don't roll your eyes just yet).

This is the reason, in the previous figure of our expanded work-flow chart, we advocate that you not only visually check your design as it progresses in Firefox and IE, but also test for validation.

Why validate?

Hey, I understand, it's easy to add some code, run a visual check in FireFox and IE, see that everything looks OK, and then flip right back to your HTML editor to add more code. After all, time is money, and you'll save that validation part until the very end. Besides, validation is just "icing on the cake". Right?

The problem with debugging based purely on visual output is, all browsers (some more grievously than others) will try their best to help you out and properly interpret less than ideal markup. One piece of invalid markup might very well look OK initially, until you add more markup and then the browser can't interpret your intentions between the two types of markup anymore. The browser will pick its own best option and display something guaranteed to be ugly.

You'll then go back and futz around with the last bit of code you added (because everything was fine until you added that last bit, so that must be the offending code), which may or may not fix the problem. The next bits of code might create other problems, and what's worse, you'll recognize a code chunk that you know should be valid. You're then frustrated, scratching your head as to why the last bit of code you added is making your template "wonky" when you know, without a doubt, it's perfectly fine code.

The worst case scenario I tend to see of this type of visual-only debugging is template developers get desperate and start randomly making all sorts of odd hacks and tweaks to their markup and CSS to get it to look right.

Miraculously, they often do get it to look right, but in only one browser. Most likely, they've inadvertently discovered what the first invalid syntax was and unwittingly applied it across all the rest of their markup and CSS. Thus, that one browser started consistently interpreting the bad syntax. The template designer then becomes convinced that the other browser is "awful" and designing these non-WYSIWYG, dynamic templates is a pain.

Avoid all that frustration. Even if it looks great in both browsers, run the code through the W3C's XHTML and CSS validators. If something turns up invalid, no matter how small or pedantic the validator's suggestion might be (and they do seem pedantic at times), incorporate the suggested fix into your markup now, before you continue working. This will keep any small syntax errors from compounding future bits of markup and code into big visual "uglies" that are hard to track down and troubleshoot.

Joomla jdoc tags and PHP

The next issue you'll most commonly run into is mistakes and typos that are created by copying-pasting Joomla 1.5 jdoc tags and other PHP code incorrectly. Fortunately, PHP does a decent job of trying to let you know in what file name and line of code in the file the offending syntax lives. Unfortunately, something about the Joomla! system doesn't always let these PHP error messages through and you'll often just get a broken template as shown in the next figure.

If your template breaks, your best bet is to open the `index.php` file and search for missing `<jdoc: ...>` or `<?php ?>` tags. Remember, PHP functions should also be followed with parenthesis followed by a semicolon, like this: `functionName();`.

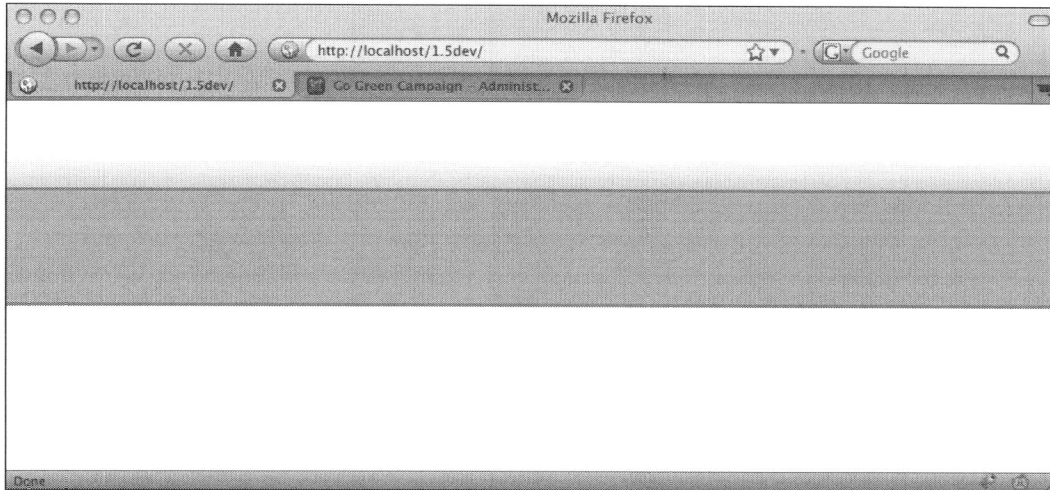

CSS quick fixes

Last, your CSS file might get fairly big, fairly quickly. It's easy to forget you already made a rule and/or just accidentally create another rule of the same name. It's all about "cascading", so whatever comes last overwrites what came first.

> **Double rules**: It's an easy mistake to make, but validating using W3C's CSS validator will point this out right away. However, this is not the case for double properties within rules. W3C's CSS validator will not point out double properties if both properties use correct syntax. This is one of the reasons the `!important` hack returns valid. (We'll discuss this hack just a little further down in this chapter under the *To hack or not to hack* section.)

Perhaps you found a site that has a nice CSS style or effect you like, and so you copied those CSS rules into your template's `style.css` sheet. Just like with XHTML markup or PHP code, it's easy to introduce errors by miscopying the bits of CSS syntax in. A small syntax error in a property towards the bottom of a rule may seem OK at first, but causes problems with properties added to the rule later. This can also affect the entire rule or even the rule after it.

Also, if you're copying CSS, be aware that older sites might be using depreciated CSS properties. It might be technically OK if they're using an older HTML DOCTYPE, but won't be OK for the XHTML DOCTYPE you're using, in terms of having a flexible and compliant design that degrades well.

Again, validating your markup and CSS as you're developing will alert you to syntax errors, depreciated properties, and duplicate rules, which could compound and cause issues down the line in your stylesheet.

Advanced troubleshooting

Take some time to understand the XHTML hierarchy. You'll start running into validation errors and CSS styling issues if you wrap a "normal" (also known as a "block") element inside an "in-line"-only element, such as putting a `header` tag (`<h1>`, `<h2>`, and so on) inside an `anchor` tag (`<a href`, `<a name`, and so on) or wrapping a `div` tag inside a `span` tag.

Avoid triggering **quirks mode** in IE. This, if nothing else, is one of the most important reasons for using the W3C HTML validator. Unfortunately, the IE browser itself doesn't seem to want to tell you if it's running in quirks mode. It doesn't seem to output that information anywhere (that I've found). However, if any part of your page or CSS isn't validating, it's a good way to trigger quirks mode in IE. Also, as I've mentioned before, IE has some well-documented wonks, and there are individuals and third parties who have created tools that exploit those wonks to determine if IE is running in quirks mode.

I've found this little JavaScript bookmarklet from David Dorward quite valuable in determining which mode IE is in (and all other browsers, which can run in quirks mode too, but don't usually display your CSS so radically different as IE does). Just drag the **QorSMode** link to your bookmarklet bar in all your testing browsers: `http://dorward.me.uk/www/bookmarklets/qors/`.

The first way to avoid quirks mode is to make sure your DOCTTYPE is valid and correct. If IE doesn't recognize the DOCTYPE (or if you have huge conflicts, such as you have an XHTML DOCTYPE but use all-cap HTML 4.0 tags in your markup), IE will default into quirks mode, and from there on out, who knows what you'll get in IE.

My template stopped centering in IE!

The most obvious thing that happens when IE goes into quirks mode is that IE will stop centering your layout in the window properly if your CSS is using the: `margin: 0 auto;` technique. If this happens, immediately fix all the validation errors in your page. Another major, obvious item is to note if your `div` layers with borders and padding are sized differently between browsers. If IE is running in quirks mode, it will incorrectly render the **box model** (we'll learn more about this in the next section), which is quite noticeable between FireFox and IE if you're using borders and padding in your `divs`. This can also cause problems with font size rendering in your template. Your fonts may appear larger than expected.

Another item to keep track of is to make sure you don't have anything that will generate any text or code above your `DOCTYPE`.

FireFox will read your page until it hits a valid `DOCTYPE` and then proceed from there, but IE will just break and go into quirks mode.

Fixing CSS across browsers

If you've been following our *debug->validate* method described in this chapter, then for all intents and purposes, your layout should look pretty spot-on between both the browsers.

Box model issues

In the event that there is a visual discrepancy between FireFox and IE, in most cases it's a box model issue arising, because you're running in quirks mode in IE. Generally, box model hacks apply to pre IE 6 browsers (IE 5.x) and IE6 if it's running in quirks mode. Again, running in quirks mode is to be preferably avoided, thus eliminating most of these issues. If your markup and CSS are validating (which means you shouldn't be triggering quirks mode in IE, but I've had people swear to me that their page validated in spite of quirks mode being activated), you might rather live with it than try to sleuth what's causing quirks mode to activate.

Basically, IE 5.x and IE6 quirks mode don't properly interpret the box model standard and, thus, "squish" your borders and padding inside your box's width, instead of adding to the width as the W3C standard recommends.

However, IE does properly add margins. This means that if you've got a `div` set to 50 pixels wide, with a 5 pixel border, 5 pixels of padding, and 10 pixels of margin, in FireFox, your `div` is actually going to be 60 pixels wide with 10 pixels of margin around it, taking up a total space of 70 pixels.

In quirks mode IE, your box is kept at 50 pixles wide (meaning it's probably taller than your FirFox `div`, because the text inside is having to wrap at 40 pixels), yet it does have 10 pixels of margin around it. You can quickly see how even a one pixel border, some padding, and a margin can start to make a big difference in layout between IE and FireFox!

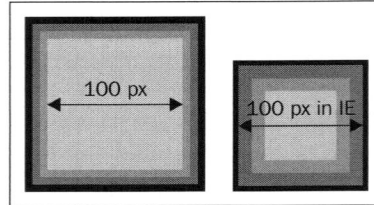

Everything is relative

Most Windows users are still predominately using IE, though Firefox and other browsers are now gaining. When it comes to validating and debugging for IE, I find that as long as I stay in strict mode and do not fall into quirks mode, I don't have too many issues with box model rendering. Occasionally, I still notice that relative CSS values, such as `%` or `.ems`, render a little differently, but that's not a box model issue, so much as an issue with how the two browser engines interpret, say 20% to be in pixels. Even so, as long as your layout doesn't look weird, it's generally OK if your template's container `div`s are a hair wider in one browser than in the other. If you're using relative values to measure everything out, your layout placement will stay intact.

What are the major browsers? According to W3schools, at the time of this writing, IE6 and IE7 together make up a little over half of the total users. Firefox comes in second. Use this link to keep up on browsing trends: `http://www.w3schools.com/browsers/browsers_stats.asp`.

As mentioned at the beginning of this chapter, you still need to look and make sure your site is rendering properly in as many browsers as you have access to. As a bonus, if you have access to multiple platforms (such as Linux or Mac, if you're on a PC), it's good to check and see how popular browsers who have distributions for those OSs look on them too.

If you're using valid markup, you'll be pleasantly surprised to find out that your site looks great in all sorts of browsers and platforms. Occasionally, if you run into a situation where something doesn't look right, you can decide if that browser is critical to your users and if you'd like to fix it.

To hack or not to hack

If for some reason, you feel you know what you're getting into and have intentionally used markup syntax that's triggering quirks mode in IE (or you just can't figure out the reason, or maybe your client insists on designing for IE5.x for Windows), then it's time for some hacks.

The cleanest hack for IE 6 is the `!important` hack. I like it because it lets CSS still render as valid. However, you should note: the `!important` value is valid syntax and meant to be used as an accessibility feature of CSS. It's not a value that was ever meant to affect design.

The fact that IE 6 does not recognize it is a bug, and though it's very simple and easy to implement, it's not recommended to be used liberally as a design fix. The understanding is that, eventually, IE will fix this bug so that it adheres to accessibility standards and then your hack will no longer work (especially if IE doesn't change anything about how it runs in quirks mode).

Remember: All CSS hacks rely on exploiting various bugs in IE to some extent and may or may not continue to work with future service patches and upgrades to IE.

To implement the `!important` hack, take the `width`, `height`, `margin`, or `padding` property that has the discrepancy in it and copy-paste a duplicate below the first property. Place the value that looks best in FireFox first, and add the `!important` value after it. Then, place the value in the duplicate property that looks best in IE below the first property. You should have something that looks like this:

```
.classRule{
    height: 100px !important;
    height: 98px;
}
```

FireFox and all other browsers will read the value with the `!important` value after it as if it were the last value in the rule. IE ignores the `!important` value and thus regular-old cascading kicks in, so it reads the actual last property value in the rule.

Other IE hacks include using the star selector bug hack (*) and the underscore hack (_). Both hacks work on the same general principle as the `!important` hack does, that IE does or doesn't recognize something that all the other browsers do or don't recognize themselves. You can find out more about the underscore hack from WellStyled.com: `http://wellstyled.com/css-underscore-hack.html`. A good overview of the star selector bug along with best ways to select a hack can be found here at sitepoint.com: `http://reference.sitepoint.com/css/workaroundsfilters`.

Be aware, those last two hacks will show up as validation errors in your CSS. Plus, the star and underscore hacks are rumored to no longer be viable in IE7. (Ahh, see! Fixing those bugs!) You must choose to use these three hacks at your discretion.

Out-of-the-box-model thinking

Your best bet is, again, to not use hacks. This is achieved in a couple of ways. First, you can break up your XHTML markup a little more. That means, for example, instead of having one div layer:

```
<div id="leftSide">...</div>
```

Having it with the assigned rule:

```
#leftSide{
width: 200px;
border: 2px;
padding: 10px;
}
```

Which is clearly going to give you problems in quirks mode in IE, because the div will stay at 200 pixels wide and squish your border and padding inside it. It would be better to tuck an extra div or other XHTML element inside the leftSide id, like so:

```
<div id="leftSide"><div>...</div></div>
```

Then, you can control the width and borders much more accurately using CSS that looks like this:

```
#leftSide{
width: 200px;
}

#leftSide div{
border: 2px;
padding: 10px;
}
```

Using a fix like this, your div will always be 200 pixels wide, despite the border and padding, in all the browsers, regardless of the browser running in quirks mode or not. Plus, your XHTML markup and CSS stays valid.

Container divs

I find that working with CSS and XHTML markup like this also keeps you from getting into other trouble. Let's say we "do the math" to figure out our column widths and margins, but then, either forget to account for borders and padding in the design or maybe just decide to add them later. In a browser like FireFox, a miscalculation or late addition like that will throw columns off, especially if their containing div is set to an exact width. This results in ugly, stacked columns. As you noted in *Chapter 2*, when we built the template mockup, I like to use clean containing divs to only control placement, width, and margins. Then, I let inner divs (which will, by default, expand to the width of the containing div) take on borders, padding, and other visual stylings. This is a good way to get your math right and keep it right, no matter what design additions may come later.

Style for IE separately with conditional comments

Your final alternative to using CSS hacks is to create two stylesheets for your template—one for general browser use and one for the IE browsers—and then IE will call in it's own style sheet.

This isn't as bad as it seems. The bulk of your CSS can stay in your main CSS file. You'll then call in this specific IE stylesheet file below your main CSS file, which will load additionally, only if the browser is IE.

In the IE stylesheet, you'll duplicate the rules and correct the properties that were not looking correct in FireFox. Because this stylesheet will load in underneath your main stylesheet, any duplicated rules will overwrite the original rules in your first stylesheet. The result is CSS styling that's perfect in FireFox and IE. However, if you run the CSS validator in IE, it will alert you to the double rules.

In your `index.php` template file, inside your `<header>` tags, add this code after your full stylesheet call:

```
...
<!--[if IE]>
    <link rel="stylesheet" type="text/css" href="ie-fix.css"
                        media="screen, projection" />
<![endif]-->
...
```

More about conditional comments: Yes it is. In the past, your best bet to loading in the proper stylesheet would have been using a server-side script to detect the browser with something such as PHP. You could use a JavaScript as well, but if someone had JavaScript disabled in his/her browser, it wouldn't work. Not everyone can be a PHP whiz; hence, I advocate this conditional comment method for loading in your two stylesheets with minimal hassle. This method is also best for keeping your two stylesheets as simple as possible (having a main one, then one with IE fixes), but you can apply all sorts of control to the conditional comment in the previous code, giving you quite a bit of power in how you dole out your CSS. For instance, you can specify what version of IE to check for: `IE5`, `IE6`, or `IE7`. You can also inverse the condition and only load in the CSS if the browser is not IE, by placing another exclamation point (`!`) in front of the IE. For example, `<!--[if !IE]> ...<![endif]>`. Learn more about this conditional CSS tag at `http://www.quirksmode.org/css/condcom.html`.

Also, please note that while I advocate using the `@import` method for bringing in stylesheets, that method will not work within the `<![if IE]>` CSS check. Use the standard link import tags that are used in this `include` method above.

One last CSS trouble-shooting technique: The best way to quickly get a handle on a rule that's gone awry is to set a border or general background color to it. You'll notice, I did this in *Chapter 2* to the initial layout. You can also use the **CSS | View Style Information** and the **Outline** tools in the Web Developer Toolbar plugin for Firefox to aid you in this. If you amend your CSS file, I suggest making the color something obvious and not part of your color scheme. Often times, using this technique will reveal quite unexpected results, such as showing that a `div` was inadvertently set somehow to just 500 wide instead of 500px wide or, perhaps, that another `div` is pushing against it in a way you didn't realize. It will quickly bring to your attention all the actual issues affecting your object's box model that need to be fixed to get your layout back in line.

The road to validation

You'll want to always validate your XHTML first. This is just as well, since W3C's CSS validator won't even look at your CSS if your XHTML isn't valid.

XHTML validation

Go to `http://validator.w3.org/`, and if your file is on a server, you can just enter in the URL address to it. If you're working locally—as I am from MAMP—from your browser, you'll need to use **Save Page As** and save an HTML file of your template's Joomla 1.5 output and upload that full HTML file output to the validator using the provided upload field. The following screenshot shows the initial result of my XHTML validation:

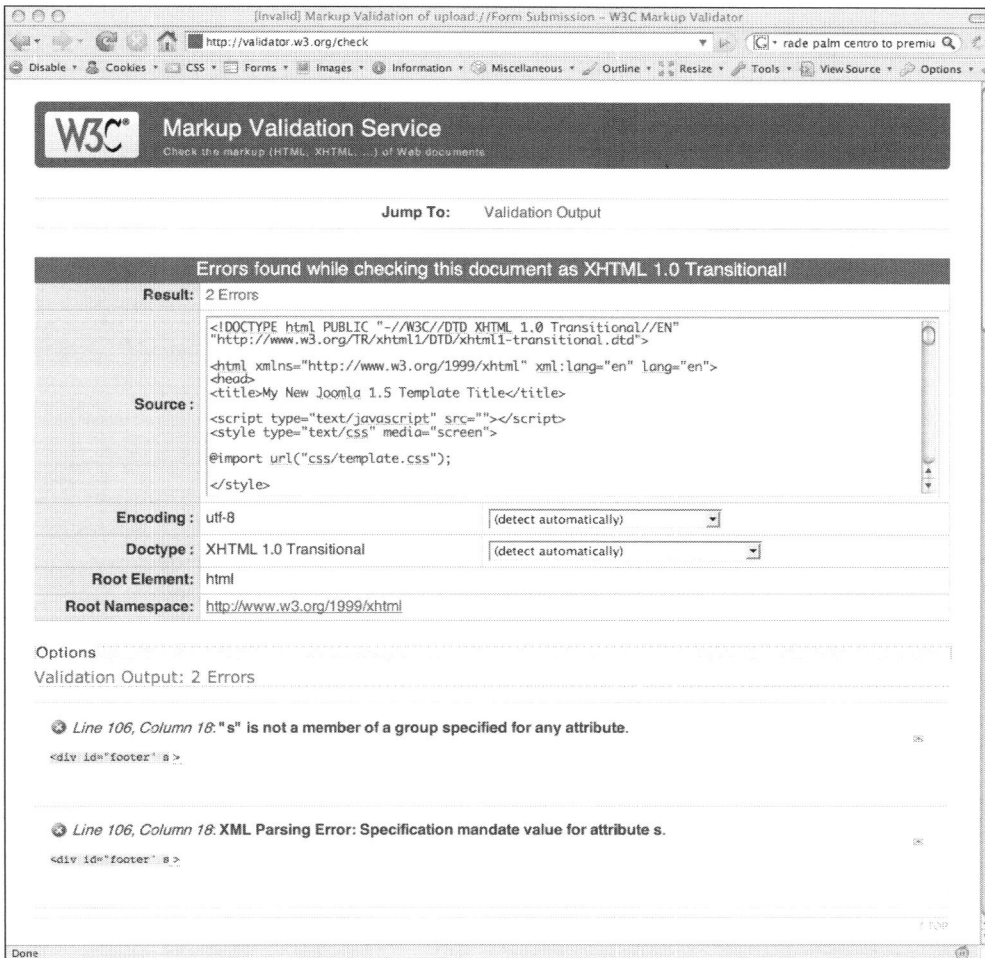

In our validator results above, you can see we have a typo in one of our `divs` (looks like an odd `s` got in there somehow), and we have an image tag that doesn't have the proper closing / in it. Wherever possible, you'll note the validator tries to tell us how to fix the error. Whenever a recommendation is made, go ahead and implement it.

We'll need to fix those two errors and run the validation again to make sure we're now validating. Don't just think you can fix the errors listed and move on without validating again. Occasionally, an error will be so grievous that it will block other errors from being picked up until it's fixed. Always *validate -> fix -> validate*, until you get a happy green bar telling you that you're good to move on.

Where's my error? The validator tells us what line the offensive code appears in, which is the reason we love HTML editors that display the line number to the left in our **Code** view. However, once your template is pulling in content from Joomla 1.5, the line the offense appears in is not necessarily the same code line in your specific template anymore. So where's the error? Well, you have to know your template files enough to recognize where the error might be. Once I know about where the error might be, I work around it by copying some unique text from the error (in my case: s>). You can also use text from an `alt` or `id` tag within the reported object. Then, use the **Find** option in your HTML editor to directly locate the error.

Ideally, when you run your XHTML through the validator, you'll get a screen with a green bar that says **This document was successfully checked as XHTML 1.0 Transitional!**.

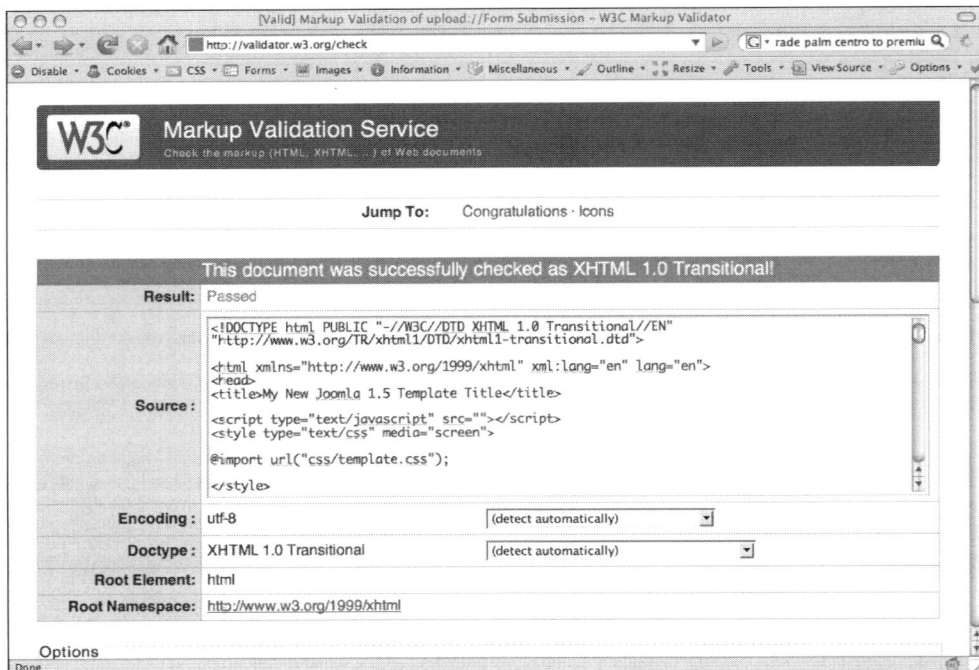

You can then move on to checking your CSS.

CSS validation

Open up another tab in your browser and go to `http://jigsaw.w3.org/css-validator/`. Again, same deal. If you're working off a server, then just enter the address of your CSS file on the development site and check the results. Otherwise, you'll have to use the **By File Upload** tab and upload a copy of your CSS file.

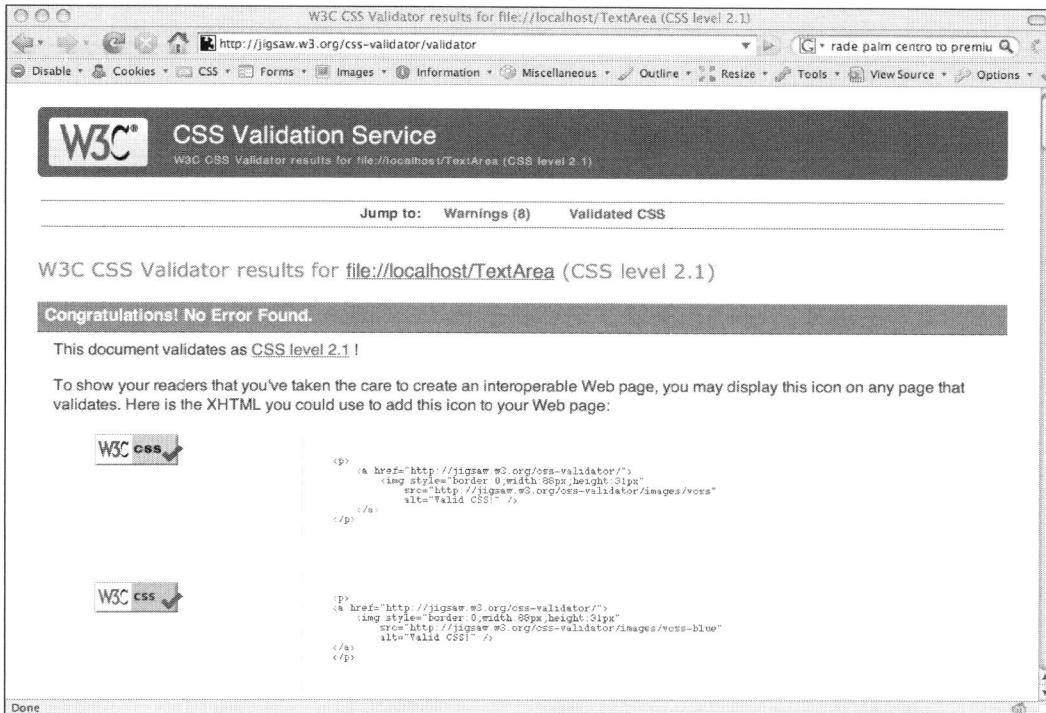

Here, you'll get to see another screen with a green bar that says **Congratulations! No Error Found.**.

If you don't get the green bar, the validator will display the offending error and again offer suggestions on how to fix it. The CSS validator will also show you the line of code the offense takes place on. This is handy, as your stylesheet is not affected by the Joomla 1.5 output, so you can go right to the line mentioned and make the suggested fix.

Here's an example of what the validator looks like if it finds errors:

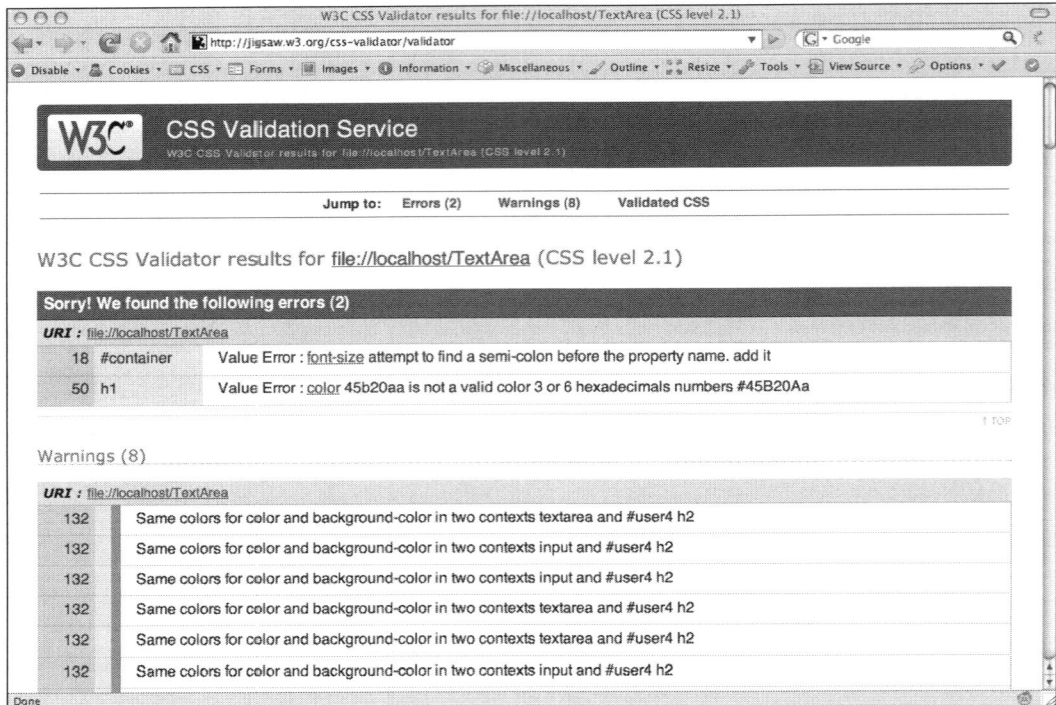

The line numbers are listed to the left of the errors and warnings.

Advanced validation

Perhaps, you've discovered (because you are talented indeed and would find something like this) that your XHTML and CSS validates, yet somehow something is still wrong with your layout. Or maybe, you're using some special JavaScripts to handle certain aspects or features of your template. W3C's XHTML and CSS tools won't validate JavaScript. If you find yourself in this situation, you're going to have to dig a little deeper to get to the root of the problem and/or make sure all aspects (such as JavaScripts) of your template's files are valid.

FireFox's JavaScript/Error Console

You can use FireFox's JavaScript/Error Console (called the JavaScript Console in 1.x and Error Console in 2.x and 3.x) to debug and validate any JavaScripts your template is using. Go to **Tools | Error Console** in your browser to activate it. You can also activate it by typing `javascript:` into your address bar and hitting *Enter* in your keyboard.

You will be pleasantly surprised to find out that the console will also spit out several warnings and errors for CSS rules that the W3C's validators probably didn't tell you about. The Error Console does hold a log of all errors it encounters for all pages you've looked at. Therefore, the best way to proceed with the Error console is to first hit **Clear** and then reload your page, to be sure you're only looking at current bugs and issues for that specific page. Here is an example of an error and warnings the console found:

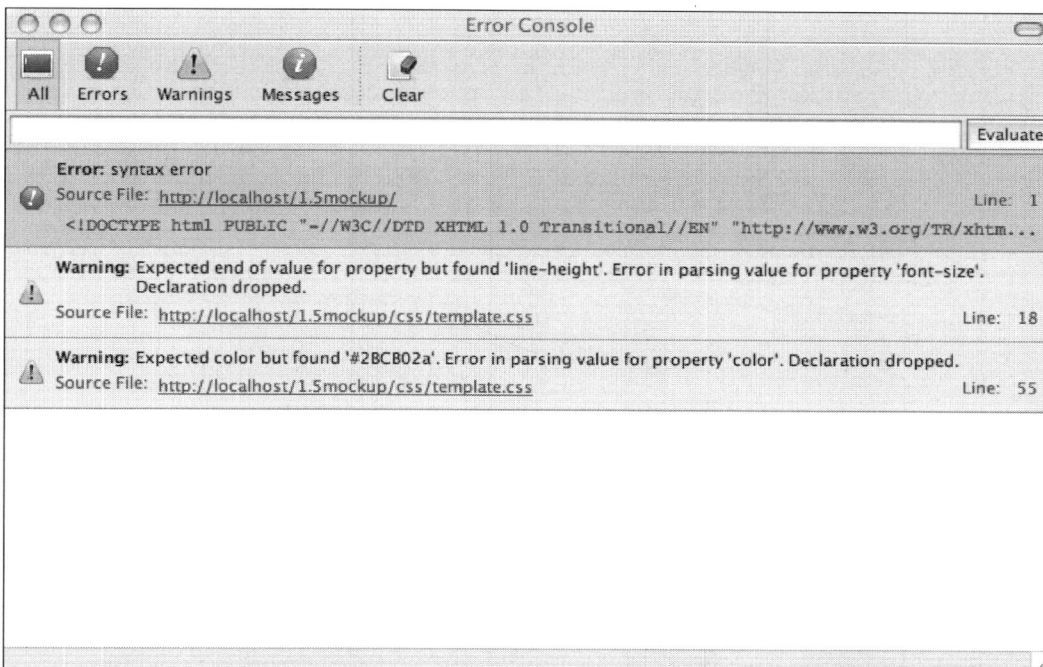

Again, the Error Console will let you know what file and line the offending code is on, so you can go right to it and make the suggested fix. In the previous screenshot, it looks like the console is notifiying me of the same issues that the CSS validator notified me of as well.

The Web Developer Toolbar

I've mentioned this tool bar a few times already. This is a great extension that adds a tool bar to your Firefox browser. The extension is also available for the Seamonkey Suite and the new Flock browser, both of which, like Firefox, are powered by the open source code of Mozilla.

Get it from here: `http://chrispederick.com/work/web-developer/`.

The tool bar lets you link directly to the DOM browsers and Error Consoles, W3C XHTML and CSS validation tools, toggle and view your CSS output in various ways, as well as lets you view and manipulate a myriad of information your site page is outputting on-the-fly. The uses of this tool bar are endless. Every time I'm developing a design, I find some feature, I'd never previously used, useful.

Validating CSS using the Web Developer Toolbar: The Web Developer Toolbar s default is for CSS2. If you're using parameters not introduced until CSS 2.1, or even CSS3, you'll want to be sure to update your Web Developer Options panel. In Firefox, go to **Tools** | **Web Developer** | **Options** | **Options**. Select the **Tools** entry from the left, and in the list of URLs on the right, edit this URL:

```
http://jigsaw.w3.org/css-validator/validator?profile=
css2&warning=2&uri=
```

To read as:

```
http://jigsaw.w3.org/css-validator/validator?profile=
css21&warning=2&uri=
```

You can see that the only difference between two URLs is that `css2` has been changed to `css21`. You can even change `css2` to `css3`.

For more information on resetting this default, see: `http://portal.hrpr.com/2007/09/20/css-validation`.

The following screenshot shows the ruler tool in the Web Developer Toolbar. Handy in that it let's you figure out exactly how many pixels wide to make a CSS property

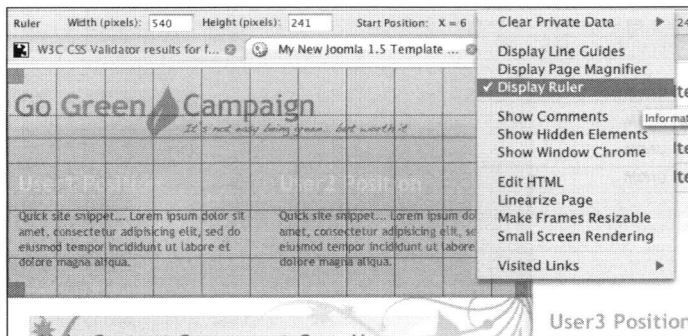

FireBug

A more robust tool is Joe Hewitt's FireBug extension for FireFox (there's a Firebug Lite version for Internet Explorer, Safari, and Opera): `http://www.getfirebug.com/`.

This extension is a powerhouse when combined with the features of the Web Developer Toolbar. Even on its own, it will find all sorts of items to debug — XHTML, CSS, JavaScript, and even little "wierdo" tidbit things happening to your DOM — on-the-fly. There's a variety of fun inspectors in this extension, and just about all of them are invaluable.

Linux and Firebug: According to *Firebug FAQ* (`http://www.getfirebug.com/faq.html`):

> *Firebug does work on Linux, but some distributions don't compile Mozilla correctly, and it is missing the components that Firebug depends on. Even more common is the case of individual Linux users compiling their own Firefox binaries incorrectly.*

Once you have Firebug installed into your browser, you can turn it off and on by hitting *F12* or going to **View | Firebug**. The following screenshot shows FireBug at work in a bottom pane of the browser:

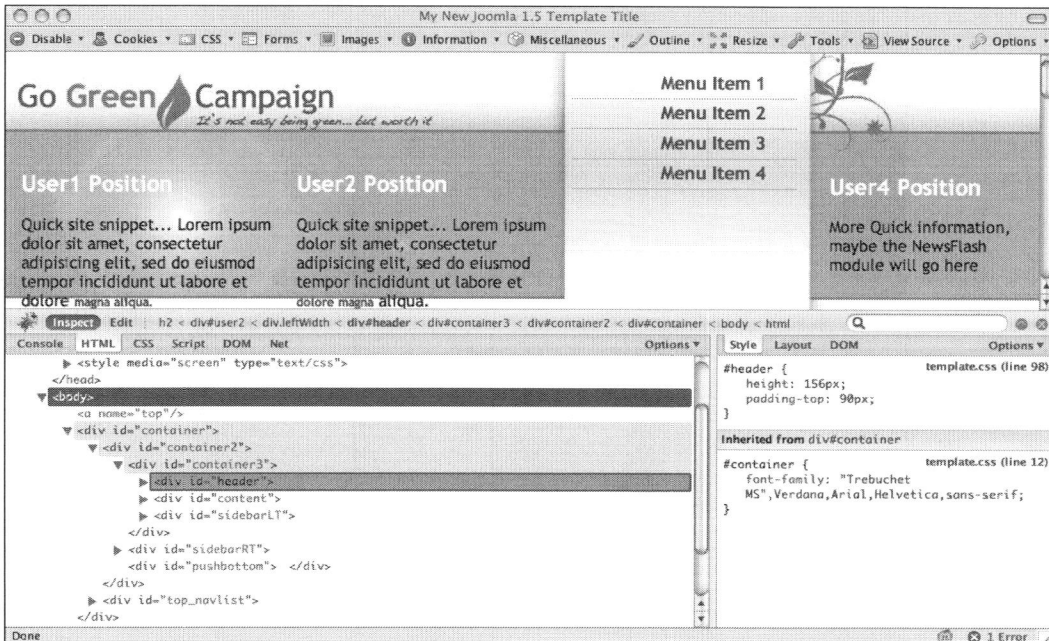

My favorite Firebug features are the options for reviewing HTML, CSS, and the DOM. Firebug will show you your box models and let you see the measurements of each ledge. Plus, the latest version of Firebug lets you make edits on-the-fly, to easily experiment with different fixes before committing them to your actual document (there are features that let you do this using the Web Developer Toolbar as well, but as you can see in the previous screenshot, I find the Firebug interface more in-depth).

DOM? I've mentioned DOM a few times in this book. Learning about the Document Object Model can really enhance your understanding of your XHTML for Joomla 1.5 templates (or any web page you design) as well as help you better understand how to effectively structure your CSS rules and write cleaner, accurate JavaScripts. Find out more from the W3Cschools: `http://w3schools.com/htmldom/default.asp`.

Checking your work in Internet Explorer

OK, remembering that you'll need to check your work in all browsers, at some point you're going to switch over and check everything out in various versions of Internet Explorer. Here are a few tools I've found useful:

Run multiple versions of IE

As much as I would love to stop supporting IE6, I have quite a few clients who just won't move up to IE7. I also have clients who've been in IE8 as a beta for quite some time already. Worse, each version of IE6, IE7, and IE8 does something completely unique and special with different CSS parameters, depending on if it's running in standard or quirks mode. Worse still, Microsoft seems to insist that you only have one IE browser on your computer system.

To get all three versions on my machine, I use TredoSoft's Multiple IE tool to install IE6. I then have IE8 as my "official IE install" and use its "compatibility view" to test for IE7.

I m on Mac with Windows XP installed on Parallels. I don't know if this install runs on Vista yet. Get Multiple IE from `http://tredosoft.com/Multiple_IE`.

IE Developer Toolbar

Although going through the methods in this chapter with the W3C validation tools and Firefox extensions will suffice, IE has a Developer Toolbar that gives you very similar access to your DOM, CSS, JavaScript, and a few other options as FireFox's Web Developer Toolbar. Sometimes it's useful (if not interesting) to be able to poke through the details on both the browsers. You can get the tool bar from Microsoft's site. You can just search in Google for "IE Developer Toolbar"; however, here is the URL: `http://www.microsoft.com/downloads/details.aspx?familyid=e59c3964-672d-4511-bb3e-2d5e1db91038&displaylang=en`.

Don't forget about the QorSMode bookmarklet

I mentioned this great little JavaScript bookmarklet earlier in this chapter. You can use it in all your testing browsers to see if you're in quirks or standards mode. `http://dorward.me.uk/www/bookmarklets/qors/`.

Extra credit: Optimizing for text and mobile browsers

If you want a better understanding of how text-only browsers or some users on mobile devices are viewing your site (not including the new iPhone or iPod Touch and similar graphical interface mobile browsers), you can use Google's mobile viewing tool to give you an idea. This may help you visualize how to better arrange your site semantically for users in these categories.

To use this Google tool, type the following into your browser:

`http://www.google.com/gwt/n?u=http://yoursitegoeshere.com`

You'll now be able to see how your complete site looks without CSS styling. You can even turn off images. Use this to think about if your Joomla 1.5 content is loading in logically and in the order of importance you prefer for your viewers. Also keep in mind, this is very similar to how a search engine bot will crawl your page from top to bottom, and thus the order in which the content will be indexed.

What about the new Mobile Safari browser?

The good news about your site and iPhone/iPod Touch users is that Mobile Safari (the mobile web browser that Apple products use) is graphical. This means the browser seems to be able to take snapshots of your site fully rendered and shrink them down into the mobile browser, allowing a user to zoom in and out on the content.

Mobile Safari attempts to be standards compliant and, apparently, does a pretty good job of it. If you've followed this book's guidance on creating W3C standards compliant XHTML markup and CSS in the creation of your template, your Joomla 1.5 site will most likely show up stunningly on an iPhone or iPod touch. The only major drawback I've seen in the Mobile Safari browser is the lack of Flash support, which is tough if your site has (or relies on) Flash content (this includes embedded YouTube, Google Video, or Jumpcut clips).

Want more info on designing for mobile devices? A List apart (as always) has some great info on designing for devices including the iPhone: `http://www.alistapart.com/articles/putyourcontentinmypocket`.

Interested in Mobile Safari? Check out this great O'Reilly Digital ShortCut by August Trometer: *Optimizing Your Website for Mobile Safari: Ensuring Your Website Works on the iPhone and iPod touch (Digital ShortCut)*. It's a digital PDF you can purchase and download from inFormIt.com: `http://www.informit.com/store/product.aspx?isbn=0321544013`.

Summary

In this chapter we reviewed the basic process to debugging and validating your template's XHTML mark up, `jdoc` tags, PHP code, and CSS. You learned how to use the W3C's XHTML and CSS validation tools. We further explored using FireFox as a valuable development tool by using its Error Console and available extensions such as the Web Developer Toolbar and Firebug.

Next, it's time to package up your design, test it, and share it with the world!

5
Your Template in Action

Now that we've got our template designed, styled, and looking great, we just have one last thing to do. It's time to share your template with your client, friends, and/or the rest of the Joomla! community.

In this chapter, we'll discuss how to properly set up your template's `templateDetails.xml` so that it installs your template into Joomla! correctly. We'll then discuss compressing your template files into the ZIP file format and running some test installations of your template package in Joomla's Administration panel.

Pay attention to the details

They don't call it the `templateDetails` file for nothing! This is where all you micro-detail-oriented types will shine. Unfortunately, I possess no detail inclinations whatsoever. The first few templates I made took several rounds of testing, as they would not install and deploy properly because I was sloppy with this file. If you're a big picture person like me, there's hope. I'll show you my tips and tricks for pulling this file together, but your first line of defense is simply to pay attention and watch what you're doing when you copy-paste over those file names.

A picture's worth a thousand words

Before we begin wrapping up our template package, we'll need one more asset—the template's preview thumbnail. You'll want to capture a screenshot of your final layout and save it to be 150 pixels high by 206 pixels wide. Why, you ask. Well, that's what everyone else seems to be doing in their template packages. Seriously, while I can't find evidence that Joomla! has any restriction on the height and width size of your thumbnail, the display panel does squish large images down and stretch small images up to fit to 206 pixels wide by 150 pixels high. You might as well make your image to those proportions so you know it won't be distorted.

You don't have to stress out if you've taken a screenshot that doesn't want to fit perfectly to 206x150. Just get it close (but not smaller) and test it. It should look good and in proportion when you roll over it in the Administration panel.

Time for action: **Create the thumbnail**

Let's create our thumbnail and make sure it displays in the Administration panel's **Extensions | Theme Manager**

Create your thumbnail in your favorite image editor, save it to about 206x150 pixels, and place your image in your template's root directory, ensuring that it is named exactly `template_thumbnail.png`. Here is what our template's thumbnail looks like:

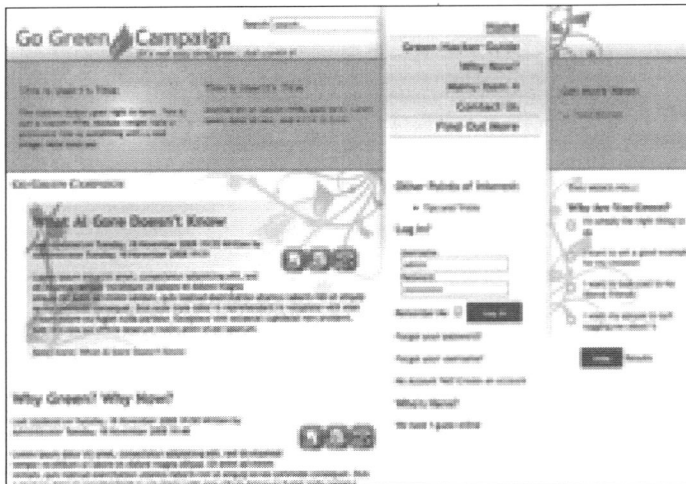

Joomla! offers previews of templates using the `template_thumbnail.png`. It's in your best interest to take advantage of that. Even though this file is touted as a "core Joomla! template file", if you don't add a thumbnail to your template's directory, as long as your `templateDetails.xml` file corresponds and doesn't have it listed, your template will still install.

Joomla! will display a **No preview available** rollover. This simply looks unprofessional. Plus, as most people will know what the template they want to activate looks like, and might not remember its name, having the `template_thumbnail.png` preview set up will help them out. Here's what not having a thumbnail will look like in the **Template Manager**:

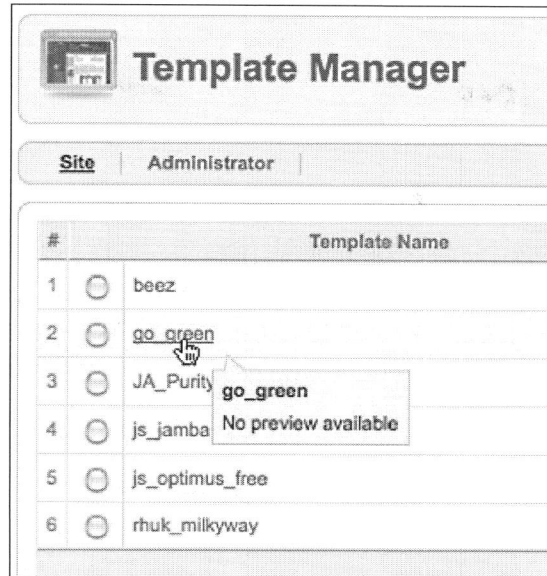

Template packaging basics

In a nutshell, there's not that much involved in getting your new template together and ready for the world. By using the default template requirements discussed in *Chapter 3* as our "base" for file reference and following good testing and validation standards, we already pretty much have a solid Joomla! 1.5 template. The next big step is making sure our `templateDetails.xml` file accurately describes and matches our template's root directory structure and we're good to go.

To make sure your template is ready to go public, run through the following steps before packaging it up:

1. Remove all unnecessary files hanging out in your template's root folder. As I work on a template, I often back up versions of my `index.php` file by renaming them with something like `index-08-12-02-v1.php` and so on. This is for quick and easy reference of test code or if I screw up and need to roll back and start over. But those backup files must be cleared out before you package up. Be sure that only the files required to run the template are left in your root directory. Don't forget to view your template one more time after deleting files to ensure that you didn't accidentally delete a file your template uses.

2. Open up the `templateDetails.xml` sheet and make sure that all the information contained in it is accurate. I had you fill parts of this in the beginning of *Chapter 3*, when we were setting up our development template directory, but I'll review in detail all the parts to fill out next.

3. ZIP it up and put it out there! Get some feedback and install it in your client's installation of Joomla!. Upload it to your own web site or to your favorite user group. The choice is yours.

The templateDetails.xml file

We very briefly discussed this in *Chapter 3*, just to get our development going, but let's review what kind of information is required in the `templateDetails.xml` file.

Quick XML syntax overview

First off, let me just point out that XML is becoming a very common file format that even most frontend web designers are finding they have to deal with more and more. If you're totally new to XML, I can't possibly go into all the details of getting started with it, but at its core, it's pretty simple. In fact, if you're all brushed up on your XHTML syntax, you're more than half way there. This is because XHTML is essentially HTML that uses XML syntax. (See? That's not so bad.)

Now, XML syntax consists of a file structure, usually called a "tree" or Document Object Model (again, we use this term in XHTML, so not so foreign), that uses all lowercase tags (sometimes referred to as nodes) and all lowercase attribute names. Attribute values must be contained within single or double quotes, like `<tagname attribute="1" .../>`. Also, all tags must close, either as a self-closing tag like `<tagname... />` (similar to an `<img... />` tag in XHTML) or a complete-close tag like `<tagname>...</tagname>`.

From the top

Now, other than the fact that in XML you can have tag names that look nothing like anything you'd place into an XHTML file, this all should seem pretty familiar. So, that's XML in a nutshell (perhaps a sunflower seed shell, but a nutshell, none-the-less). Let's take this `templateDetails.xml` file from the top, the very top:

1. ```
<?xml version="1.0" encoding="utf-8"?>
```

This line will appear in every XML document you encounter or create. The version attribute value may change and the encoding attribute value (which denotes the types of characters the document should display) may not always be `utf-8`, but this line is essential to declaring an XML file. (`utf-8` is a safer way to go, but if you're sure you'll only be using Latin characters, you can change it to `iso-8859-1`.)

2. ```
<!DOCTYPE install PUBLIC "-//Joomla!  1.5//DTD template 1.0//
   EN" "http://dev.Joomla! .org/xml/1.5/template-install.dtd">
```

You don't need to add this line, but it's great that Joomla! took the time to create a **DTD (Document Type Declaration**, that is, DOCTYPE). It's a great way to double-check and validate your `templateDetails.xml` file for any illegal values.

> **What is this DTD business**? This should look familiar, as we used a DOCTYPE line in our `index.php` file. As I mentioned, XHTML "borrows" its syntax from XML. Many HTML/code editors will already help you to ensure your XML file stays well formed. Meaning, you should be able to use your editor's syntax checker and be alerted if your file has any missing tags, mis-matched tags or missing quote marks from attributes.
>
> By adding this DOCTYPE line to your XML file, you can further validate your XML file by making sure it doesn't contain any tag names, attributes, or values that Joomla! doesn't allow in the `templateDetails.xml` file. This DTD works exactly the same way the XHTML 1.0 Transitional DTD DOCTYPE line works in our `index.php` file and is what enabled us to use the W3C's validator on our template. You can use it here too. Simply go to the `http://validator.w3.org/` site we discussed in *Chapter 4* and paste your XML in. Any errors should come right up and let you know how to fix them.
>
> For those of you who don't have a syntax checker in your HTML/code editor, this performs a syntax check as well. If you paste in XML without a DOCTYPE line, the W3C validator will simply check your XML syntax for well formedness.

Descriptive tags

We'll now take a look at what each type of tag in the `templateDetails.xml` file does.

1. First, we start up with the actual XML tree structure. The root node is `<install>`, and if you scroll all the way down to the bottom, you'll find its closing tag `</install>`. It has a couple of key attributes, `version` and `type`:

   `<install version="1.5" type="template">`

   This lets Joomla!'s backend code know that it's a template that's being installed (components, modules, and plugins each have XML files with a similar tag in them) and that the template was designed ideally for Joomla! 1.5.

2. Next up is the `<name>` node:

   `<name>go_green</name>`

   I mentioned in *Chapter 3*, to be careful and enter the name of your template exactly as you named your template's root directory. This node will be used as instructions for Joomla! to create the directory it installs your template into from the final ZIP file. Thus, you must also be sure to not enter a name with characters that would be illegal to use as a directory file name. So, no forward or back slashes, carrots, pipes, stars, quotes, blank spaces, ampersands, exclamation points, or colons!

   > **Remember**: In addition to blank spaces, these characters are bad: `\/:*?!"<>|`. Do not use them in your `name` node.

3. We're now ready for the `<creationDate>` node:

   `<creationDate>12/22/08</creationDate>`

   I've experimented with several different date formats in this node: `2008-12-22`, `December 22, 2008`, and so on—they all seem to validate. Whatever format you prefer, just make sure it makes sense and people can tell when the template was made.

4. Next comes the `<author>` node:

   `<author>Tessa Blakeley Silver</author>`

5. In addition to your name fill out the `<authorEmail>` node, it's nice to add how people can get in touch with you or any support services you have in place if they have questions about the template.

   `<authorEmail>tessa@hyper3media.com</authorEmail>`

6. The `<authorUrl>` tag can be the URL of the site that template is for (if it's a custom design, but most likely it is going to be your personal or company's URL), where people can find out about you and perhaps look at more of your templates and/or other services and products you might offer (use this node as a little free advertising)

   `<authorUrl>http://www.hyper3media.com</authorUrl>`

7. Any copyright information you'd like to include goes into this tag. Generally, you'll place in the year, maybe the month that you made the template, and your or your company's name. You may wish to include "See CreativeCommons License" or "All Rights Reserved" at the end of this if you intend to keep control of the design for whatever reason. If you intend for the template to be completely free to the public, you can just leave this tag empty and include the specific licensing information in the license tag below.

   `<copyright>`© **2008 Tessa Blakeley Silver**`</copyright>`

8. In addition to the copyright, which assigns you as the creator and owner of the template and its design, you'll probably want to fill out the license information—be it a custom license you create that limits the use of the template (especially if you sell it commercially) or a GNU GPL or Creative Commons license. I'll cover copyrights and licensing in more detail in just a few moments.

   `<license>`**Go Green Joomla! 1.5 Template by Tessa Blakeley Silver for Packt Publishing is licensed under a Creative Commons Attribution 3.0 United States License**`</license>`

9. Next, you have the `<version>` tag. Most software and web application/template development is based on a *Change Significance* versioning system, and most tend to use the GNU's two/three digit system of *major.minor.revision*. So, if this is your template's first debut, you may want to put `1.0` in the `<version>` tags. If the template has been changed, had bugs fixed, or is "reincarnated" in any way, you may feel a higher version is appropriate (say, `1.2.8` or `2.0`). Of course, if you feel the template is not finished and is a beta release, you may want to place a sub version like 0.5 (or whichever set of numbers you feel accurately describe the template's current development status).

   `<version>`**1.0**`</version>`

> **More on software versioning**: For more information on understanding and assigning version numbers to your templates, check out Wikipedia: http://en.wikipedia.org/wiki/Software_versioning.

10. Last, you'll want to add a quick description of what the template looks like, any specific purpose it's best suited for and or any other template it's based off of or inspired by.

```
<description>A green, leafy, XHTML 1.0 Transitional, CSS2
Table-less template, best suited for ecologically oriented and
alternative energy sites</description>
```

Copyright and licensing?

In steps 7 and 8 that we just discussed, we entered some basic copyright and licensing information. Most people think these are exclusive; for example: if you copyright a template, that means only you can distribute it and you can't add a GNU GPL for free distribution to it, or if you license it for free distribution, then you can't copyright it. This isn't true. Copyrighting and licensing work hand in hand, even when you're giving it all away freely to the public. First off, an unregistered copyright is generated automatically the instance you create (or perform or publish) your work. You and only you are allowed to license it. (Your decedents can license it too if you register the copyright: `http://www.copyright.gov/register/`). I find it doesn't hurt to fill out the copyright information, as it clarifies you as the clear designer and creator. You can then license and distribute your templates in any way you wish.

You'll find that most Joomla! templates you find for free on the Web use the GNU GPL. If you're not familiar with the GNU GPL, you can learn more about it here: `http://www.gnu.org/copyleft/gpl.html`.

You may wish to do the same thing with your template, if you want it to be freely distributed, available to all, and changeable by all with no permissions necessary, as long as they acknowledge you.

If you've created a completely original design that you intend to sell commercially, or just want to be able to grant permission for any other possible use, you'll want to place the specific copyright information and the name of the person or organization that holds the copyright. Something like © 2008 Your Name, All Rights Reserved is generally recognized as legal with or without any formal copyright filing procedures. You can then leave the license tags empty or enter a quick description and URL address to a full license and distribution agreement that you and your lawyer have come up with.

This book's template has been created for Packt Publishing for educational purposes, and the GNU GPL is more than adequate. Though, as a designer that fell into programming, I feel the text is a bit "software-ish" and "tech-heavy", so I'm going to redistribute the Go Green Campaign template under a more general, public-friendly Creative Commons license: `http://creativecommons.org`.

I'll use the CreativeCommons license tool to assist me in selecting an appropriate license (`http://creativecommons.org/license/`):

I'll, of course, allow sharing of the template and let others "remix" or make modifications, as long as they "share alike", which means derive new templates from this template with proper credit. However, I will prevent it from being sold commercially by another entity (commercial sites are welcome to download it and use it as-is). This means that no one can legally take the template package and offer it for sale or use it in a way that generates income for them without my permission. If they reuse or redesign the package in any other non-commercial way, they're free to do so. They're simply required to give me and Packt Publishing credit where credit is due.

My licensing agreement looks like this: Go Green Joomla! 1.5 Template by Tessa Blakeley Silver for Packt Publishing is licensed under a Creative Commons Attribution 3.0 United States License.

The end result is a license that keeps to the spirit of the GNU GPL, but is much easier to understand. It tells the user up front that it allows sharing, which is important to me for educational purposes and prevents commercial distribution without permission and, by requiring share-alike, encourages a continued friendly Joomla!-esque atmosphere of open source collaboration. It also expressly states the version number of the license, making it very easy for anyone to look up and read in detail.

The Creative Commons site now also offers versions of the GNU /GPL and GNU LGPL (as well as Public domain and BSD licenses) that have been re-written for humans, lawyers, and machines. Ultimately, the choice is yours to pick the license you feel most accurately represents the spirit in which you would like to see your work distributed and shared within your Joomla! community.

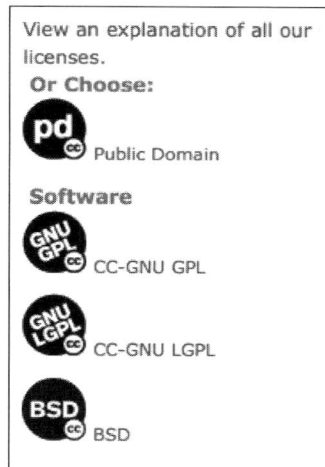

View an explanation of all our licenses.
Or Choose:

pd Public Domain

Software

CC-GNU GPL

CC-GNU LGPL

BSD

File, position, and param tags

We're now ready to look at the filename and position tags in the templateDetails.xml file.

1. First up, the filename tags are wrapped inside a set of parent tags. If you have filename tags that are not wrapped inside the `<files></files>` tags, you'll be creating a corrupted template package.

A quick sample of your files should look something like this:

```
<files>
    <filename>index.html</filename>
    <filename>index.php</filename>
    <filename>css/template.css</filename>
    <filename>css/index.html</filename>
    <filename>params.ini</filename>
    <filename>templateDetails.xml</filename>
    <filename>template_thumbnail.png</filename>
</files>
```

Self reference?

You might think it's odd that you have to include the `templateDetails.xml` file within the `filename` list inside your `templateDetails.xml` file, but you have to do it. So, don't forget.

index.html?

When looking through the default templates that come with your installation of Joomla! 1.5, you'll notice that each directory in the template has an `index.html` file in it. If you open that file, you'll see it's blank. This is a good practice to get into. Some servers have their `.htaccess` set up to display the contents of directoriesxs that do not have an `index.html` file in them. Adding these files is a precaution you can take to make sure that nosy hackers can't snoop through your template files and find a way to exploit your template or Joomla! installation.

2. The same thing goes for the `position` location tags. We added these module position locations in *Chapter 3*, but you need to make sure they're located within `<positions></positions>` tags.

A quick sample of your positions should look like this:

```
<positions>
    <position>left</position>
    <position>right</position>
    <position>top</position>
    <position>breadcrumb</position>
    <position>user1</position>
    <position>user2</position>
    <position>user3</position>
    <position>user4</position>
    <position>user5</position>
    <position>debug</position>
    <position>syndicate</position>
</positions>
```

3. Your files are listed in paths that are relative to the template's root. That means anything in the root is simply listed like so:

```
<filename>index.php</filename>
```

4. And anything that is inside a directory, like images or CSS is listed like so:

```
<filename>css/template.css</filename>
```

You must get every file that is listed in the root, and in each directory listed inside `<filename>` tags, using their relative path.

This unfortunately can mean a lot of tedious clicking on filenames, copy-pasting over into your `templateDetails.xml` file. If your template only has a few files supporting it, this is fine (incentive to keep your template as clean and elegant as possible). However, if you have a lot of files in your template and want to be sure you get them all (rather than packaging up and having an error, only to have to try and figure out what you're missing), you have a few options.

Because I'm comfortable with a little PHP, I wrote my own script that lists files within a single directory. This is not all-encompassing, as, once I drop it in the root of my template and copy-paste my root files, it means I have to update line **5** of the script and point it to each directory within my template: `images`, `css` (and `js` if I use JavaScript toolkits).

Time for action:

1. Here is the script in detail. Line **5** has been highlighted. I usually place this script into the root of my template and name the file as `remove.php` (so it stands out at me and I know I have to remove it prior to packaging; also, this means it won't list in the files when you run the script). This file is available in *Chapter 5*'s code packet called `remove.php`.

```
<h2>Remove this file prior to packaging your template!</h2>

<?php

// change this value to the template directory where files are
                                                    stored.

$dir="images"; //"." = root
if ($dir_list = opendir($dir)){
    if ($dir == "."){
      $dir = "";
    }else{
       $dir = $dir."/";
    }//if/else

    while(($filename = readdir($dir_list)) !== false){
```

```
//makes sure only files and their relative path to the root are
                                                                listed

    if ($filename != ".DS_Store" && $filename != "." && $filename
!= ".." && $filename != "remove.php" && $filename != "css" &&
$filename != "html" && $filename != "images" && $filename !=
"js"){
?>

//the follcwing displays in html so you can copy and paste into
                                    your templateDetails.xml file:
&lt;filename&gt;<?php echo $dir; ?><?php echo $filename;
                                    ?>&lt;/filename&gt;<br/>

<?php
    }//if
    }//while
closedir($dir_list);
}//if
?>
```

2. I then make sure to run the script once on the root by specifying " . " for the $dir variable, and then copy-paste the results into my templateDetials. xml file (being sure to overwrite everything listed in the <files>...</ files> tags if I'm using another template's templateDetails.xml file to help me out!).

3. Now, I repeat this process by changing the $dir="." ; line to first $dir="images"; , then $dir="css"; , and last $dir="js"; if I've created those directories in my template.

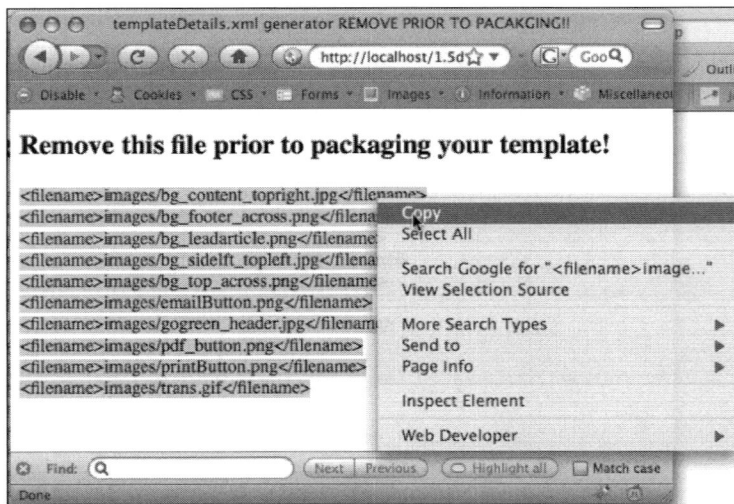

What about the html directory?

Last, we have all the files inside the `html` directory to contend with. While you can use the script in the previous screenshot pointing it to each directory within the `html` directory again, this can get tedious. The point of this filename listing is to get each file that supports your template documented. You can't just stop at a directory that might have more files within it.

Time for action: **Updating the** `templateDetails.xml` **file**

We'll now need to update our `templateDetails.xml` file with all of the Beez template information. Each and every file needs to be properly listed with its correct relative path in order for the template to install correctly. You'll want to take some care in making sure these files are included in their entirety in the `templateDetails.xml` file.

Open up the Beez `templateDetails.xml` file and copy all the filenames and paths that start with `html` into `templateDetails.xml` file.

> **Don't do this**: `<filename>html/com_contact</filename>`. The `com_contact` folder within the `html` folder has two more directories within it and **three** more files per directory! All of those files and their paths must be listed in your `templateDetails.xml` file. Copy the html file listings from the `Beez templateDetails.xml` folder to be certain you've listed all of them.

Param tags

Let's take a look at our action here.

Time for action: **Creating the** `params` **tag options**

We'll cover taking advantage of these tags in *Chapter 9*, but for now, I like to make sure the root tags are there for when you're ready to upgrade the template.

The last thing I like to be sure to add to my `templateDetails.xml` file is to leave the parent tags for `param` options:

```
<params>
</params>
```

While we don't have a `params.ini` file set up or any parameters to specify at this time, it's OK to have the parent tags there. We'll cover extending our Joomla! template with a `params.ini` file and making use of these tags in *Chapter 9*.

Third-party tools: While my script makes things easier for me, it simply might not do so for you. There are some third-party tools that can help you generate your `templateDetails.xml` file. You can search through the extensions link on Joomla!'s site: `http://extensions.Joomla!.org/`. Be sure to check that the tools you try out generate Joomla! 1.5 `templateDetails` files (not just Joomla! 1.0 or Mambo `templateDetails` files).

Joomla! XML: The best tool I've come across so far is called Joomla! XML. Unfortunately (for me), it only runs on Windows (and has run OK on my Mac Parallels XP so far). It has some great features and even remembers your basic info. If you're truly uncomfortable with XML and/or you're going to be creating lots of Joomla! templates, this application is just great. And it's free for private use. The author would appreciate donations if you're using it to generate commercial templates: `http://www.younic.de/Joomla!-template-xml`.

ZIP it up!

We're now ready to ZIP up our template files and test an installation of our template package. "Zipping" is the file compression type Joomla! requires. If you're a Windows PC user, chances are, you're very familiar with zipping files. If you're a Mac user, it's just as easy. As a new Mac user, I was thrilled to discover its built-in support for creating ZIP archives similar to Widows XP (and I assume Vista). Select your template's folder and right-click, or use *Ctrl*+click, to select **Create Archive**.

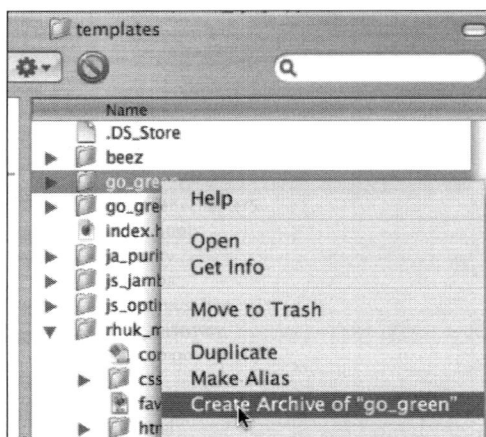

Even if you're working off a server, rather than locally, it's probably best if you download your template's directory and ZIP it up on your local machine. Plus, you'll want to test your install, and most everyone will be uploading your file off their local machine into the Joomla! Administration panel's **Template Manager**.

No way to ZIP?

If you're on an older computer and don't have compression software, you'll have to take a little tour of the Internet to find the very best ZIP solution for you. There are tons of free archiving and compression tools that offer the ZIP format.

So let's start with the obvious. If you don't have any ZIP compression tools, head over to `http://www.stuffit.com/`. You'll find STUFFIT software is available for Mac or PC and lets you compress and expand several different types of formats, including `.zip`. The standard edition is most likely all you'll ever need, and while there's nothing wrong with purchasing good commercial software, you'll have plenty of time to play with the trial version. The trial period for the standard software is 15 days, but you might find that it lasts longer than that (especially if you're patient while the continue trial button loads). If you're on a PC, you also have WinZip as an option: `http://www.winzip.com/`, where again, you're given a trial period that does seem to last longer than the suggested 45 days.

WinZip and STUFFIT are considered "industry standard" software. They've been around for a good while and are stable products that, for under $50, you can't go too wrong with.

Come on, where's the free Open Source stuff? If you must have truly free compression software and are on a PC, there is 7-Zip: `http://www.7-zip.org/`. I've only minimally played around with 7-Zip, but it does create and expand ZIP files, and can even compress in a new format (called 7z) that gets better compression than standard ZIP files. Unfortunately, not too many people are readily using the 7z format yet, and Joomla! can't install any template or extension that isn't in the ZIP format, so make sure you're creating a standard ZIP version of your template when you use it.

Each compression utility has its own interface and procedures for creating a standard .zip file. I'll assume that you have one, or have chosen one from the options discussed, and have made yourself familiar with how to use it. The following screenshot illustrates the files in your template's root directory being zipped into a ZIP file.

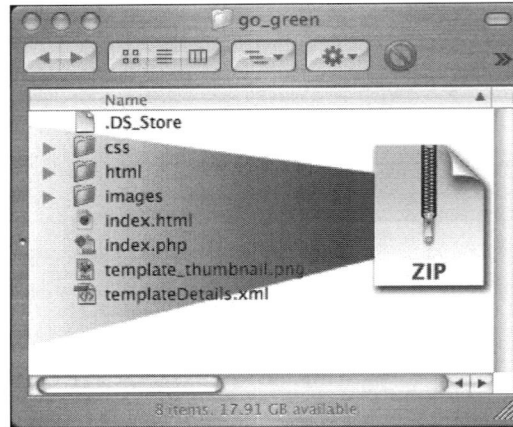

One last test

You're now ready to test the package. Start from scratch. If at all possible, don't install the template back into your sandbox installation (especially if it's on your local machine). If, for some reason, your sandbox is all you have, I recommend you rename your existing development template directory or back it up (so you're sure to be testing your package).

Ideally, you'll want to install your template on a web server installation, preferably the one where the template is going to be used (if it's a custom design for a single client) or under the circumstances you feel your template's users are most likely to use (for example, if you're going to post your template for download on the Web, then test your template on an installation of Joomla!, installed on a shared/virtual hosting provider, which most people use).

Don't assume the ZIP file you made is going to unzip or unpack properly within Joomla! (files have been known to corrupt). Follow the procedure you know your client will be using or the procedure someone finding your template on the Web will perform.

1. If applicable, download the ZIP file from wherever it will be accessible from the Web.

2. In your Joomla! Administrator panel, go to **Extensions | Install / Uninstall**, and follow the steps on the screen to install your template.

3. If you receive a **Successful!** screen, go to **Extensions | Template Manager**, and select the template and make sure it displays properly.

4. If you receive an **Error!** screen, proceed to the next section to read up on possible troubleshooting causes and their solutions.

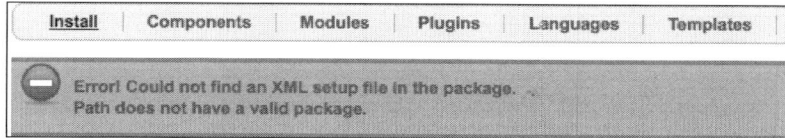

Install	Components	Modules	Plugins	Languages	Templates

Error! Could not find an XML setup file in the package.
Path does not have a valid package.

Troubleshooting installations

The most common problems you'll run into with installation errors are caused by the following:

- An invalid `templateDetails.xml` file. Use the W3C validator (`http://validator.w3.org/`) to check if your syntax and tag/node names are set up properly.

- You listed a file in your `templateDetails.xml` file that doesn't exist in your template's directory (or is misplaced within the directory).

- You gave your template the same name as another template already installed.

- You forgot to add a file to the template's directory that's listed in your `templateDetails.xml` file. This is difficult, as, depending on the file, you'll probably get a "success" screen. You'll need to look through your template carefully to make sure all images, CSS styles, and any JavaScript functions are showing up and executing properly.

Remember, you can't always believe what you see

While the error messages on Joomla's install panel are fairly helpful, not listing a file that's needed will actually show you a success message, although your template will be broken, so you'll need to sleuth out what files are missing. Also, having an invalid XML file will tell you that the `templateDetails.xml` file does not exist—well, it does, but you have to discover why it's not validated.

With the successful installation and testing of your template, you now have an understanding of the entire Joomla! template development process, from conception to packaging.

Get some feedback and track it.

You're not quite done! Great design doesn't happen in a vacuum. If you've developed your template for private use by a client, then you've probably already gone through a rigorous process of feedback and changes during the template's development. But if you're developing a template for commercial sale, free distribution to people, or even just for yourself, you'll want to get some feedback.

How much feedback you require is up to you. You might just want to email a handful of friends and ask them what they think. If you plan to widely distribute your template freely or commercially, you really should offer a way for people to review a demo of template and post comments about it.

At first glance, if you're happy with something, you might not want anyone else's input. Having to hear criticism is hard. However, let me take a moment to digress and introduce you to a scientific term called "emergence". It basically dictates that "we" is smarter than "me". It's the basis behind a lot of things, from how ants form food routes for their colonies to how people in urban areas create neighborhoods niches and why the Web is transforming itself into a huge social network. As far as how this phenomenon is related to feedback, if you have a group of people guess how many jelly beans are in a jar, the average of everyone's answer will be closer to the exact amount than anyone's single guess. Now, design aesthetics are a lot more ambiguous than the correct number of jelly beans in a jar, but using this principle in receiving feedback is still something your template can really take advantage of.

See how people use your template. You'll be surprised with the situations and circumstances they attempt to use it in, which you would have never thought of on your own. After several feedback comments, you'll probably be able to detect patterns: what kind of hosting they're using, what kind of sites (discussed in *Chapter 2*) they are applying it to, and, most importantly, what in the template is working really well for them and what drawbacks are they encountering.

You'll be able to offer version upgrades to your template by being able to see if your template needs any tweaks or additions made to it. More importantly, you'll also see if there's anything in your template that can be parred down, removed, and simplified. Remember: more isn't always better! Just remember to update your `templateDetails.xml` file, especially if you have added and/or deleted any files, images, module positions, and as you'll find out later, parameters.

Summary

In this chapter we reviewed describing our template in the `templateDetails.xml` file and how to package up your finished template into a working ZIP file that anyone should be able to upload into their own Joomla! installation.

Congratulations, you now know about getting a Joomla! template design off that coffee shop napkin and into the world! In the next few chapters, we'll get down to the nitty-gritty of getting things done quickly with our template markup reference and cookbook chapters. We'll cover key design tips and cool "how-tos", such as how to set up dynamic drop-down menus, best practices for integrating Flash, AJAX techniques, useful Joomla! extensions, and more.

6
Joomla! 1.5 Template Reference

Now that you've had some hands-on experience with making templates, you've probably noticed that Joomla! outputs quite a bit of CSS class and id rules. Even if you intend to control much of that output with **module chrome** and **template overrides**, it's helpful to know where to look for and how to set up those overrides.

You can always use your DOM Source Inspector to see what's wrapped around markup that you're currently working with, but clearly, it will be helpful to have a heads-up on what to look for within the DOM as well.

We'll use this chapter to go over jdoc tags for templates, the standard CSS class and id rules that Joomla! outputs, how module and template override files are organized, as well as useful Joomla! PHP code you can use in your template to aid in making it more user-friendly and dynamic. Of course, wherever possible, I'll let you know the relevant Joomla! documentation links to bookmark, to give you in-depth detail and save you a little time searching through the Joomla! documentation site and the Web.

Last, take note that I'll mention how these Joomla! 1.5 items differ in use from a Joomla! 1.0 template, so that those of you looking to update a Joomla! 1.0 template to 1.5 can quickly get a handle on what to update in your templates and what new features to add.

Consider this chapter your "cheat sheet".

Jdoc include tags

I've mentioned a few times that the jdoc include tags are new to Joomla! 1.5 templates. Previously in Joomla! 1.0, more complicated, abstract PHP code, originally created for Mambo, was used. The jdoc tags are much cleaner, visually make sense (no more guessing what attribute values like "-3" mean), and, thus, are much easier to remember.

Site header information tag

This is pretty simple: the tag outputs all the appropriate meta tags and header information that corresponds to your site and each individual page:

```
<jdoc:include type="head" />
```

Joomla! 1.0 to 1.5 conversion

If you're converting a 1.0 template to 1.5, you'll replace this PHP function in your 1.0 template's header with the above jdoc tag:

```
<head>
...
<?php mosShowHead(); ?>
...
```

The component include tag

Wherever you place this include, all component content will appear (from articles to poll results to contact forms, and so on):

```
<jdoc:include type="component" />
```

Joomla! 1.0 to 1.5 conversion

The 1.0 equivalent of this tag is the mosMainBody function. You'll replace this PHP function with the above jdoc include:

```
<?php mosMainBody(); ?>
```

Module position tags

With module tags, we have a few options to work with. So, we can control what modules load into the area, thus assigning their positions as well as what style to output the module content with:

```
<jdoc:include type="modules" name="position" style="styleName" />
```

Module position styles

In the `jdoc include` example above, within the `style` attribute, you can place one of the following six style names to various effect:

Style name	Effect	Sample
none or raw	Modules are displayed in plain text, without titles.	Content
xhtml	Modules are displayed wrapped in a single `<div>` tag, with titles in `<h3>` header tags. (This is preferred for most applications of Joomla.)	`<div class="moduletable">` `<h3>`**Title**`</h3>` **Content** `</div>`
rounded	Modules are displayed wrapped in several `<div>` tags with titles in `<h3>` header tags, allowing for more complex CSS styling, such as the container techniques discussed in detail in Chapter 4 or applying stretchable, rounded corners.	`<div class="module">` `<div>` `<div>` `<div>` `<h3>`**Title**`</h3>` **Content** `</div>` `</div>` `</div>` `</div>`
table	Modules are displayed in a table with a single row column. This is also the default setting. You'll never really need to use it.	`<table class="moduletable" cellpadding="0" cellspacing="0">` `<tbody>` `<tr>` `<th>`**Title**`</th>` `</tr>` `<tr>` `<td>`**Content**`</td>` `</tr>` `</tbody>` `</table>`

Style name	Effect	Sample

horiz	Modules are again displayed in a table with multiple column rows, giving it the effect of being displayed horizontally, rather than vertically like the default.	`<table>`
		`<tbody>`
		`<tr>`
		`<td align="top">`
		`<table cellpadding="0"`
		`cellspacing="0"`
		`class="moduletable">`
		`<tbody>`
		`<tr>`
		`<th`
		`valign="top">Title</th>`
		`</tr>`
		`<tr>`
		`<td>`**Content**`</td>`
		`</tr>`
		`</tbody>`
		`</table>`
		`</td>`
		`<!--next table cell`
		`starts-`
		`->`
		`<td align="top">`
		`<table cellpadding="0"`
		`cellspacing="0"`
		`class="moduletable">`
		`<tbody>`
		`<tr>`
		`<th`
		`valign="top">Title</th>`
		`</tr>`
		`<tr>`
		`<td>`**Content**`</td>`
		`</tr>`
		`</tbody>`
		`</table>`
		`</td>`
		`</tr>`
		`</tbody>`
		`</table>`

outline	This is used to preview modules and help aid in module position names.	In your Administration panel, go to **Extenstions | Template Manager | yourTemplate | Preview** for a sample of this output.

Joomla! 1.0 to 1.5

For those of you trying to update a 1.0 template, replace your old
mosLoadModules tag:

```
<?php mosLoadModules ( 'modName', styleNumber); ?>
```

With the new jdoc include:

```
<jdoc:include type="modules" name="positionName" style="styleName" />
```

Where modName is located in your mosLoadModule tag. Be sure to replace it with the
module postionName in your jdoc include tag, and where your styleNumber was
in your mosLoadModule tag, replace it with the corresponding styleName in your
jdoc include tag. The following will help you match up and select the appropriate
style name:

- table = 0 (this still is the default)
- horiz = 1
- none (or raw) = -1
- xhtml = -2
- rounded = -3

Menu output options

Very similar to 1.0, Joomla! 1.5 does need a little special attention to menu output.
Yes, menus are modules, and yes, even though you set your module position to
output rounded or xhtml, you might want to log in to your admin panel and
make sure that your menus are outputting the XHTML markup you desire.

The default for Joomla! 1.5 is now **List**, which will also display nested lists for
multi-level menu items (the **Extend** extension is no longer needed). However, if
you're upgrading a 1.0 template and need the menu to output in a horizontal or
vertical table, you'll need to assign the correct XHTML output in the menu's
Module Manager.

Go to **Extensions | Module Manager** and select the relevant menu item.

On the far right, select the appropriate **Menu Style** from the drop-down list. Your choices are **List, Legacy - Vertical, Legacy - Horizontal**, and **Legacy - Flat List** (note: this won't include nested lists; not recommended). The following screenshot illustrates selecting the menu style.

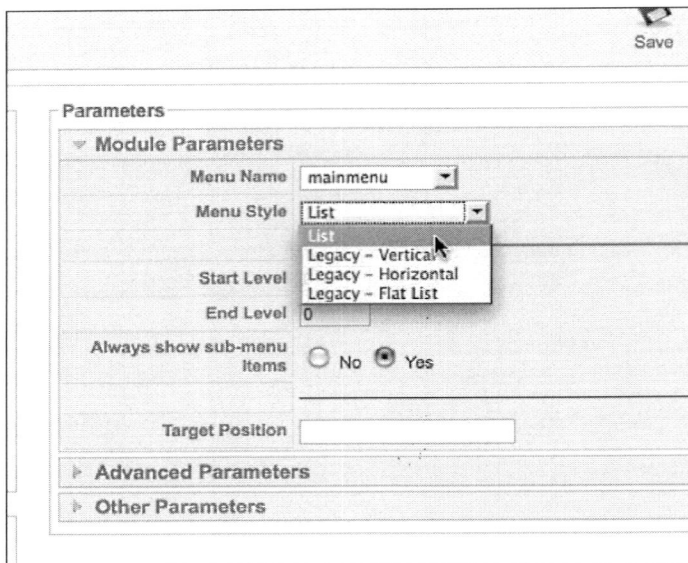

- **List**: This will output your menus in clean WC3-compliant lists and nest any submenu items a parent or top-level or root menu item may have. This is highly recommended, as it allows your menus to be easily (and beautifully) styled with CSS, degrade gracefully in older browsers and yet still appear functional in older, text-based browsers. (Many mobile-and disability-focused browsers are text-based and strip out CSS styles.)

- **Legacy - Vertical**: This option will display the top-level menu items only in a table format that stacks vertically. You'll probably select this only if you're using an older 1.0 that you've upgraded to 1.5 or installed in Joomla! 1.5's "legacy mode".

- **Legacy - Horizontal**: This option will display the top-level menu items only in a table that extends out horizontally. You'll probably select this only if you're using an older 1.0 that you've upgraded to 1.5 or installed in Joomla! 1.5's legacy mode.

- **Legacy - Flat List**: This option does display in a W3C-compliant list mode, yet only displays the top-level menu items. Again, you'll probably select this only if you're using an older 1.0 that you've upgraded to 1.5 or installed in Joomla! 1.5's legacy mode.

Using overrides

As mentioned in *Chapter 3*, template overrides are specialized files the Joomla! system checks for in your template's html folder. Template overrides include module chrome and **component overrides**. If Joomla! discovers that a particular file exists, for a specific module or component, in your template's html folder, Joomla! will reference that file's output, rather than its core output. The most common approach is to use the Beez template overrides, if you'd like to have truly accessible, table-less XTHML output from Joomla!. You can also create your own files.

Of course, the Joomla! system is not "psychic"! You can't just create an override and place it anywhere in your template directory, named anything you want, and hope Joomla! figures out your intentions. There is a specific folder and order placement you have to follow in order for Joomla! to understand that your file is intended to override specific core output. We'll take a closer look at this next.

Module overrides and chrome

In the earlier jdoc section, when we looked at module tags and layout control, we noted that you can specify rounded, xhtml, horiz, and vert styles. You can also easily set up additional chrome by editing or creating a file within the html directory, inside the appropriate mod_moduleName folder.

Inside the html directory, the following files are available to set up your own module chrome (see the next screenshot): modules.php, mod_search/default.php, mod_poll/default.php, mod_login/default.php, mod_latestnews/default.php, mod_newsflash/_item.php, default.php, horiz.php, and vert.php.

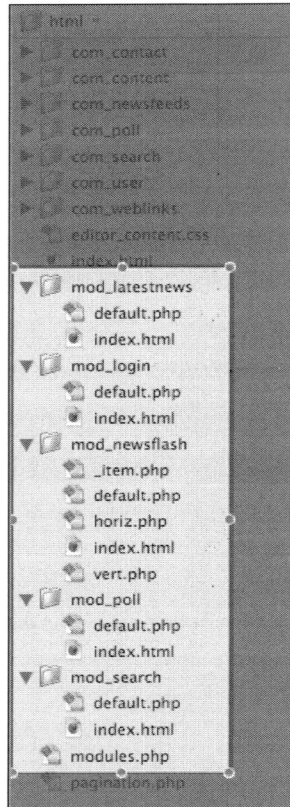

Keep in mind, while the stated folder structure is essential to follow, and each folder should have a default.php file in it, you can also create additional helper or view files if needed to support that layout. Notice that the Beez template mod_newsflash override takes advantage of this. Again, the purpose of overrides is to separate out the Joomla! CMS core from your site's presentation. This means you can change how your content output from the components and modules are displayed, but any updates to Joomla's core system will not require you to change your files (or it shouldn't; I can't guarantee the Joomla! development team will never produce a core system change that stops working with the API hooks used in the template overrides or module chrome, but that is the goal). This aspect gets a bit beyond the scope of this title, but if you'd like to know more, please reference the Joomla! documentation site: http://docs.joomla.org/Understanding_Output_Overrides.

How module chrome works

If you open up the Beez `module.php` file, you'll notice (under quite a bit of useful comments) some PHP code that looks like this (starting around line **24**):

```php
function modChrome_beezDivision($module, &$params, &$attribs)
{
    $headerLevel = isset($attribs['headerLevel']) ? (int)
                            $attribs['headerLevel'] : 3;
    if (!empty ($module->content)) : ?>
        <div class="moduletable<?php echo $params-
                    >get('moduleclass_sfx'); ?>">
            <?php if ($module->showtitle) : ?>
                <h<?php echo $headerLevel; ?>><?php echo $module->title;
                                    ?></h<?php echo $headerLevel; ?>>
            <?php endif; ?>
            <?php echo $module->content; ?>
        </div>
    <?php endif;
}
```

You would reference this chrome override by calling the second half of the function name, after `modChrome`: `modChrome_beezDivision`. You would then reference `beezDivision` in your `jdoc` module position style tag in the following fashion:

```
<jdoc:include type="modules" name="user1" style="beezDivision" />
```

Your template will now call in this particular chrome override, as opposed to the standard `xhtml` style previously called in. Unfortunately, for display purposes, this chrome override is not really that much different from the `xhtml` chrome style.

That's OK, if we change the last value of the `$headerLevel` variable from 3 to 2 (about line **26** in the `module.php` file) like so:

```php
$headerLevel = isset($attribs['headerLevel']) ? (int)
                        $attribs['headerLevel'] : 2;
```

We can quickly see the end result in our template's `user1` module position, as the header is now an `h2` instead of an `h3` tag (see the following screenshot):

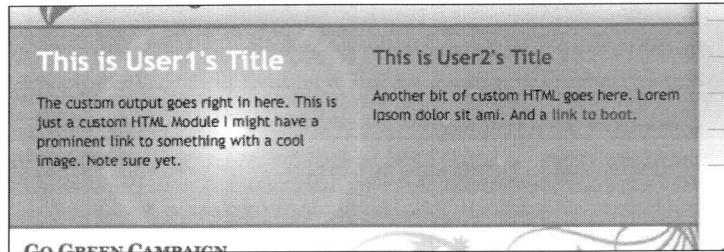

From this example, you can see how to expand and start creating your own module chrome. You can, basically, copy the above `beezDivision` function, paste it underneath the existing function, and tweak the `$headerLevel` variable as well as any XHTML markup you see surrounding the Joomla! PHP code.

To really construct module chrome from scratch, I would recommend you be comfortable with PHP and understand the various variable and pJoomla! parameter you can use. You can find out more about these by referencing this page in the Joomla! documentation: `http://docs.joomla.org/Applying_custom_module_chrome`.

Don't confuse module chrome with module overrides! You'll note in the previous screenshot, showing the `html` directory with its module override directories, that in addition to the `modules.php` page, there are module overrides for specific module types. You can tweak, adjust, or write up these views from scratch, in addition to the chrome. The chrome that we just tweaked above is for general output, and most module views that you tweak will also end up being pulled, so to speak, through the chrome. For example, you may tweak the poll's module view (remember, the poll also has a component view) to be in an ordered list instead of an unordered list. That view, with the ordered list, will then also get pulled through the special chrome you set up, wrapping it in the `header` and `div` tags you specified.

Component overrides

Similar to module chrome and overrides, component overrides require that you copy in (or create from scratch) files inside specially named directories inside your `html` directory. The following screenshot displays these component override directories and files:

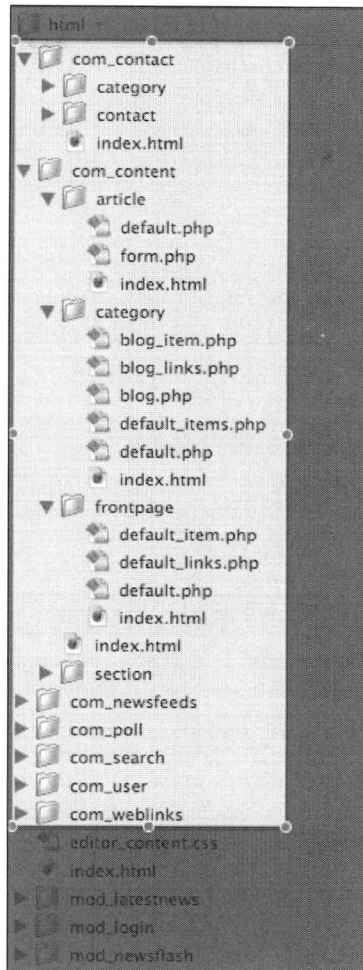

Also similar to module view overrides, component overrides just simply need to be there. If they're not there, Joomla! automatically reverts to its core output. In *Chapter 9*, we'll take a look at tweaking a component override for the article pages output. And once again, similar to module view overrides and module chrome, really whipping up component overrides from scratch requires a deeper understanding of Joomla! 1.5 and PHP than a book for creating templates aimed primarily at web designers can really get into.

After taking a look at our modest but very useful tweak in *Chapter 9*, if you feel your eye for PHP syntax is pretty good and you'd like to try your hand at more component overrides, be sure to check out that Understanding Output Overrides in the Joomla! documentaion: `http://docs.joomla.org/Understanding_Output_Overrides`.

Pagination

You can also override and tweak your pagination layout with a file called
pagination.php inside the html folder. Be aware, this file is entirely PHP. You can
look through it and easily see the XHTML markup to tweak, but be careful! The
XHTML markup is being built up and outputted inside the $html variable in PHP. If
you accidentally delete or overwrite any of the PHP syntax surrounding the XHTML,
you'll break this file. Having a good eye for PHP syntax is a must for tweaking this file.

Additional template information

OK, we've already been chatting about how useful it is to, at the very least, have
that eye for PHP syntax. It's, of course, even more useful to have a little PHP under
your belt. I'm going to quickly stray even further into PHP development, and then
come right back to templating and Joomla! basics. (Promise!) Even if you have no
interest whatsoever in PHP development, bear with me, this little bit of background
information on Joomla! 1.5 may help you better understand controlling your template.

Joomla! 1.5 was rebuilt using **object-oriented programming**, also affectionately
called as **OOP**. One advantage of OOP is that you can use design patterns to aid in
development. Joomla! 1.5 heavily relies on a design pattern called the **Model View
Controller** or **MVC** pattern. The MVC design pattern ensures that separate files
containing specific PHP code are used to tell the content management system (the
CMS) three main things. Mainly: what its purpose and core function is (the *Model*),
how to control visual display (aka the *View*), and how to do specific things such as
update, delete, and edit content, and set CMS administration preferences, and so on
(the *Control*).

Now, what the heck does this mean to you as a template designer? To start, as we
saw above, we're no longer constrained to that core Joomla! table output. The "View"
of MVC is indeed separate from the rest of the system, and thus, I don't have to go
through all sorts of advanced discussions about how to hack tables out of the Joomla!
system in a way that makes your CMS vulnerable to being incompatible with
updates and has nothing to do with your template.

The next feature is that within this OOP, MVC framework, your whole template
can be referenced as an "object", and that simply means it can be referenced in your
index.php file with PHP code using the $this->propertyName variable. We've
already taken advantage of it several times in our template, mostly to help target
our template directory using the baseurl property name. That is:

```
<link rel="stylesheet" href="<?php echo $this->baseurl; ?>/templates/
                    go_green/css/template.css" type="text/css" />
```

The following are additional template properties you might find useful in dynamically enhancing your template:

```php
<?php echo $this->base; ?> // outputs the full http:// path not just
the url name
<?php echo $this->_file; ?> // outputs the server path to the file
called in (not the same as the url path!) i.e.: /~user/httpdocs/
1.5dev/templates/go_green/index.php
<?php echo $this->title; ?> //outputs the Article Title
<?php echo $this->description; ?> //outputs the Article Description
<?php echo $this->template; ?> //outputs the template's Name
```

For a more complete listing of what's available in your template's object array, check out the Joomla! documentation: http://docs.joomla.org/Objects%2C_methods_and_properties_available_from_your_template.

You'll also find the countModules method useful for helping you set up dynamic layouts for collapsible columns. We'll cover how to use this method in detail in *Chapter 7*.

```php
$this->countModules('positionName'));
```

You'd replace positionName with the name of the module position you want to count the modules in; that is, right, user1, left, footer, and so on.

For more information on the countModules method, check out these links in the Joomla! documentation:

- http://docs.joomla.org/JDocumentHTML/countModules
- http://docs.joomla.org/Operators_for_use_with_the_countModules_function

Common Joomla! CSS

As you can see, via template overrides, you can pretty much define any CSS ids or classes you want. For those of you who are into creating and tweaking template overrides, unless you're going to create a highly custom, private, not-for-the-public template, my recommendation is you continue to use Joomla's general CSS ids and classes for component and module output as much as possible.

This is a good way to ensure your template is familiar to other Joomla! administrators, especially if you want to offer your template to the public or for commercial sale. It's easy for them to look up and customize CSS rules rather than forcing them to discover all the new and interestingly-named CSS ids and classes you created. For those of us working with Joomla's core output or the Beez template overrides (which attempts to use Joomla's standard CSS), here is a list of some of the most common CSS ids and classes. Those of you familiar with Joomla! 1.0 template design will be pleased to find these haven't really changed.

This list has been put together after a bit of research and a lot of experimentation with the Web Developer Toolbar CSS tools. It is probably not complete, but if you account for these items in your CSS rules, you'll be pretty well covered for most Joomla! projects, and it will be easy to spot any ids or classes not covered here and add them to your CSS sheet.

The Joomla.org forum has a post with a fairly comprehensive list, most of which you'll recognize here (although it does have some items on it that I don't seem to pick up in my template with the Beez overrides), so it's definitely worth checking out: http://forum.joomla.org/viewtopic.php?t=125508.

Joomla! 1.5 CSS ids

#active_menu	This is generated by the type="modules" include. Use it to style and control the currently selected main menu item.
#blockrandom	This is generated by the type="component" include when you're using the wrapper. This is the iFrame's id.
#contact_email_copy	This is generated by the type="component" include when you're in the contact form page view. This is a field name id.
#contact_text	This is generated by the type="component" include when you're in the contact form page view. This is a field name id.
#emailForm	This is generated by the type="component" include when you're in the contact form page view. This is a field name id.
#mainlevel	This is generated by the type="modules" include. Use it to style and control the main menu div holding each main menu item.
#mod_login_password	This is generated by the type="modules" include. This is a field name id.
#mod_login_remember	This is generated by the type="modules" include. This is a field name id.

`#mod_login_username`	This is generated by the `type="modules"` include. This is a field name `id`.
`#poll`	This is generated by the `type="modules"` include by the poll module. You can control the placement of the entire `id` with this.
`#search_ordering`	This is generated by the `type="component"` include when you're in the search form page view. This is a field name `id`.
`#search_searchword`	This is generated by the `type="component"` include when you're in the search form page view. This is a field name `id`.
`#searchphraseall`	This is generated by the `type="component"` include when you're in the search form page view. This is a field name `id`.
`#searchphraseany`	This is generated by the `type="component"` include when you're in the search form page view. This is a field name `id`.
`#searchphraseexact`	This is generated by the `type="component"` include when you're in the search form page view. This is a field name `id`.
`#voteid1,#voteid2,#voteid3`, and so on	This is generated by the `type="modules"` include. This is generated by the poll module and are field name `id`s for the radio buttons.

Joomla! 1.5 CSS classes

`.article_separator`	This is generated by the `type="component"` include. You can style the space/separations between articles in the blog or news flash views.
`.back_button`	This is generated by the `type="component"` include code. It's used to style the main back button, which is similar to hitting the back button in your browser.
`.blog`	This is generated by the `type="component"` include if you're in blog view.
`.blog_more`	This is generated by the `type="component"` include if you're in blog view. It indicates there are more blog stories in the links below.
`.blogsection`	This is generated by the `type="component"` include if you're in blog view. It formats additional blog links.
`.button`	This is generated by the `type="modules"` include. Use it to consistently style and control buttons generated by any of the modules.

.buttonheading	This is generated by the type="component" include if you're in blog view. Use this to control the layout and style of the PDF, email, and print controls.
.category	This is generated by the type="component" include code if you're in blog view. Use it to control the layout and style of links to categories such as "Latest News" or "Popular" or "Most Read".
.componentheading	This is generated by the type="component" include if you're in latest news or blog view.
.contact_email	This is generated by the type="component" include code when you're in the contact form page view. Use it to control the overall placement and style of all the contact form elements.
.content_rating	This is generated by the type="component" include as well as the type="modules" include. Style the ratings output of the content that has been voted on.
.content_vote	This is generated by the type="component" include as well as the type="modules" include. Style the link or button that allows the user to vote on the content.
.contentdescription	This is generated by the type="component" include as well as the type="modules" include. Style the descriptions of the content that can be voted on.
.contentheading	This is generated by the type="component" include. Use it to style the titles of articles and headings.
.contentpaneopen	This is generated by the type="component" include as well as the type="modules" include. It indicates the start of the content.
.contenttoc	This is generated by the type="component" include code. Use it to style the TOC listings some content may generate.
.createdate	This is generated by the type="component" include as well as the type="modules" include. It controls the style of the displayed creation date of an article or a blog entry.
.fase4rdf	This is generated by the type="component" include. It's part of a great type of dynamic formatting class offered and lets you style the news RSS feeds you can set up through Joomla.
.frontpageheader	This is generated by the type="component" include. If you're using the home page module, style the front page headers with this class.
.inputbox	This is generated by the type="component" include as well as the type="modules" include. Use this to consistently style and control all form fields generated by the mosMainBody or a module.

`.latestnews`	This is generated by the `type="modules"` code. The `class` is wrapped around a list of latest news links, which you can control with additional rule calls; that is, `.latestnews td` or `.latestnews li`, depending on the output options you've chosen.
`.mainlevel`	This is generated by the `type="modules"` include. It lets you style and control main menu items displayed in the `#mainlevel` id.
`.modifydate`	This is generated by the `type="component"` include. It accompanies date information if an article has been modified.
`.module`	This `class` is generated by the `type="modules"` include when using the `"rounded"` style option.
`.moduletable`	This `class` is generated by the `type="modules"` include when using the `table`, `horiz`, `none`, or `xhtml` style options.
`.mosimage`	This is generated by the `type="component"` include. Use it to control and style images placed with articles.
`.mosimage_caption`	This is generated by the `type="component"` include. Use it to control and style image captions placed with articles.
`.mostread`	This is generated by the `type="modules"` code. It is similar to `.latestnews`. The `class` is wrapped around a list of latest news links, which you can control with additional rule calls; that is, `.latestnews td` or `.latestnews li`, depending on the output options you've chosen.
`.newsfeed`	This is generated by the `type="component"` include in the News Feeds view. Use it to control and style the overall news feed display.
`.newsfeeddate`	This is generated by the `type="component"` include in the News Feeds view. Use it to control and style the news feed displayed dates.
`.newsfeedheading`	This is generated by the `type="component"` include in the News Feeds view. Use it to control and style the news feed headers.
`.pagenav`	This is generated by the `type="component"` include. Use it to control and style the overall placement of next and previous page navigation.
`.pagenav_next`	This is generated by the `type="component"` include. Use it to control and style the next page button.
`.pagenav_prev`	This is generated by the `type="component"` include. Use it to control and style the previous page button.
`.pagenavbar`	This is generated by the `type="component"` include. Use it to control and style the overall placement of next and previous page navigation.
`.pagenavcounter`	This is generated by the `type="component"` include. Use it to control and style the overall placement of the page counter under the navigation.

[171]

.pathway	This class is generated by the mospathway(); include.
.polls	This is generated by the type="modules" include. This is generated by the poll module, and you can use it to set alternating backgrounds for your poll-select items.
.pollsborder	This is generated by the type="modules" include. This is generated by the poll module, and you can use it to style the outside border of the module. Not to be confused with the .pollstableborder class!
.pollstableborder	This is generated by the type="modules" include. This is generated by the poll module, and you can use it to style the border of the table generated by the module.
.readon	This is generated by the type="component" include as well as the type="modules" include. Use this to consistently style and control all the "Read More" links for truncated news, news flashes, and blog items.
.search	This is generated by the type="modules" include. This is generated by the search module, and you can use it to control and style the main search field.
.sectionentry1	This is generated by the type="modules" include. This is generated by the poll module, and you can use it to set alternating backgrounds for your poll-select items.
.sectionentry2	This is generated by the type="modules" include. This is generated by the poll module, and you can use it to set alternating backgrounds for your poll-select items.
.sectionheader	This is generated by the type="component" include as well as the type="modules" include. You can use it to control section header titles displayed by modules and content.
.small	This is generated by the type="component" include as well as the type="modules" include. It's used to denote author names and other data related to an article or blog post.
.smalldark	This is generated by the type="component" include as well as the type="modules" include.
.sublevel	This is generated by the type="component" include as well as the type="modules" include. It's also used to denote sub items of navigation.
.syndicate	This is generated by the type="modules" include. Use this to style the syndicate button layout or borders of your syndicate module.
.syndicate_text	This is generated by the type="modules" include. Use this to style the syndicate layout if you're using text instead of buttons.
.text_area	This is generated by the type="component" include. Use it to control and style the text areas of forms much like the .inputbox class.

Joomla! 1.0 to 1.5 conversion

The fact that Joomla! has left its core CSS `ids` and `classes` alone is a great aid in helping you update 1.0 templates to 1.5. Once you've changed your legacy `mos...` tags to the new, appropriate `jdoc include` tags, you should find that your CSS is able to style just fine. Of course, if you went from a table-based layout to a table-less layout with overrides, you'll need to tweak your CSS to affect `divs` with those same CSS rules instead of tables, which can be a little different, but the general bulk of the work shouldn't be too bad.

Template parameters

Joomla! 1.5 allows you to pass parameters from the Administration panel to your template, giving your Joomla! administrator additional control over the template in some very useful ways. We'll cover how to set up a simple parameter function in detail in *Chapter 9*. For your reference, the essentials you need to know are covered in the next few sections.

Define a parameter in the templateDetails.xml file

You'll want to place your parameter definitions within `<param>` tags inside the `<params>...</params>` tags at the bottom of the `templateDetails.xml` file before the closing `</install>` tag. For example:

```
<install>

...

<params>
    <param name="logoType" type="list" default="image" label="Logo
                            type" description="Type of Logo">
        <option value="graphicHead">Graphic</option>
        <option value="textHead">Text</option>
    </param>
    <param name="logoText" type="text" default="" size="50"
        label="Logo text" description="Your Logo Text" />
    <param name="sloganText" type="text" default="" size="50"
            label="Slogan" description="Your Slogan Text" />
</params>
...

</install>
```

Retrieve a parameter in the template file

Most importantly, you'll need to create a `params.ini` file and make sure it is writeable (Joomla! will install your template, and if this file is included in your `templateDetails.xml` file, install it to be writable, if the server allows.) The `params.ini` file is key, as that's where the results will be stored for later retrieval by the template.

To retrieve a parameter within your `index.php` page, place the following code were you'd like the parameter to be displayed or referenced by PHP code.

```php
<?php $myParam = $this->params->get( 'parameterName' ); ?>
```

The `parameterName` will be whatever you specify it to be in your `templateDetails.xml` file. So, based on my sample code above, the parameter name can be `logoType`, `logoText`, or `sloganText`.

Useful standard parameter types

Here are the most useful types I've used in a template:

- **text**:
```xml
<param name="parameterName" type="text" default="Some text"
       label="Enter some text" description="" size="10" />
```

- **textarea**:
```xml
<param name="parameterName" type="textarea" default="default"
 label="Enter some text" description="" rows="10" cols="5" />
```

- **list**:
```xml
<param name="parameterName" type="list" default="" label="Select
                                       an item" description="">
  <option value="item1">Item 1</option>
  <option value="item2">Item 2</option>
</param>
```

- **radio buttons**:
```xml
<param name="parameterName" type="radio" default="0" label="Select
                                   an option" description="">
  <option value="0">1</option>
  <option value="1">2</option>
</param>
```

- **hidden variable**:

```
<param name="parameterName" type="hidden" default="" />
```

- **calendar display**:

```
<param name="parameterName" type="calendar" default="5-30-2009"
label="Select your birth date!" description="" format="%d-%m-%Y"
/>
```

Joomla's documentation site has a great tutorial on template parameters, which includes a full list of standard parameter types and how to implement them: `http://docs.joomla.org/Tutorial:Template_parameters`.

Again, be sure to check out *Chapter 9*, where we'll implement a parameter function into our case study template.

Summary

We've taken a look at the essentials you'll need most to constantly look up, from `jdoc include` tags and standard CSS output, to overrides, chrome, and template parameters. I've also included key points to be noted for all you template developers upgrading 1.0 templates to 1.5. Dog-ear this chapter for handy reference, and let's get ready to start cooking. First up: dynamic layouts, drop-down menus, and Flash.

7
Dynamic Layouts, Menus, and Interactive Elements

In this chapter we're going to take our Go Green Campaign template and enhance it. We'll start with adding dynamic layout capabilities to our template. Joomla! allows you to set up **conditional statements** in your `index.php` file, using some basic PHP. This will give our template's layout some powerful flexibility, not to mention it makes it easy to switch up the "hum-drum" boringness of having the same three columns on every page. Next, we'll move on to drop-down menus, slick Flash headers, YouTube embeds, and other interactive Flash content.

Aside from the PHP conditional statements in our layout, most of the techniques I'm about to discuss in this chapter (and the next) are often used inappropriately and needlessly, not to mention they can create issues with usability and accessibility standards, but I'll try to cover how to integrate them as elegantly and usably as possible.

"Don't Make Me Think: A Common Sense Approach to Website Usability", *Steve Krug, New Riders Press*, is an excellent book on web site design for usability and testing that anyone who has anything to do with web site development or design can greatly benefit from. You'll learn why people leave web sites, how to make your site more usable and accessible, and even how to survive those executive design whims (without the use of a hammer). You can find out more at Steve's site: `http://www.sensible.com/`.

DIY or extensions?

In this chapter and the next, I'll discuss how to create some of these techniques yourself but will also direct you to comparable extensions or, in the case of more complex techniques, show you extensions that do the job and point you in the direction for learning more about doing it yourself. As to the question: should I use extensions or do it myself? That depends on a few things, such as:

- Time available
- Your technical comfort level
- The level of control you want over the template
- If your template is unique for use on a single site or if you plan on a wide distribution of it

If you're new to web development, especially using PHP, and/or you just don't have the time to create a completely custom solution, Joomla!! extensions are a great way for you to go. If you've been developing with various web technologies for a while, and you want to have exact, detailed control over your template, then you should be able to implement and further customize any of the solutions discussed in the next few chapters.

The other consideration is usage of your template. If you're developing a template that is for a specific client to only be used on his/her site, then you might want to implement a solution directly into your template. This will enable you to have detailed control over its display via your template pages and `template.css` sheet. If, on the other hand, you plan to sell your template commercially or, otherwise let it be widely distributed, your best bet is to make it as extension-friendly as possible. (By "extension-friendly", I simply mean, test it with popular extensions to make sure they work well with your template. You can go to `http://extensions.joomla.org` and sort by "popular extensions". SiteGround has a comprehensive list of popular Joomla! 1.5 extensions as well: `http://www.siteground.com/joomla_extensions.htm`.) This way, your template users have greater flexibility in how they end up using your template and aren't "locked in" to using any features you've enabled the template with.

Dynamic layouts

There's no extension shortcut for this. You have to make sure your template is properly set up to handle conditional statements. This is a good enhancement to add, as Joomla! administrators can choose to have different modules in different positions for different pages and also choose not to have any modules assigned to positions on certain pages. The way our template currently stands, if no modules are assigned to the `user3` or `right` positions, a blank column will sit there, taking up space and looking odd and somewhat ugly.

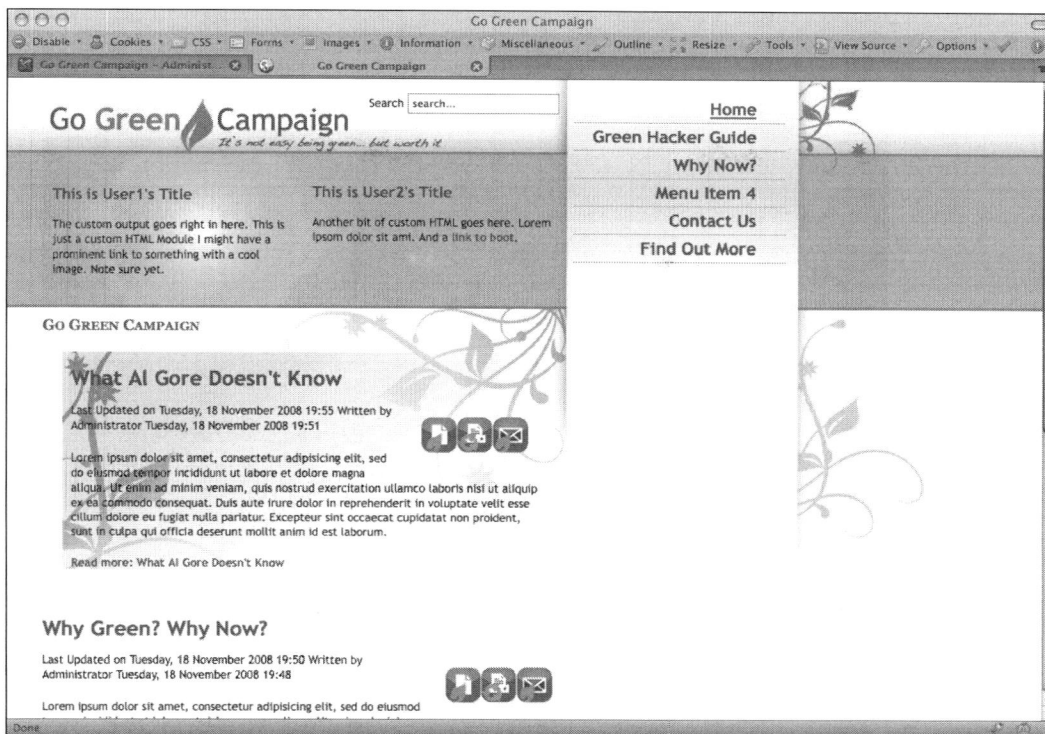

What we would like to have happen is, ideally, if no modules are assigned to user3, then the content module expands to take over that column. If no modules are assigned to the user3 position and to the right position, then the content module can take over both columns. This will work well, as I've taken the time to set up my header image so that if the middle and far-right columns are removed, taking with them the extended shadows and vines background images, the top area of the header will still look great and appear to merge with the white background instead of extending over it, creating an area for columns.

Now the way our layout is set up, if there are modules assigned to the user3 position but not to the right position, then the right position will remain blank. However, as it's on the far edge of our layout, this will not seem as odd or broken as it does when there are no modules assigned to the user3 position.

We can handle this with a few pieces of PHP code that work with Joomla's backend.

PHP syntax

We discussed in *Chapter 3* a little bit about PHP syntax. First off, you'll want to make sure that all your PHP statements are wrapped in the following tags:

```
<?php //statements ?>
```

Then, within those tags, we'll want to check a Joomla! function that is called countModules(). This function will tell us if there are or aren't any modules assigned to the module position for the page that has just loaded in the browser.

In order to check this, we'll construct an if statement and have it check our two module positions.

PHP if/else conditional statements

Let's see how these conditional statements are used.

Time for action: Adding an if/else **statement**

Let's add in the required code to set up an if/else statement with PHP in our index.php file.

1. Starting just under the closing </div><!--//header--> tags, which should be around line **55**, the first thing we'll check for is if the user3 position doesn't have any modules assigned but the right position does. If this comes back as "true", we'll want to tell our template what to do:

```
...
<?php if (!$this->countModules('user3') and ($this-
                      >countModules('right')): ?>
<!--there are no user 3 items-->
<!-- Begin #contentWide -->
<div id="contentWide">
<!--//start Joomla! component-->
<jdoc:include type="component" />
<!--//end Joomla! component-->
</div><!-- //contentWide -->
</div><!--//container3-->
<!-- #right sidebar -->
<div id="sidebarRT">
<div id="user4">
<!--//start user4 mod-->
<jdoc:include type="modules" name="user4" style="xhtml" />
<!--//end user4 mod-->
</div><!--//user4-->
<div id="right">
```

```
<!--//start right mod-->
<jdoc:include type="modules" name="right" style="xhtml" />
<!--//end right mod-->
</div><!--//right-->
</div><!--//sidebarRT -->
...
```

2. Note that by placing an exclamation point (!) in front of the `user3` position check, we're telling PHP and Joomla! to confirm there are no modules assigned. By not placing the exclamation point in front of the `right` position check, we're telling PHP and Joomla! to confirm the result to have modules assigned.

3. If those statements, negative for `user3` and positive for `right`, come back as "true", the XHTML `div` code and `jdoc` tags we located underneath the PHP statement will be rendered in the browser.

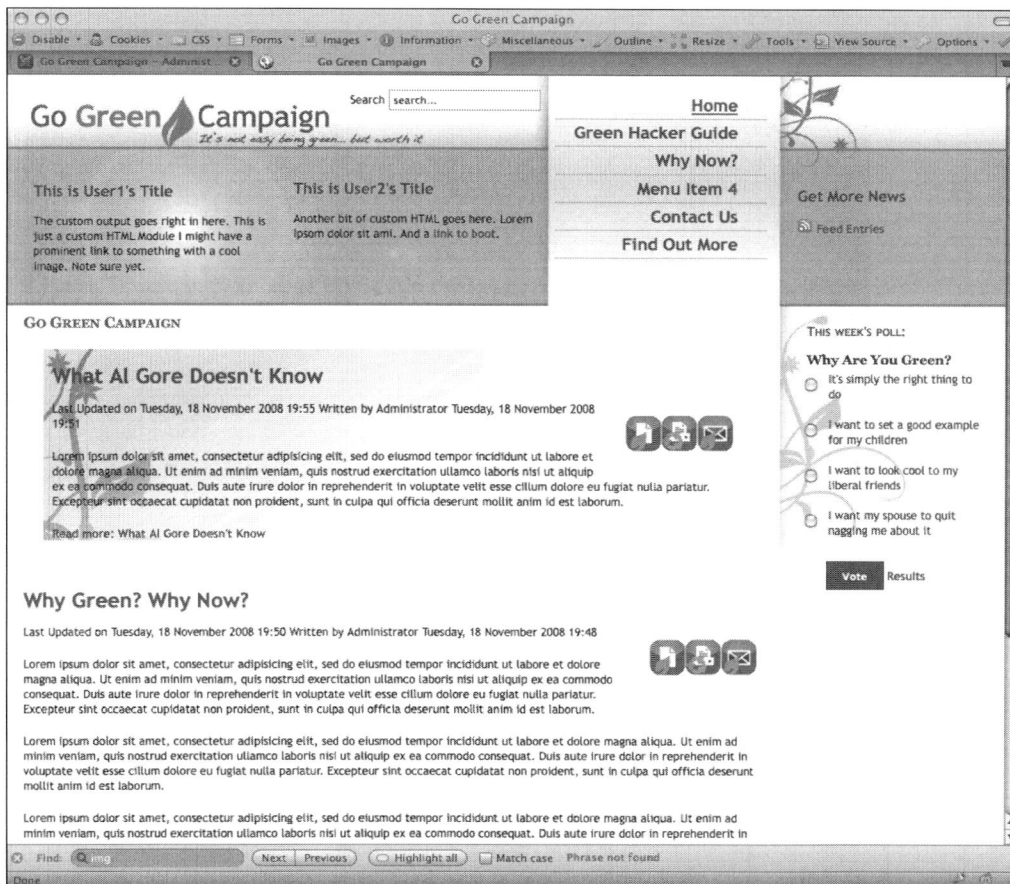

4. But what if they come back "false"? Perhaps user3 came back negative for modules and the right position did too! If that's the case, we'd want the content area to stretch all the way across the screen. Let's check for that by combining both position checks into one countModules function:

```
...
<?php  elseif (!$this->countModules('user3 and right')): ?>
<!--there are no user3 AND no right modules-->
<!-- Begin #fullScreen -->
<div id="fullScreen">
<!--//start Joomla! component-->
<jdoc:include type="component" />
<!--//end Joomla! component-->
</div><!-- //fullScreen -->
</div><!--//container3-->
...
```

5. Note that, above, I was able to make a more elegant check by taking advantage of the countModules function's built-in logic operators, whereas before, to ensure that user3 didn't have any modules assigned but right did, I separated them out into two countModule checks.

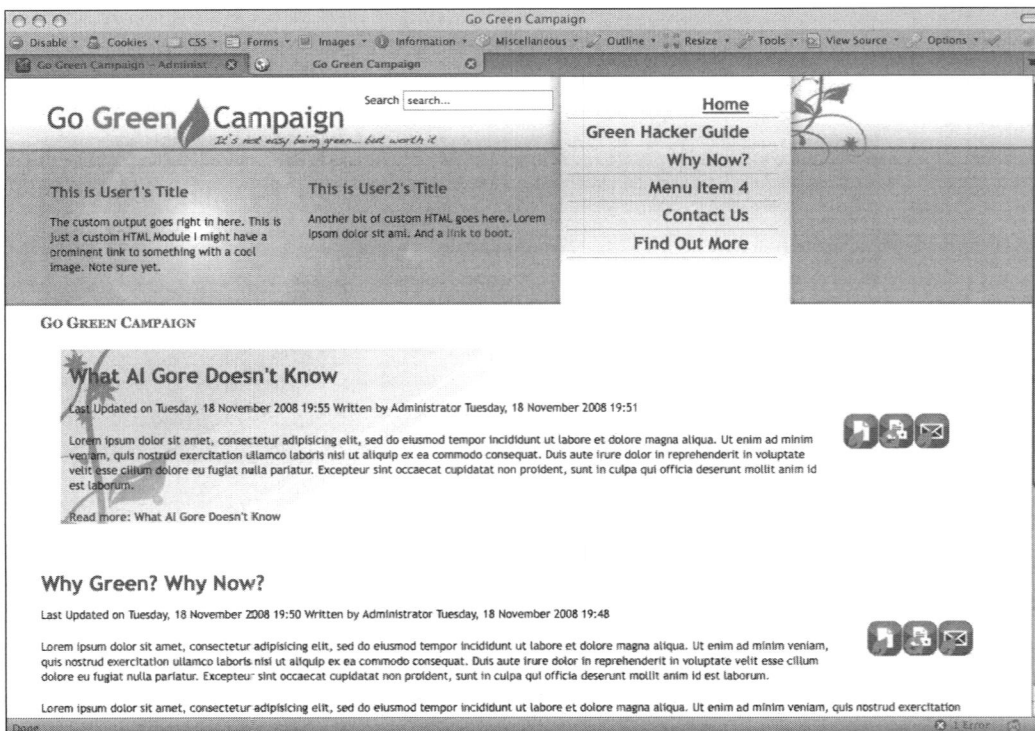

6. What if there are modules in both positions? We can use logic to assume that if the requirements of the two `if`/`else` statements above are not met, then that means either both positions have modules assigned or, at the very least, `user3` has modules assigned. And if `user3` has modules assigned to it, then we want our layout to stay as it is. We don't have to do a full `countModules` check, we just say that if anything else comes back no matter what it is, do the following:

```
...
<?php else;?>
<!--//there is at least user3 modules-->

<!-- Begin #content -->
<div id="content">

<!--//start Joomla! component-->
<jdoc:include type="component" />
<!--//end Joomla! component-->

</div><!-- //content -->

<!-- #left sidebar -->
<div id="sidebarLT">

<div id="user3">

<!--//start user3 mod-->
<jdoc:include type="modules" name="user3" style="xhtml" />
<!--//end user3 mod-->

</div><!--//user3-->

</div><!--//sidebarLT   -->

</div><!--//container3-->

<!-- #right sidebar -->
<div id="sidebarRT">

<div id="user4">

<!--//start user4 mod-->
<jdoc:include type="modules" name="user4" style="xhtml" />
<!--//end user4 mod-->

</div><!--//user4-->

<div id="right">

<!--//start right mod-->
<jdoc:include type="modules" name="right" style="xhtml" />
```

```
<!--//end right mod-->

</div><!--//right-->

</div><!--//sidebarRT -->
...
```

Above, you'll see that our XHTML markup and `jdoc` tags are exactly the same as our original layout.

7. Lastly, we want PHP to stop asking Joomla! questions! To make sure that happens, we'll need to end this `if/else` statement we've set up:

```
...
<?php endif; ?>
...
```

Update your CSS

We'll now take a look at updating the `template.css` file with the new `container ids`.

Time for action: Updating the CSS

Now that you've handled the PHP, XHTML, and `jdoc` markup, you'll need to make sure your stylesheet can handle the `div` containers we just set up.

I've set up the following rules for `contentWide` and `fullScreen` underneath my `content id` rules in my `template.css` file:

```
...
#contentWide {
    margin:0;
    width: 775px;
    float:left;
}
#fullScreen {
    margin:0;
    width: 990px;
    float:left;
}
...
```

And there you have it! You can use the `countModules()` function in combination with PHP `if/else` statements to check for a variety of returns, not just "true" or "false" answers. As you might have deducted from the function's name containing the word `count`, you can determine how many modules are loaded into each position.

As I showed you above, you can check for multiple positions within a single function and compare how many modules are in each position. You can also perform basic math functions on the results. OK, all this may seem a little too much to think about at first, but as you become more sophisticated and creative with your template layouts, you will see how this function alone gives you unbelievable flexibility in determining how you set up your template for rich and varied dynamic layouts.

> **Find out more**: To learn more about the `countModules()` function, check out Joomla!'s documentation:
> `http://docs.Joomla.org/JDocumentHTML/countModules.`

Dynamic menus

This is the nice thing about Joomla!—it's all dynamic. Once you install Joomla! and design a great template for it, anyone with the right level of administrative capability can log into the Administration panel and add, edit, and delete content, menu items, and other modules. But generally, when people ask for dynamic menus, what they really want are those appearing and disappearing drop-down menus, which, I believe, they like because they quickly give a site a very "busy" feel.

I must add my own disclaimer; I don't like drop downs. Before you get on my case, I will say it's not that they're "wrong" or "bad", they just don't meet my own aesthetics, and I personally find them non-user-friendly. I'd prefer to see a menu system that, if it requires sub sections, displays them somewhere consistently on the page, either by having a vertical navigation expand to display sub sections underneath or, if a horizontal menu is used, showing additional sub sections in a set location on the page.

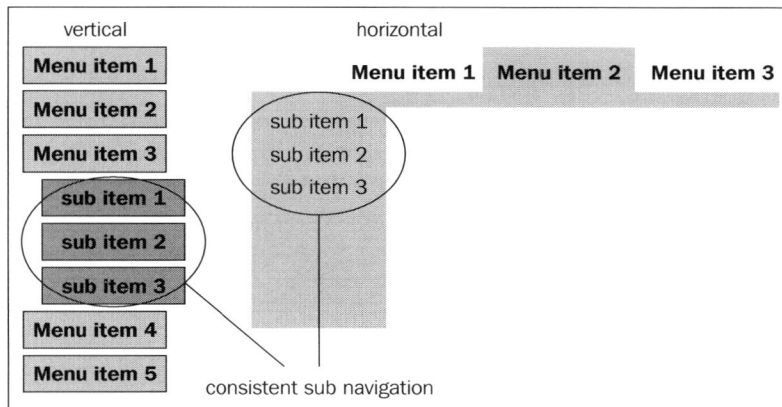

I like to be able to look around and see: "OK, I'm in the **New Items** | **Cool Dink** section, and I can also check out **Red Dinks** and **Retro Dinks** within this section". Having to constantly go back up to the menu and drop down the options to remind myself of what's available and what my next move might be is annoying. Still haven't convinced you not to use drop downs? OK, read on!

Drop-down menus

I was especially negative about drop-down menus, as the solutions I used to run across required bulky JavaScripting or the use of Flash, which does not create very clean, semantic, SEO-friendly (or accessible) XHTML markup. Luckily, a few years ago, Patrick Griffiths and Dan Webb came up with the **Suckerfish** method.

This Suckerfish method is wonderful, because it takes valid, semantically-accurate, unordered lists (Joomla! 1.5's favorite) and, using almost pure CSS, creates drop downs. The drop downs are not tab accessible, but they will simply display as a single, clear, unordered list to older browsers that don't support the required CSS.

> IE6, per usual, poses a problem or two for us, so there is some minimal DOM JavaScripting needed to compensate and achieve the correct effect in that browser.

If you haven't heard of or worked with the suckerfish method, I recommend you go on line and read Dan and Patrick's article in detail: http://alistapart.com/articles/dropdowns.

More recently, Patrick and Dan have revisited this method with *Son of Suckerfish*, which offers multiple levels and an even further parred-down DOM JavaScript. Check it out here: http://www.htmldog.com/articles/suckerfish/dropdowns/.

I also suggest you playing around with the sample code provided in these articles so that you understand exactly how it works. Go on, read it! When you get back, I'll review how to apply this method to your Joomla! template.

DIY Suckerfish menus in Joomla! 1.5

If you've read up on Patrick and Dan's method, you can see the essential part of this effect is getting your menu items to show up as unordered lists with sub or nested unordered lists. Once you do, the rest of the magic can be easily handled by finessing the CSS that Patrick and Dan suggest into your Joomla! template's CSS and placing the DOM script in your index.php template's header tags. Seriously, that's it!

The really good news is, as long as you use the XHTML style in your `jdoc` module position tags, Joomla! already outputs your content's pages and their sub pages using unordered lists. Right-clicking on our page link in Firefox to **View Selected Source** and checking the DOM inspector shows us that the menu is in fact being displayed using an unordered list.

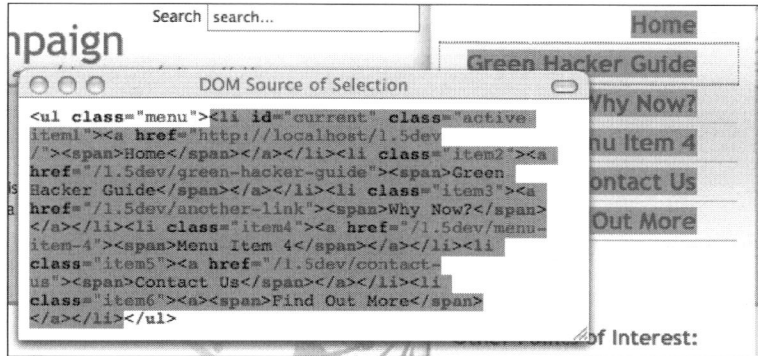

Now you can go into your Joomla! Administration panel and add as many menu items and submenu items as you'd like via the main menu module. By going to **Menu | Main Menu**, you'll be able to add menu items as we did in *Chapter 3*. By using the **Parent Item** option box, you can specify which existing menu item to set as the parent to your new menu item. The following screenshot illustrates selecting a parent menu item for a new menu item:

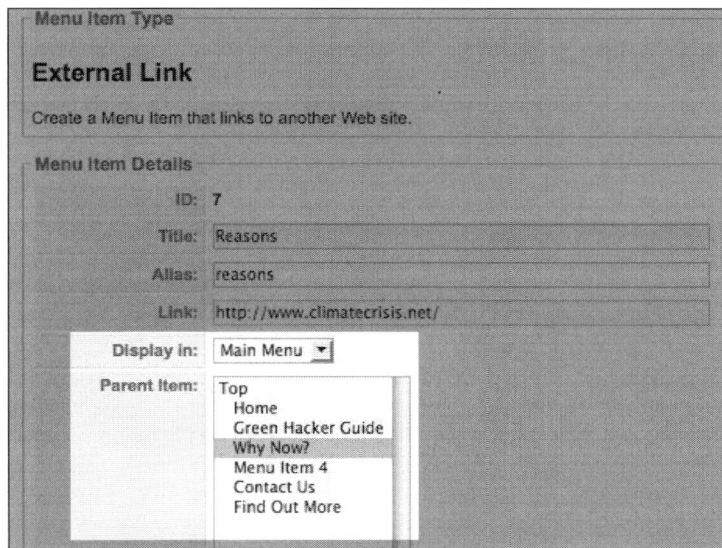

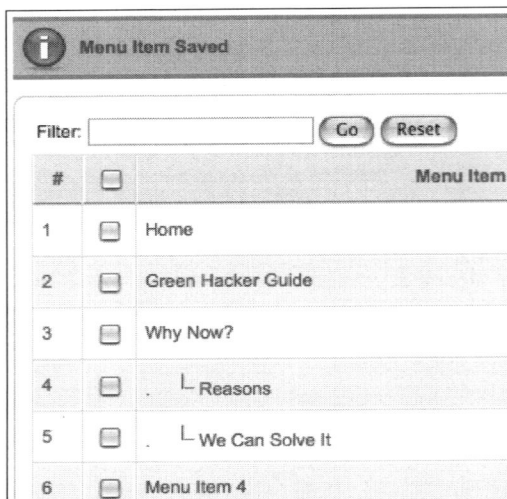

Once you've added submenu items to existing menu items, you'll be able to use the DOM Source Selection Viewer to see that your menu is displayed with unordered lists and sub-lists.

Applying the CSS to Joomla!

We're going to be using the new and improved Son of Suckerfish method so that, if need be our menu can handle multi-level drop downs. To start, I'll take Dan's and Patrick's suggested code for vertical menus and adjust it a bit to fit my CSS class names. I'll also make an adjustment to the CSS, as my menu will need to drop down to the left, not the right. Their vertical menu sample can be found here: `http://www.htmldog.com/articles/suckerfish/dropdowns/example/vertical.html`.

Before I tweak the CSS to fit my template, there's one more consideration to make: in Joomla!, our menu item's `ul` has a class called `.menu`. The trouble is, all menu lists that Joomla! outputs will have the `.menu` class. I only want my main menu to render out with Suckerfish CSS rules, so I'll take advantage of Joomla!'s ability to add a class suffix to a module.

Time for action: **Suckerfish CSS**

Let's now take a look at adding the Suckerfish CSS to Joomla:

1. Go to **Extensions | Module Manager** and select your main menu module.

2. On the right side of the screen, select **Advanced Parameters**, add the suffix `_sf` for "Suckerfish" to the module, and hit **Save**.

    The following screenshot shows where in the **Parameters** section to add the suffix in the **Module Manager**:

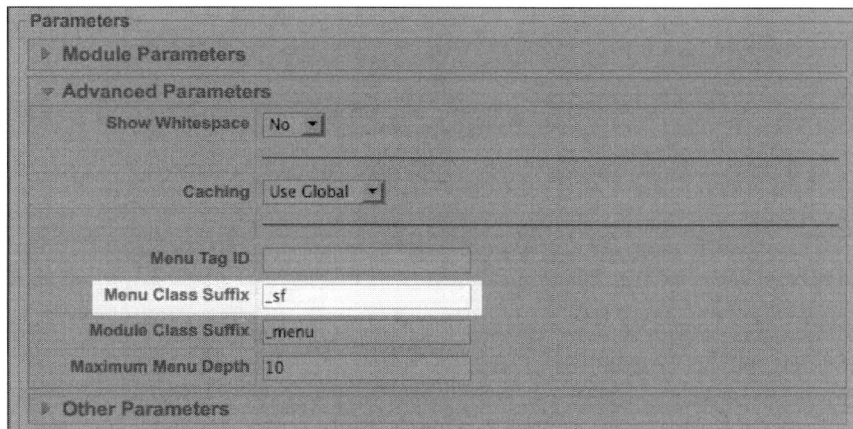

Now that it's taken care of, I'll note that my main menu isn't styled anymore. To quickly remedy that, I'll need to update the CSS rules that reference the `.menu` class as well as insert the following styles:

```
...
/*////////// NAV //////////*/
#top_navlist {
    position: absolute;
    top: 15px;
    margin-left: 550px;
    /*border: 1px solid #ffff00;*/
}

#top_navlist h3{
```

```
        display: none;
    }
    .menu_sf, .menu_sf ul { /* all lists */
        padding: 0;
        margin: 0;
        list-style: none;
        float : left;
        width: 220px;
        font-family: "Trebuchet MS", Verdana, Arial, Helvetica, sans-serif;
        /*font-variant: small-caps;*/
    }
    .menu_sf li { /* all list items */
        position : relative;
        float : left;
        line-height : 1.25em;
        margin-bottom : -1px;
    }
    .menu_sf li a {
        width: 190px;
        line-height: 30px;
        display : block;
        color : #0059B2;
        font-weight : bold;
        font-size: 18px;
        text-decoration : none;
        text-align: right;
        /*background-color : white;*/
        border-bottom : 1px solid #9FD780;
        /*padding : 0 0.5em;*/
        padding-right: 30px;
    }
    /* suckerfish dropdowns */
    .menu_sf li ul { /* second-level lists */
        position : absolute;
        left: -999em;
        margin-left : -214px;
        margin-top : -28px;
    }
    .menu_sf li ul ul { /* third-and-above-level lists */
        right: -999em;
    }
    .menu_sf li ul {
        background-color : white;
        width: 213px;
        border: 1px solid #818749;
```

```
}
.menu_sf li ul li a{
   width: 200px;
   padding : 0 7px;
   border-bottom : 1px solid #999999;
}
.menu_sf li a:hover {
   color : #999999;
}
.menu_sf #current a{
   color: #666666;
   text-decoration: underline;
}
.menu_sf #current ul li a{
   text-decoration:none;
   color:#000000;
}
.menu_sf #current ul li a:hover{
   color : #999999;
}
.menu_sf li:hover ul ul, .menu_sf li:hover ul ul ul, .menu_sf
                                           li.sfhover ul ul,
.menu_sf li.sfhover ul ul ul {
   left: -999em;
}
.menu_sf li:hover ul, .menu_sf li li:hover ul, .menu_sf li li li:hover
ul, .menu_sf li.sfhover ul, .menu_sf li li.sfhover ul, .menu_sf li li
li.sfhover ul { /* lists nested under hovered list items */
   left: auto;
}
...
```

Applying the DOM Script to Joomla!

The last bit is the JavaScript, so the hover works in IE6. I call it DOM scripting or the DOM script, but it's basically just a JavaScript that rewrites your markup (how your DOM is being perceived by IE6) on-the-fly. This drop-down effect relies on the CSS hover attribute; IE6 only recognizes the hover attribute if it is applied to an entity (link). IE7 has fixed this limitation and works similarly to FireFox and other browsers. Dan's and Patrick's script appends the additional .sfhover class to the li items in only IE6.

You'll need to add this script to your `index.php` file, inside the `header` tags. The thing to remember here is that Dan and Patrick named their `ul`'s id as `nav` and that's what this script is looking for. Our `ul`'s id is named `top_navlist`; so, by simply switching out `document.getElementById("nav");` to `document.getElementById("navlist");`, you're good to roll in IE.

Time for action: Applying the DOM script

The following script will make your drop downs work in IE6.

The full script in your header tags should look like this (I prefer to tuck it into an include `.js` file and reference it in my `index.php` file with a JavaScript `include`: `<script type="text/javascript" src="<?php echo $this->baseurl; ?>/templates/go_green/js/suckerfish.js"></script>`):

```
<script type="text/javascript"><!--//--><![CDATA[//--><!--
sfHover = function() {
   var sfEls = document.getElementById("top_navlist").
                        getElementsByTagName("LI");
   for (var i=0; i<sfEls.length; i++) {
      sfEls[i].onmouseover=function() {
         this.className+=" sfhover";
      }
      sfEls[i].onmouseout=function() {
         this.className=this.className.replace(new RegExp("
                                 sfhover\\b"), "");
      }
   }
}
if (window.attachEvent) window.attachEvent("onload", sfHover);
//--><!]]></script>
```

Note that the `document.getElementById` must reference the id (not class name) of the wrapping `div` you placed your module within. For demonstration purposes, I've kept the CSS pretty bare bones and ugly, but when we check this out in our browser we now see:

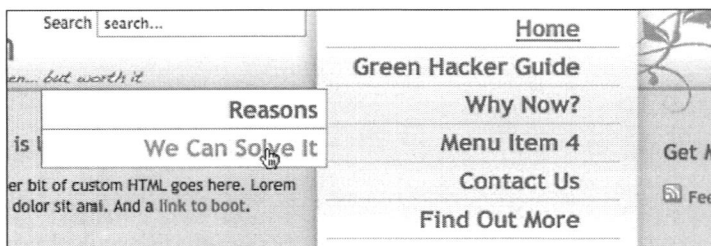

It's working! Remember, with the above code, you can have drop-down menus that go three-levels deep (Dan's and Patrik's HTML Dog article shows you how to make it handle as many levels as you'd like).

Control those drop-down levels

No matter how cool Suckerfish drop downs are, refrain from going overboard on those levels! Cascading levels can become really tedious for a user to dragg a mouse through and turn a site with a "busy feel" into a total mess. You'll find that with a little care, you can easily organize your site's page content so that it only requires two levels. From there, if you really need it, you can add an occasional third level without creating too much user distraction.

At this point, all that's left is fixing up the CSS to make it look exactly the way you want. You've now just added, semantic, SEO and accessible-as-possible (and yes, W3C compliant) dynamic drop-down menus in Joomla!.

Drop-down menu extensions. Now you're probably already thinking: "wait, this is Joomla!, maybe there's an extension", and you'd be right! Searching the "Extensions" section of the Joomla.org site, you'll find two well-heeded extensions for implementing Suckerfish-inspired drop downs:. `http://extensions.Joomla.org/extensions/core-enhancements/menu-systems/drop-&-tab-menus`.

My two favorites are:

Extended Menu: Daniel Ecer's menu uses the Suckerfish method and offers a way to display them in several options. I discussed this extension in the Joomla! 1.0 book, and it is fully native in Joomla! 1.5 as well: `http://extensions.Joomla.org/extensions/core-enhancements/menu-systems/drop-&-tab-menus/163/details`.

Superfish Dropdown Menu: Cy Moris has taken "Superfish", which is the Suckerfish menu enhanced with a tasteful Jquery fade effect that degrades elegantly in browsers that are older and/or have JavaScripting turned off: `http://extensions.Joomla.org/extensions/core-enhancements/menu-systems/drop-&-tab-menus/6731/details`.

Flash-ize It

Adobe Flash: It's come quite a long way since my first experience with it as a Macromedia product (Version 2 in 1997). Yet still, it does not adhere to W3C standards, requires a plugin to view, and, above all, is a pretty pricey proprietary product. So why is everyone so hot on using it? Love it or hate it, Flash is here to stay. It does have a few advantages, which we'll take a quick look at.

The Flash player plugin does boast the highest saturation rate around (way above other media player extensions), and now readily accommodates audio and video, which many video sites, most notably YouTube, take advantage of. It's pretty easy to add and upgrade it for all major browsers. The price may seem prohibitive at first, but once you're in for the initial purchase, additional upgrades are reasonably priced. Plus, many third-party software companies offer very cheap authoring tools that allow you to create animations and author content using the Flash player format (in most cases, no one need to know you're using the $50 version of Swish and not the $800 Flash CS4 to create your content).

Above all, it can do so much more than just play video and audio (like most extensions). You can create seriously rich and interactive content, even entire applications with it, and the best part is, no matter what you create with it, it is going to look and work exactly the same on all browsers and platforms. These are just a few of the reasons so many developers choose to build content and applications for the Flash player.

Oh, and did I mention you can easily make awesome, visually-slick video-and audio-filled stuff with it? Yeah, that's the reason your client wants you to put it in their site.

Flash in your template

A common requested use of Flash is usually in the form of a snazzy header within the template of a site, the idea being that various relevant and/or random photographs or designs load into the header with some super cool animation (and possibly audio) every time a page loads or a section changes.

I'm going to assume if you're using anything that requires the Flash player, you're pretty comfy with generating content for it. So, we're not going to focus on any Flash timeline tricks or ActionScripting. We'll simply cover getting your Flash content into your Joomla! template.

For the most part, you can simply take the HTML object embed code that Flash (or other third-party tools) will generate for you and paste it directly into the header area of your Joomla! `index.php` template file.

I use a very basic embed method, based on the "Satay" method. This method works well with the ObjectSwap version check and ActiveX Restriction workaround that we'll get to in the next section of this chapter).

What's the Satay method? It's a slightly cleaner way to embed your Flash movies while still supporting web standards. Drew McLellan discusses its development in detail in his article: `http://www.alistapart.com/articles/flashsatay`. This method was fine on its own until IE6 decided to include its ActiveX Security Restriction. Nowadays, your best bet is to just implement the ObjectSwap method, which we'll discuss below.

Placing Flash content directly into your Joomla! template is really only useful if you're the only person who will ever be administrating the Joomla! site with this content, or you're positive the Flash content is purely part of the template's design and not something any Joomla! Administrator would ever want to control. If you plan to release your Joomla! template to the public, you really should consider displaying your Flash content via the CMS, either in a module or in the content area. This will also save you the trouble of having to update your templateDetails.xml file, if you plan to distribute the template.

Time for action: Adding a swf file to your template

You can use the swf file included in this book's code packet (`http://www.packtpub.com/files/code/7160_Code.zip`) or one you've created on your own.

1. Create a new directory in your template, called flash, and place the swf file in it. Then, include this code inside your header div in your index.php template file:

```
...
<object data="<?php echo $this->baseurl  ?>/templates
/go_green/flash/green-flash-sample.swf" type="application/x-
shockwave-flash" width="280" height="50">

  <param name="movie" value="<?php echo $this->baseurl ?>/
      templates/go_green/flash/green-flash-sample.swf" />
  <param name="menu" value="false" />
  <param name="wmode" value="transparent" />
  <param name="quality" value="best" />

</object>
...
```

2. Add this `id` rule to your stylesheet (I placed it just below my other `header` and `intHeader` `id` rules):

```
...
#flashHold{
  float: right;
  margin-top: 12px;
  margin-right: 47px;
}
...
```

> Be sure to place the full path to your `swf` file in the `src` and `value` parameters for the embed tags! Store your Flash file inside your template folder and link to it directly. I like to use the `<?php echo $this->baseurl ?>` Joomla! PHP code to lead me up to my template location. This will ensure that your `swf` file loads properly.

As long as you take care to make sure the `div` is positioned correctly, the object embed code has the correct height and width of your Flash file, and you're not accidentally overwriting any parts of the template that contain Joomla! `jdoc` tags or other valuable PHP code, you're good to go.

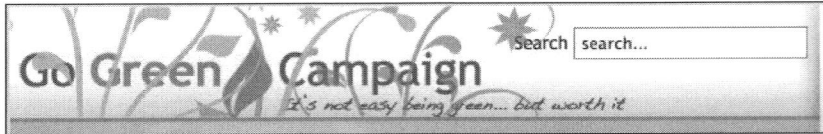

Pass Flash a Joomla! variable

So now you've popped a nice Flash header into your template. Here's a quick trick to make it all the more impressive:

If you'd like to keep track of what page, post, or category your Joomla! user has clicked on and display a relevant image or animation in the header, you can pass your Flash `swf` file a variable from Joomla! using PHP.

The PHP variable `$Itemid` is used by Joomla! to denote specific page content. If you're using the Joomla! default URL strings, you will probably notice something like this in your address bar:

```
http://localhost/1.5dev/index.php?option=com_content&view=article&id=
3&Itemid=2
```

If you've set Joomla!'s SEO Settings to use search-engine-friendly URLs, you will notice something like the following:

```
http://localhost/1.5dev/green-hacker-guide
```

The SEO-friendly URLs are definitely preferred, especially for a live site. However, if you turn them off temporarily, you'll be able to click through your content and notice what `Itemids` are assigned to the different menu items on your site. Jot down a few numbers and then you can turn your SEO-friendly URLs back on.

That `Itemid=` at the end of the URL we noted above, can be accessed in your template as a PHP variable. In the past, with Joomla! 1.0, if you coded up `<?php echo $Itemid; ?>` in your template, the result would be the number "2" displaying in your site (or the number of whatever menu item you clicked on).

The same principle can be used in Joomla! 1.5. However, Joomla! has beefed up its security so that its "non-friendly" URLs can't be exploited quite so easily. You have to do a little "coaxing" to target any of the variables you find in your Joomla! 1.5 site's URLs.

Calling the variables via a small PHP function and assigning them to a new variable does the trick:

```php
<?php
   function getItemid(){
     global $Itemid;
     return $Itemid;
   }
   $newItemid = getItemid();
?>
```

You can now call `$newItemid` anywhere in your Joomla! template with a simple PHP echo statement.

Time for action: Prepping the Flash file

Let's set up a Flash file to accept our Joomla! variable.

1.   In your Flash authoring program, set up a series of animations or images that will load or play based on a variable set in the root timeline called `itemID`.

2.   You'll pass this variable to your ActionScript.

3. In my example FLA if the `itemID` variable does not equal 3, then the main animation will play, but if the variable returns 3, then the visibility of the movie clip containing the question marks in it will be set to `true`. (`itemID 3` is the "Why Now" link in my Joomla! 1.5 case study. `itemID` might be named differently in your project. You can set it to any `itemID` value you want for your own template.)

Time for more action: **Passing the variable to the** `swf` **file**

Now, let's get our PHP variable into our `swf` file. In your object embed code, where your `swfs` are called, be sure to add this code:

```
<object data="http://wpdev25.eternalurbanyouth.com/wp-content/
templates/oo_magazine/flash/ooflash-sample.swf"
      type="application/x-shockwave-flash"
      width="338"
      height="150">

      FlashVars="itemID=<?echo newItemid;?>">

   <param name="movie" value="http://wpdev25.eternalurbanyouth.com/wp-
          content/templates/oo_magazine/flash/ooflash-sample.swf?" />
   <param name="menu" value="false" />

    <param name="FlashVars" value="itemID=<?echo newItemid;?>"/>

   <param name='wmode" value="transparent" />
   <param name='quality" value="best" />
</object>
```

Using this method, every time someone loads a page or clicks a link on your site that is within the "Why Now" item link, PHP will render the template tag as (or, whatever the `$newItemid;` for that page is):

```
itemID=3
```

So, your Flash file's ActionScript is going to look for a variable in the `_root` or `_level0` called `itemID`, and, based on that value, do whatever you told it to do. This could be calling an ActionScript function, or a `gotoAndPlay()`, to send it to a frame and animate—whatever you want the `.swf` file to do. Here's a screenshot of our leafy header animation after the "Why Now" link (aka `itemID 3`) was selected:

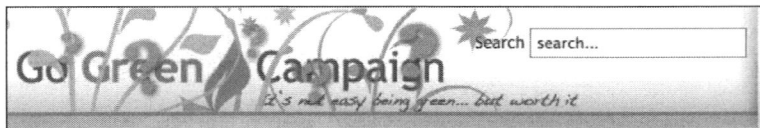

More fun with CSS

If you look at the final template package for this chapter (`http://www.packtpub.com/files/code/7160_Code.zip`), I've included the original `green-flash-sample.fla`. You'll notice if you open up the `.fla` (created in Flash CS3), it has a standard white background. If you look at my embed code, you'll note that I've set my `wmode` parameter to `transparent`. This way, my animation is working with my CSS background. Rather than beef up my `swf`'s file size with another Go Green logo, I simply animate over what's already there. Even if my animation "hangs" or never loads, the user's perception and experience of the page is not hampered. You can also use this trick as a "cheater's preloader". In your stylesheet, assign the `div` that holds your Flash object embed tags, a background image of an animating preloading GIF, or some other image that indicates the user should expect something to load. The user will see this background image until your flash file starts to play and covers it up. My favorite site to get and create custom loading GIFs is `http://www.ajaxload.info/`.

The ObjectSwap method for Flash

What about users who don't have Flash installed or have an old version that won't support your content? What about users who are still using IE6 with its silly ActiveX Restriction? By amending your object embed code with this following solution, your template will gracefully handle users who do not have Flash. If you've used the "overlay" method above, they'll simply see the CSS background image and probably know nothing is wrong. This method lets you add in a line of text or a static image as an alternate, so people who don't have the extension/correct version installed are either served up alternative content and they're none-the-wiser, or served up content that nicely explains that they need the Flash player and directs them toward getting it. Most importantly, this method also nicely handles IE's Active X restrictions.

What is the Active X Restriction? In 2006, the IE browser upgraded its security, so users now have to validate content that shows up in the Flash player (or any player) via MicroSoft's ActiveX Controls. Your Flash content will start to play, but there will be this "grey outline" around the player area, which may or may not mess up your design. If your content is interactive, then people will need to click to activate it. This is annoying but the ObjectSwap method is an excellent workaround for it.

Essentially, you need to include your Flash content via a JavaScript include file. I used to use my own custom JavaScript, which was great for new content, but not so great for all my old content that's already out there (who wants to go rewrite all his/her object embed tags as JavaScript includes?). The ObjectSwap method relieves this burden. You simply include your Flash with the Satay method embed and make sure your template calls the objectswap.js file via a JavaScript include in your header tags. You can learn more about this method from SitePoint: http://www.sitepoint.com/article/activex-activation-issue-ie.

Time for action: Adding the ObjectSwap script

It helps to understand a little bit of JavaScript, but even if you don't, this is a great script that will very easily allow you to activate Flash movies for ActiveX and make it much easier to update older content from past projects without stripping out the original object embed tags. And because it's so simple, it fits right into a Joomla! template page without any stress.

1. You'll simply copy the JavaScript include line into your header.php and/or index.php header tags:

   ```
   <script type="text/javascript" src="<?php echo $this->baseurl; ?>/
                templates/your_template_name/js/objectSwap.js"> </script>
   ```

2. You'll then include the objectswap.js file with your template template files, by placing the file inside your template folder. As you can see by my path above, I like to make a js folder inside my template folder and place .js files inside there. Be sure to update your templateDetails.xml file with all new files you add to your template.

3. Be sure to read the article at the link provided above. Download the example files here:

   ```
   http://www.sitepoint.com/examples/objectswap/objectswap.zip
   ```

More good news! It looks like Microsoft is planning to remove the "click to activate" requirement for IE's newer versions. Eventually, IE6 will go away, and we'll all live happily ever after with IE8 and beyond. Even after this happens, as mentioned above, the objectswap.js is a great way to handle not having Flash installed or having a version that is too old.

Good developer's tip

Even if you loath IE (as a lot of us web developers tend to), it is an industry standard browser, and you have to work with it. I've found Microsoft's IE blog (`http://blogs.msdn.com/ie/`) extremely useful in keeping tabs on IE so that I can better develop CSS based-templates for it. While you're at it, go ahead and subscribe to the RSS feeds for Firefox (`http://developer.mozilla.org/devnews/`), Safari (`http://developer.apple.com/internet/safari/`), and your other favorite browsers. You'll be surprised at the insight you can glean, which can come in extremely handy if you ever need to debug CSS or JavaScripts for one of those browsers.

Yes, of course, there're extensions: This won't help you too much if you're planning on using Flash in your template. For Flash in your Joomla! posts and pages, Jim Penaloza has written a great little extension using the SWFObject method detailed above. You can find out more about it here: `http://extensions.Joomla.org/extensions/5871/details`.

Flash in Joomla! content or modules

For Flash content that's going to go into a specific Joomla! module or article/content page, there's pretty much only one way to go about it: get an extension.

Many of the sites I'm working on are putting up their videos of commercials, conferences, presentations, and just plain fun and silliness on YouTube, then embedding the files on their own sites.

YouTube is great! For this book's project, I was able to use the site's search functionality to quickly find the relevant video snippet of Al Gore discussing his movie *An Inconvenient Truth*, and to the right of the video play area, I quickly found the options for linking to YouTube page or embedding the file. Wanting to embed the Flash video on my site, I selected the code from the **Embed** field on the YouTube's site just to the right of the video display.

Now the fun begins. If you've spent any time at all with a Joomla! project and attempted to place any specific markup into an article, you've probably realized pretty quickly the frustrating limitations of the TinyMCE WYSIWYG editor. In the past, for Joomla! 1.0 sites, the XHTML/CSS savvy administrator could turn off the TinyMCE editor and place in custom markup without much difficulty.

The TinyMCE WYSIWYG editor is a little too "helpful", and I'm not sure why it even has that cute little "HTML" button option in it, as whatever special markup you place in there, it is just going to be overwritten with whatever TinyMCE "thinks" the markup should be—which is pretty limited. Flash embed tags are definitely not in this WYSIWYG's vocabulary! The following screenshot illustrates attempting to turn off the TinyMCE editor in my **User Parameters**:

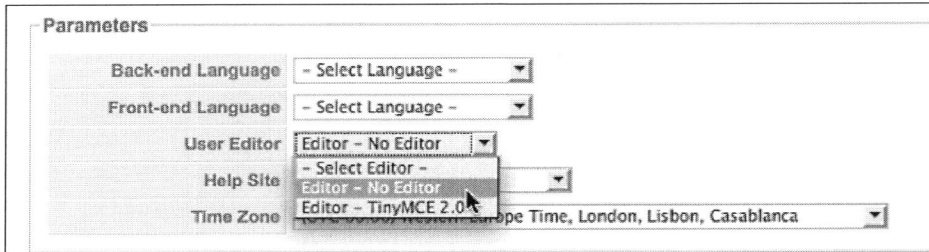

However, after turning off this editor in Joomla! 1.5 and going to the **Content | Article Manager**, I attempted to place in my YouTube embed tag.

I placed the embed code in my non-WYSIWYG editing screen as shown in the following screenshot:

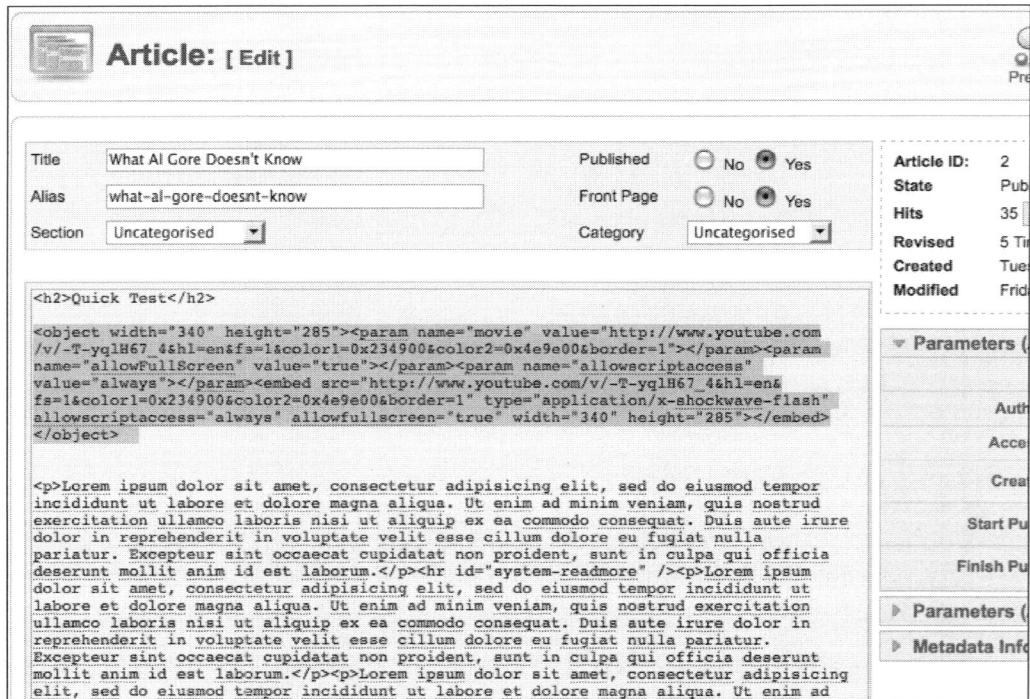

Trouble is, after hitting **Save**, Joomla! still stripped out the `<object>` `<embed>` parts of the tag, leaving only the `<params>` list. This resulted in no video showing and a broken layout.

I even tried turning the TinyMCE editor back on and using the **Insert Embeded Media** button. I mean, it must be there for a reason, right? Using this feature, I pasted in the URL to the YouTube file. This looked promising as the wizard box displayed my video and allowed me to select some options for it:

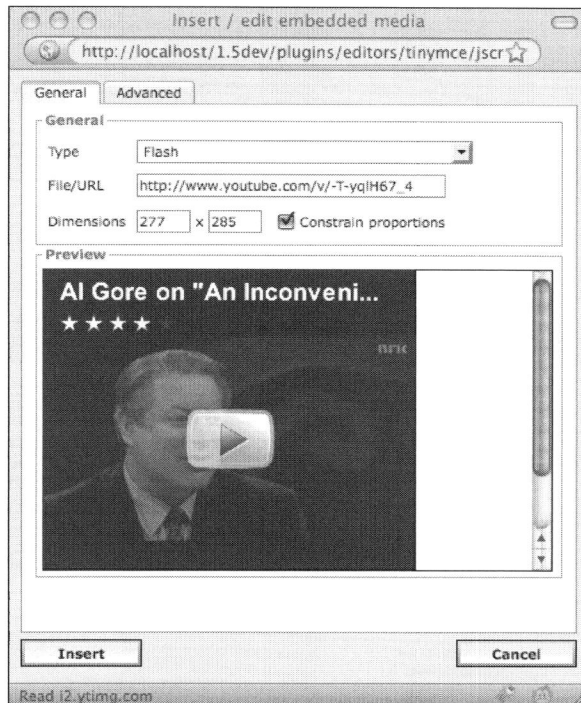

Alas, it was of no use. Once hitting **Insert** and then **Save** in the article panel, I returned to my site only to find no Flash video and a very broken layout:

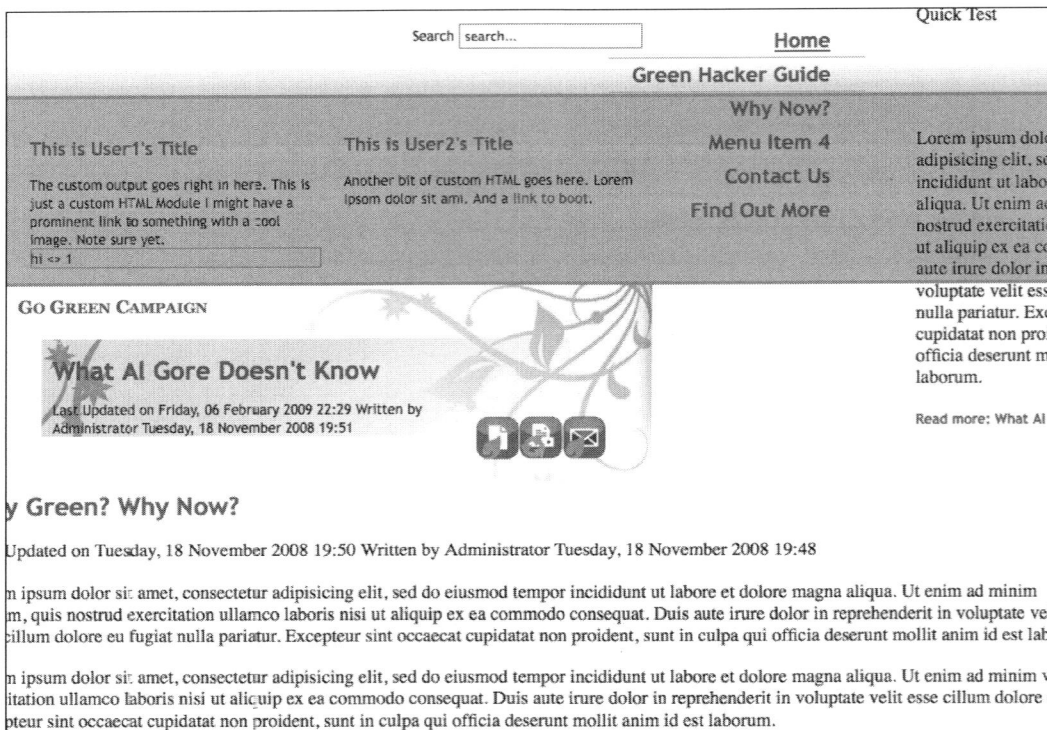

Yuck! This to me, as much as I like Joomla!, is a bit of a drawback on Joomla's part. Video swapping is common place these days, and lots of open source CMSs use some variant of the TinyMCE editor and don't have this issue with entering custom markup and embed tags into content.

Ah, but in the world of open source, many good souls have recognized this issue, and there are many, many extensions you can easily implement to embed Flash into your Joomla! content. As far as easily getting Flash video into your site, I really like Cory Webb's plugin, which can be found along with instructions to use it here:

```
http://www.howtojoomla.net/2008072390/how-tos/mambots/plugins/how-to-
embed-a-youtube-video-into-an-article-in-Joomla-15
```

After downloading this plugin and going to **Extensions | Install/Uninstall**, the plugin installed just fine. As shown in the following screenshot, I then went to **Extensions | Plugin Manager** and enabled it.

> You'll find that installing most extensions—be they components, modules, or plugins—into Joomla! 1.5 is this easy. They're also just as easily unpublished and deleted. Don't be afraid to try the extensions I suggest and do searches to find your solutions to your site's specific needs.

I then simply pasted the main link from my YouTube page into my content.

The end result was, surprisingly (after all the trouble I'd just gone through), perfect:

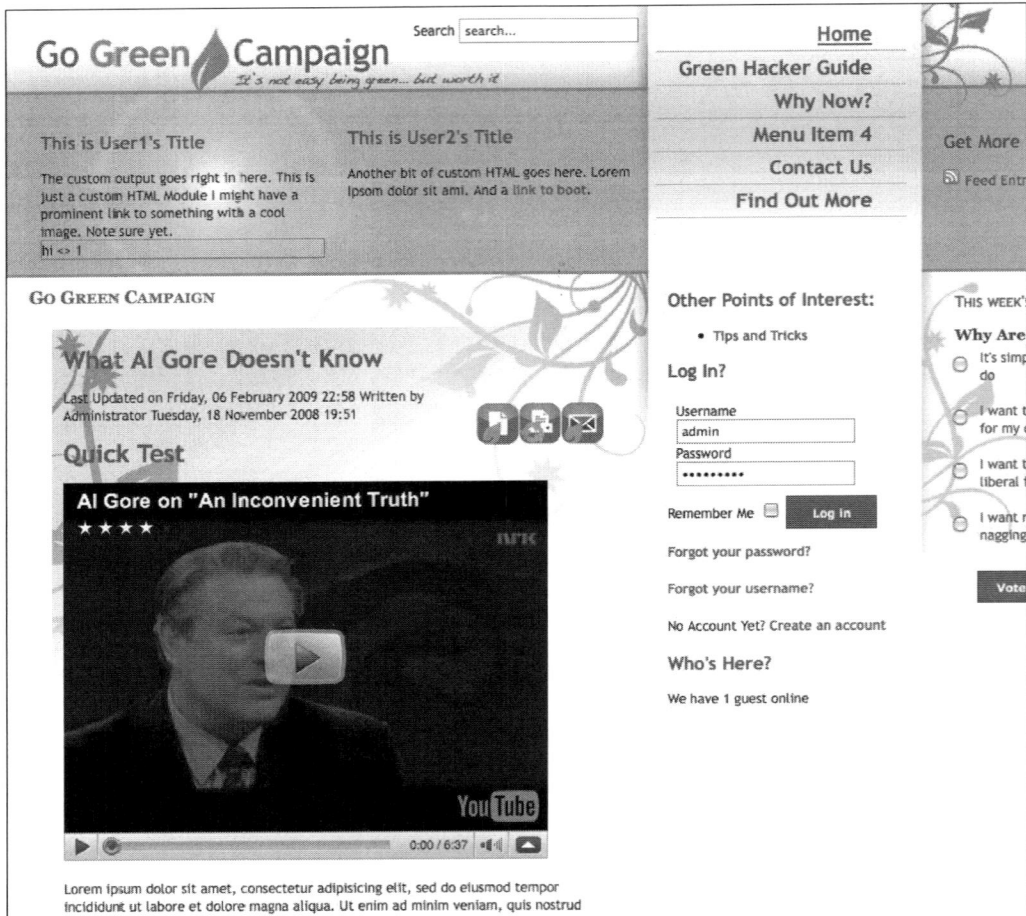

Want more Flash? Despite my warnings at the beginning of this chapter, if you still want to add more interesting Flash to your site, there's a host of Flash-based Joomla! extensions that allow you to easily embed Flash content and features into your Joomla! site and use the Administration panel to easily customize and update your Flash content. For more video-content-embedding extensions, check out this link: `http://extensions.Joomla!.org/extensions/search/1/youtube`.

Even more Flash: There are great extensions for other Flash content, such as photo galleries and your own files. My personal favorite is the Ozio photo gallery extension, which is an easy install and offers a host of "skins": `http://oziogallery.Joomla.it/index.php?option=com_content&view=article&id=38&Itemid=40&lang=en`. Check out the extensions directory for more Flash: `http://extensions.Joomla.org/index.php?option=com_mtree&task=listcats&cat_id=2023&Itemid=35`.

Summary

In this chapter we've looked at creating a dynamic layout with collapsable columns and getting drop-down Suckerfish menus and Flash content quickly and painlessly into your Joomla! template and content. Next up: Getting AJAX with dynamic interactive forms into your Joomla! project.

8
AJAX/Dynamic Content and Interactive Forms

AJAX: an acronym that Jesse James Garret of AdaptivePath.com came up with in 2005. Just a few short years later, it seems like every site has a "taste" of AJAX in it. If you're totally new to AJAX, I'll just point out that, at its core, AJAX is nothing very scary or horrendous. AJAX isn't even a new technology or language.

Essentially, AJAX stands for: Asynchronous JavaScript and XML, and it is the technique of using JavaScript and XML to send and receive data between a web browser and a web server. The biggest advantage this technique has is that you can dynamically update a piece of content on your web page or web form with data from the server (preferably formatted in XML), without forcing the entire page to reload. The implementation of this technique has made it obvious to many web developers that they can start making advanced web applications (sometimes called RIAs — Rich Interface Applications) that work and feel more like software applications than web pages.

Keep in mind that the word AJAX is starting to have its own meaning (as you'll also note its occasional use here as well as all over the Web as a proper noun rather than an all-cap acronym). For example, a Microsoft web developer may use VBScript instead of JavaScript to serve up Microsoft Access database data that is transformed into JSON (not XML) using a .NET server-side script. Today, that guy's site would still be considered an AJAX site rather than an "AVAJ" site (yep, AJAX just sounds cooler).

In fact, it's getting to the point where just about anything on a web site (that isn't in Flash) that slides, moves, fades, or pops up without rendering a new browser window is considered an "Ajaxy" site. In truth, a large portion of these sites don't truly qualify as using AJAX, they're just using straight-up JavaScripting. Generally, if you use cool JavaScripts in your Joomla! site, it will probably be considered Ajaxy, despite not being asynchronous or using any XML.

We're going to take a look at the most popular methods to get you going with AJAX in Joomla!—using extensions and plugins, in order to help you include dynamic self-updating content and create interactive forms in your Joomla! site. While we're at it, we'll also look at some cool JavaScript toolkits, libraries, and scripts you can use to appear Ajaxy.

Want more info on this AJAX business? The w3schools site has an excellent introduction to AJAX, explaining it in straightforward simple terms. They even have a couple of great tutorials that are fun and easy to accomplish even if you only have a little HTML, JavaScript and server-side script (PHP or ASP) experience (no XML experience required): `http://w3schools.com/ajax/`.

Preparing for dynamic content and interactive forms

Gone are the days of clicking, submitting, and waiting for the next page to load, or manually compiling your own content from all your various online identities to post in your site.

A web page using AJAX techniques (if applied properly) will give the user a smoother and leaner experience. Click on a drop-down option and check-box menus underneath are immediately updated with the relevant choices—no submitting, no waiting. Complicated forms that, in the past, took two or three screens to process can be reduced into one convenient screen by implementing the form with AJAX.

As wonderful as this all sounds, I must again offer a quick disclaimer: I understand that, like with drop-down menus and Flash, you may want AJAX to be in your site, or your clients are demanding that AJAX be in their sites. Just keep in mind, AJAX techniques are best used in situations where they truly benefit a user's experience of a page; for example, being able to painlessly add relevant content via an extension or cutting a lengthy web process form down from three pages to one. In a nutshell, using an AJAX technique simply to say your site is an AJAX site is probably not a good idea.

You should be aware that, if not implemented properly, some uses of AJAX can compromise the security of your site. You may inadvertently end up disabling key web browser features (such as back buttons or the history manager). Then there's all the basic usability and accessibility issues that JavaScript in general can bring to a site.

Some screen readers may not be able to read a new screen area that's been generated by JavaScript. If you cater to users who rely on tabbing through content, navigation may be compromised once new content is updated. There are also interface design problems that AJAX brings to the table (and Flash developers can commiserate). Many times, in trying to limit screen real estate and simplify a process, developers actually end up creating a form or interface that is unnecessarily complex and confusing, especially when your user is expecting a web page to, well, act like a normal web page.

> **Remember to check in with Don't Make Me Think**: This is the Steve Krug book I recommended in *Chapter 7* for help with any interface usability questions you may run into
>
> **Really interested in taking on AJAX**? For you programmers, I highly recommend *"AJAX and PHP: Building Responsive Web Applications"*, *Cristian Darie, Bogdan Brinzarea, Filip Chereches-Tosa, and Mihai Bucica, Packt Publishing*. In it, you'll learn the ins and outs of AJAX development, including handling security issues. You'll also do some very cool stuff, such as make your own Google-style auto-suggest form and a drag-and-drop sortable list (and that's just two of the many fun things to learn in the book).

So, that said, you're now all equally warned and armed with all the knowledgeable resources I can think to throw at you. Let's get to it: how exactly do you go about getting something Ajaxy into your Joomla! site?

Joomla! extensions

Essentially, this book is primarily about creating a Joomla! template and not about PHP, JavaScript, or the specific inner workings of Joomla's MySQL databases. Thus, we're going to focus on installing and integrating some extensions that can help aid you in adding AJAX functionality to your site. (Never fear; in a bit, we will take a look at a few easy-to-implement JavaScript libraries and a plugin that can easily "AJAX-ify" your site and template.)

Keep in mind, extensions are not part of your template. They are additional files with Joomla!-compatible PHP code, which are installed separately into their own directories in your Joomla! 1.5 installation. Once installed, they are available to be used with any template that is also installed in your Joomla! installation.

Even though these are not part of your template, you might have to prepare your template to be fully compatible with them. Some extensions may have their own stylesheets, which are installed in their extension directory. Once you've installed an extension, you may want to go into your own template's stylesheet so that it nicely displays XHTML objects and content that the extension may output into your site.

We covered what extensions are in *Chapter 2* in some detail, but to refresh your memory, I'll remind you that extensions are any component, module or plugin that you install into your Joomla! 1.5 installation.

Components control content that displays in the main `type="component"` `jdoc` tag in your template. Note that components may also have module settings and the ability to display content in assigned module positions. The poll component is a good example of a component that also has module settings.

Modules are usually smaller and lighter and only display in module positions.

Plugins generally help you out more on the backend of your site, say to switch WYSIWYG editors or with enabling OpenID logins, but as we'll see, some plugins can affect the display of your site to users as well.

Deciding where AJAX is best used

On the whole, we're going to look at the most popular places where AJAX can really aid and enrich your site's user experience. We'll start with users adding comments to articles and pages and streamlining that process. We'll then take a look at a nice plugin that can enhance pagination for people reading long articles on your site.

We'll then move on to the RSS Reader module, which can enhance the content in your modules (and even makes your users have fun arranging them). Finally, we'll realize that AJAX isn't just for impressing your site users. You, as an administrator, can (and do) take advantage of AJAX as well.

Please note: These extensions were chosen by me based on the following criteria:

1. They provided some useful enhancement to a basic site.

2. They, at the time of this writing, were free and received very good feedback on Joomla!.org's extensions site: `http://extensions.Joomla.org`.

In the next few pages, I'll walk you through installing these extensions and discuss any interesting insights for doing so, and benefits of their enhancements (and some drawbacks). But you must use the extension links provided to make sure you download the latest stable versions of these extensions and follow the extension author's installation guides when installing these into your Joomla! site. If you run into any problems installing these extensions, please contact the extension's author for support. Always be sure to take the normal precaution of backing up your site before installation, at least for any non-stable extensions you may decide to try.

Installing the Joomla! comment component

Chances are, if you've invested in Joomla! 1.5 as your CMS, you need some powerful capabilities. Easy commenting with "captcha" images to reduce spam is always helpful:

```
http://extensions.Joomla!.org/extensions/contacts-&-feedback/
comments/4389/details
```

To install this extension (and the other few coming up), you have to basically go to **Extensions | Install/Uninstall** and upload the extension's ZIP file. You'll then proceed to the plugin, component, and/or modules panel and activate the extension so that it is ready to be implemented on your site.

Upon installing this comment component, to my surprise, it told me that it was for an older version of Joomla! Everything on the download page seemed to indicate it worked with 1.5. The installation error did mention that I just needed to activate the **System Legacy** plugin and it would work. So I did, and the comment form appeared on all my article pages. This may seem like a step backward, but for extensions like this, which are very useful, if they work well and stay stable in Legacy Mode, a developer may have made the decision to leave well enough alone. The developer will most likely eventually upgrade the extension (especially if Legacy Mode goes away in future versions of Joomla!). Just be sure to sign up for updates or check back on any extensions you use if you do upgrade your site. You should do this regardless of whether your extensions run natively or in Legacy Mode.

The advantage of AJAX in a comment form is that a user isn't distracted and comments' post smoothly and right away (a bit of instant gratification for the user, even if you never "confirm" the post and it never gets actually published for other viewers). This extension outputs tables, but for the ease of handling robust comments and having a great admin area to manage them, I'll make do. The following screenshot shows the Joomla! comment component appearing in an article page:

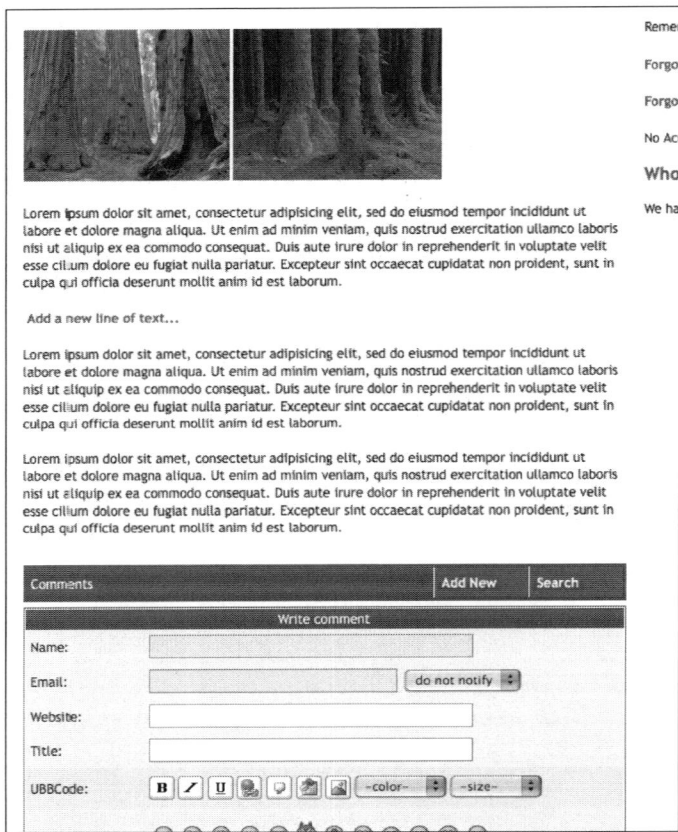

As you can see in my previous image, I have some strong styles that are trying to override the component's styles. A closer look at the output HTML will give me some class names and objects that I can target with CSS. The administration panel's **Component | Joomla! Comment | Other Component** settings page also allows quite a few customization options. The **Layout** tab also offers several included style sheets to select from as well as the option to copy the CSS sheet out to my template's directory (the component will do this automatically). This way, I can amend it with my own specific CSS, giving my comment form a better fit with my template's design.

Installing the core design Ajax Pagebreak plugin

If your site has long articles that get broken down regularly in to three or more pages, Pagebreak is a nice plugin that uses Ajax to smoothly load the next page. It's a useful feature that will also leave your site users with a little "oh wow" expression.

```
http://www.greatJoomla!.com/news/plugins/demo-core-design-ajax-
pagebreak-plugin.html
```

After successfully installing this plugin, I headed over to the **Extensions | Plugin Manager** and activated it.

I then beefed out an article (with Lorem Ipsum) and added page breaks to it on the Home Page. It's hard to see in a screenshot, but it appears below the **Prev** and **Next** links without a full browser redraw. I've set my site up with SEO-friendly URLs, and this plugin does amend the URLs with a string; that is, `http://yoururl.com/1.5dev/menu-item-4?start=1`. I'm not sure how this will really affect the SEO "friendliness" value of my URL, but it does give me a specific URL to give to people if I want to send them to a targeted page, which is very good for accessibility. One thing to note, the first page of the article is the original URL; that is, `http://yoururl.com/1.5dev/menu-item-4`. The second page then appends `?start=1,` the third page becomes `?start=2`, and so on. Just be aware that when sending links out to people, it is always best to pull the URL directly from the site so that you know it's correct!

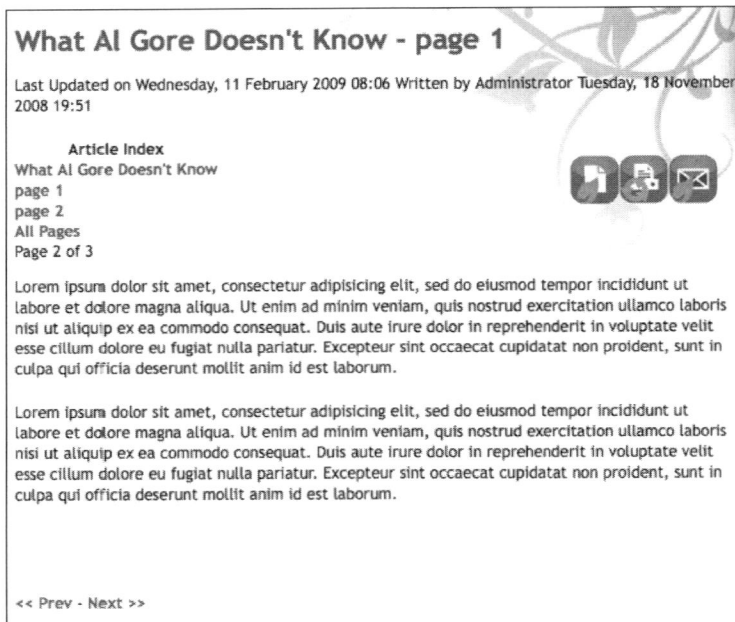

Installing the AJAX RSS Reader Version 3 with Draggable Divs module

RSS feeds are a great way to bring together a wide variety of content as well as bring all your or your organization's "social network happenings" to one place in your own site. I like to use RSS feeds to get people interested in knowing what an organization is doing (or tweeting), or reading, and so on. Having links and lists of what's currently going on can compel users to link to you, join your group, follow you, and become a friend, a fan, or whatever.

This AJAX powered module has the extra feature of being draggable and somewhat editable. This is a nice way to draw a user in to the feeds and let them play with them and arrange the information to their taste. Sometimes, sorting and reorganizing makes you see connections and possibilities that you didn't see before. The next image may seem confusing, but it's a screenshot of the top `div` box being dragged and dropped.

```
http://extensions.Joomla!.org/extensions/394/details
```

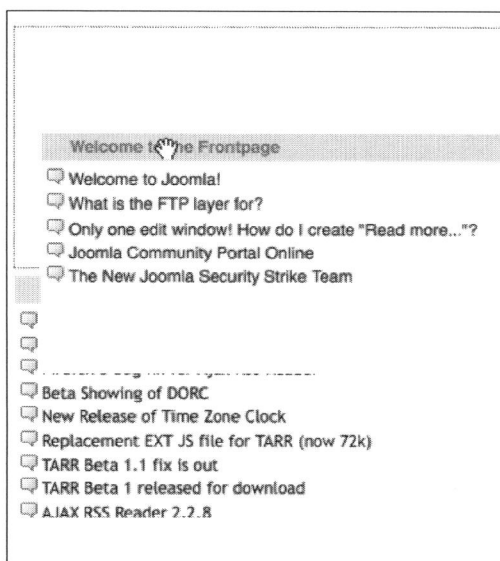

AJAX: It's not just for your site's users

I've already mentioned, when applied properly, how AJAX can aid in interface usability. Joomla! attempts to take advantage of this within its Administration panel by enhancing it with relevant information and compressing multiple page forms into one single screen area. Here's a quick look at how Joomla! already uses AJAX to enhance its Administration panel forms:

The following image shows how the image uploader uses a "lightbox" `div` layer effect so that you can keep track of where you are in the content editor.

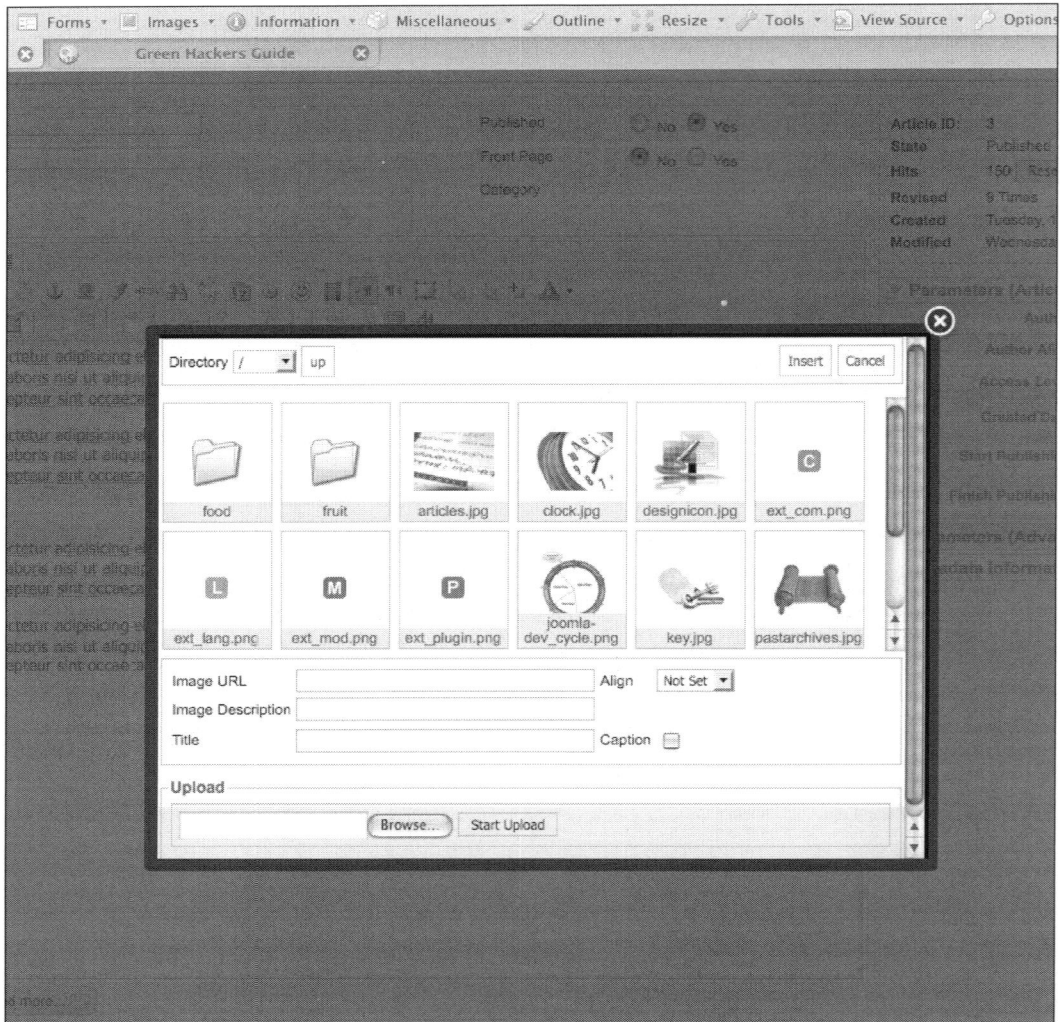

In the next image, you can see how Joomla! helps keep the administration area cleared up by using smooth-sliding accordion panels. This helps you see everything on one page and have access to just what you need, when you need it.

```
Article ID:    3
State          Published
Hits           156  Reset
Revised        10 Times
Created        Tuesday, 18 November 2008 19:55
Modified       Wednesday, 11 February 2009 06:21
```

▷ Parameters (Article)

▽ Parameters (Advanced)

Show Title	Use Global ▾
Title Linkable	Use Global ▾
Intro Text	Use Global ▾
Section Name	Use Global ▾
Section Title Linkable	Use Global ▾
Category Title	Use Global ▾
Category Title Linkable	Use Global ▾
Article Rating	Use Global ▾
Author Name	Use Global ▾
Created Date and Time	Use Global ▾
Modified Date and Time	Use Global ▾
PDF Icon	Use Global ▾
Print Icon	Use Global ▾
E-mail Icon	Use Global ▾
Content Language	– Select Language – ▾
Key Reference	
Alternative *Read more:* text	

▷ Metadata Information

The AJAX factor

Aside from the many interface-enhancing, time-saving benefits of Ajax, sometimes you do just want to "wow" your site visitors. It's easy to give your site an Ajaxy feel, regardless of asynchronously updating it with server-side XML, just by sprucing up your interface with some snappy JavaScripts. The easiest way to get many of these effects is to reference a JavaScript library (sometimes called a toolkit or framework, depending on how robust the provider feels the code is). A few of the leading favorites in the AJAX community (in no particular order) are:

- Script.alico.us: `http://script.aculo.us/`
- Prototype: `http://www.prototypejs.org/`
- jQuery: `http://jquery.com/`

There're also:

- MooTools: http://mootools.net/
- moo.fx: http://moofx.mad4milk.net/

Prototype is more of a framework and Script.alico.us is more of an add-on toolkit or set of libraries for neat effects. In fact, Script.alico.us references the Prototype framework, so your best bet is probably to use Script.alico.us, but if you do work with it, be sure to check out Prototype's site and try to understand what that framework does.

moo.fx is the smallest JavaScript effects library (boasting a 3k footprint), but again, it needs to be supported by the MooTools or Prototype frameworks.

jQuery is my personal favorite. It pretty much stands on its own without needing to be backed up by a more robust framework such as Prototype. Yet, you can still do some very robust things with it, such as manipulating data and the DOM. Plus, it's packed with the ability to do neat and cute visual effects similar to Script.alico.us or moo.fx.

Using JavaScript libraries such as the above, you'll be able to implement their features and effects with simple calls into your Joomla! posts and pages.

JavaScript component/plugin scripts

The fun doesn't stop there! What's that? You don't have time to go read up on how to use a JavaScript library such as jQuery? Never fear! There are many other JavaScript effect plugins that are built using the above libraries.

One of the most popular scripts out there that makes a big hit on any web site is Lightbox JS: http://www.huddletogether.com/projects/lightbox2/.

Lightbox JS is a simple, unobtrusive script used to overlay images on the current page. It's great, but it uses both the Prototype and Script.alico.us libraries to achieve its effects. Unfortunately, I've found Lightbox JS was a bit limited in terms of using it with a CMS that has a WYSIWYG editor like TinyMCE (although that didn't stop clients from wanting it on their site).

The problem

If you'll remember from *Chapter 7*, we had an issue with getting custom markup into our TinyMCE WYSIWYG editor. I then attempted to turn off the TinyMCE editor and found that even after using the plain text area editor, Joomla! modified my custom XHTML.

The same problem holds for Lightbox JS. While simple to add to your template, in order for Lightbox JS to work, you need to add a custom `rel="lightbox"` attribute to each `<a href...` tag that will call an image into the lightbox. While turning off the TinyMCE editor actually works here, and keeps the `rel="lightbox"` in tact after hitting **Save**, it only does so as long as the TinyMCE editor stays turned off.

This means: setting up quick Lightbox JS gallery images for clients in content pages only to have them constantly, inadvertently, mess them up and break them because they'd open up the content using their user logins, which, of course, are set to use the TinyMCE editor.

Upon loading the content from the database into the edit screen, TinyMCE likes to help out and do some cleaning up for you. That `rel="lightbox"` attribute in any links in the page sometimes drops out (and sometimes it stays; if you have several links to images, some may break and others may work). The client then calls me to fix the problem (upset, as they have to call me, and they thought they'd be the ones maintaining their own site).

While I'd like to get upset with my non-XHTML savvy clients, the truth is this is exactly the reason they've invested in the Joomla! CMS. They need an easy way to manage large sites with perhaps multiple editors, many of whom don't have the foggiest idea what an HTML tag is.

Enter jQuery lightBox

jQuery lightBox by Leandro Vieira Pinho is very similar to Lightbox JS in that it has that very nice, smooth animation. On the plus side, it uses only the jQuery library. On the plus plus side, it doesn't require any custom markup to your `<a href...` tags. You can download it from here:

`http://leandrovieira.com/projects/jquery/lightbox/`

Time for action: Adding jQuery to your template

This is an extremely easy-to-implement plugin. (Don't get confused, this is not a Joomla! plugin. jQuery refers to packaged scripts that use its library as plugins).

After downloading it, add the key `.js` and `.css` files inside your Joomla! template's `<header>` tags:

```
...
<script type="text/javascript" src="<?php echo $this->baseurl;
                ?>/templates/go_green/js/jquery.js"></script>

<script type="text/javascript" src="<?php echo $this->baseurl;
    ?>/templates/go_green/js/jquery.lightbox-0.5.js"></script>
...
```

You'll also add in a call to the jQuery lightBox CSS file:

```
...
<link rel="stylesheet" type="text/css" href="<?php echo $this-
>baseurl; ?>/templates/go_green/css/jquery.lightbox-0.5.css"
media="screen" />
...
```

Don't forget to upload the images in the ZIP package to your template's image directory and update the `jquery.lightbox-0.5.js` files image paths in line's **30** to **34**:

```
...
        imageLoading:       'templates/go_green/images/lightbox-ico-
loading.gif',      // (string) Path and the name of the loading icon

        imageBtnPrev:       'templates/go_green/images/lightbox-btn-
prev.gif',      // (string) Path and the name of the prev button
image

        imageBtnNext:       'templates/go_green/images/lightbox-btn-
next.gif',      // (string) Path and the name of the next button
image

        imageBtnClose:      'templates/go_green/images/lightbox-btn-
close.gif',      // (string) Path and the name of the close btn

        imageBlank:         'templates/go_green/images/lightbox-blank.
gif',           // (string) Path and the name of a blank image
(one pixel)
...
```

> Alternatively, you can upload the jQuery lightBox images into the `images` folder; that is, in the root of your Joomla! installation. You then won't need to edit the `jquery.lightbox-0.5.js` file. However, if you package your template up for other people to use, the images will not come over with your template and the script may appear broken.

Now, we're ready to activate the jQuery lightBox plugin. This is the beauty of jQuery. It has a robust DOM and CSS selector feature, and that means we don't have to put any special `class` or `rel` tags in our markup. We can generally target `<a href` links by placing a small jQuery JavaScript in our header (below our `.js` and `.css` file calls) like so:

```
...
<script type="text/javascript">
$(function() {
    $('#page a').lightBox(); // Select all links in an XHTML area with
page ID
```

```
});
</script>
...
```

This will work for all our article pages, because in *Chapter 3* we implemented the Beez template override files and all articles are wrapped in a `div` with a `#page id`.

Now you can create an article or content page in your Administration panel using the easy method of creating an article and adding content to it.

I uploaded the images via Joomla's built-in image uploader, which you can find at the bottom of the content editor. I then inserted my thumbnail version into the page and created a link to the image using the link editor in TinyMCE's editing options.

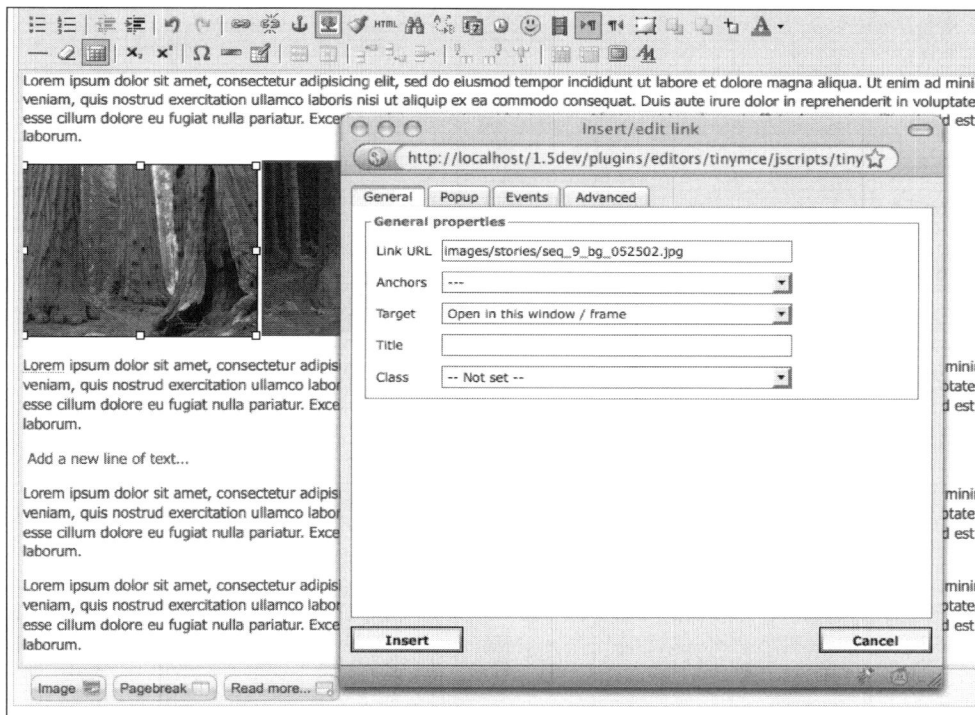

That's it!

But wait! Unfortunately, there's a small drawback: because I'm targeting the a href links inside the #page div, my **PDF**, **print**, and **email** buttons are activating the lightBox. As you can see by the following screenshot, the results are "interesting":

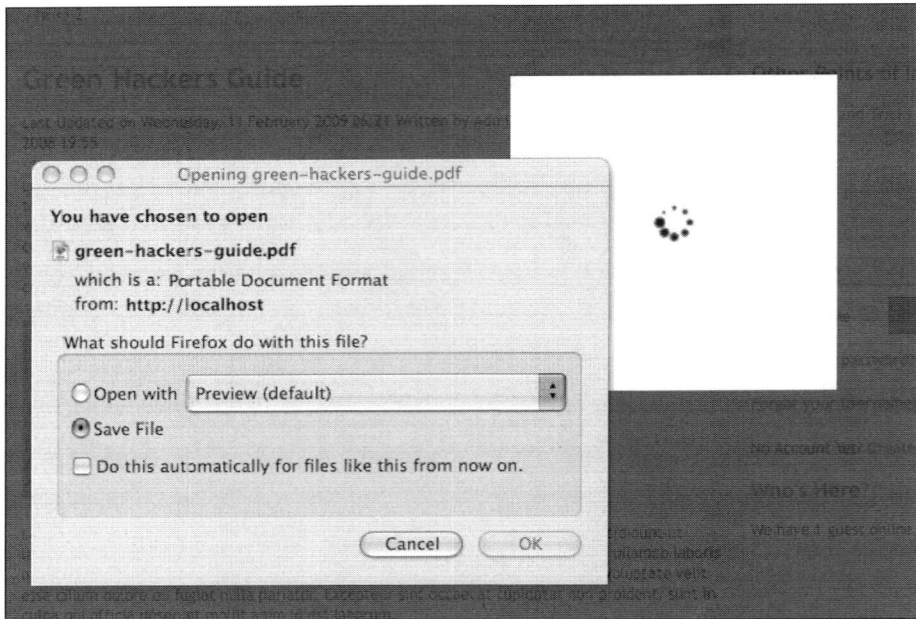

This is easily remedied if you know a bit about jQuery's selectors.

First off, we'll simply target the area we want to focus in on a bit more:

```
$('#page p a').lightBox();
```

This will only activate a hrefs inside p (paragraph) tags. This doesn't fix our problem, as those button links happen to be wrapped inside paragraph tags too. However, they do have a class called .buttonheading associated with them. So, we'll select a href's inside p tags that *do not* contain the class .buttonheading, as follows:

```
$('#page p:not(.buttonheading) a').lightBox();
```

This is great. The **PDF**, **print**, and **email** buttons now work. But I know my clients. They're going to create articles, and using nothing but the WYSIWYG editor, with no clue as to what markup they're actually creating. They will not only upload images with links for the lightBox, but probably also will throw in a bunch of other links to other stuff that shouldn't kick off the lightBox. The nerve! They can be so "link-happy" sometimes. Well, that's OK too. We'll simply amend the a selector a bit:

```
$('#page p:not(.buttonheading) a:has(img)').lightBox();
```

By adding `a:has(img)`, only the `<a href...` tags that wrap around images will activate the jQuery lightBox plugin.

You now have a fool-proof lightBoxing method that the most sloppy HTML mess-making WYSIWYGing editors will be hard pressed to break! The following image shows the lightbox at work in the template:

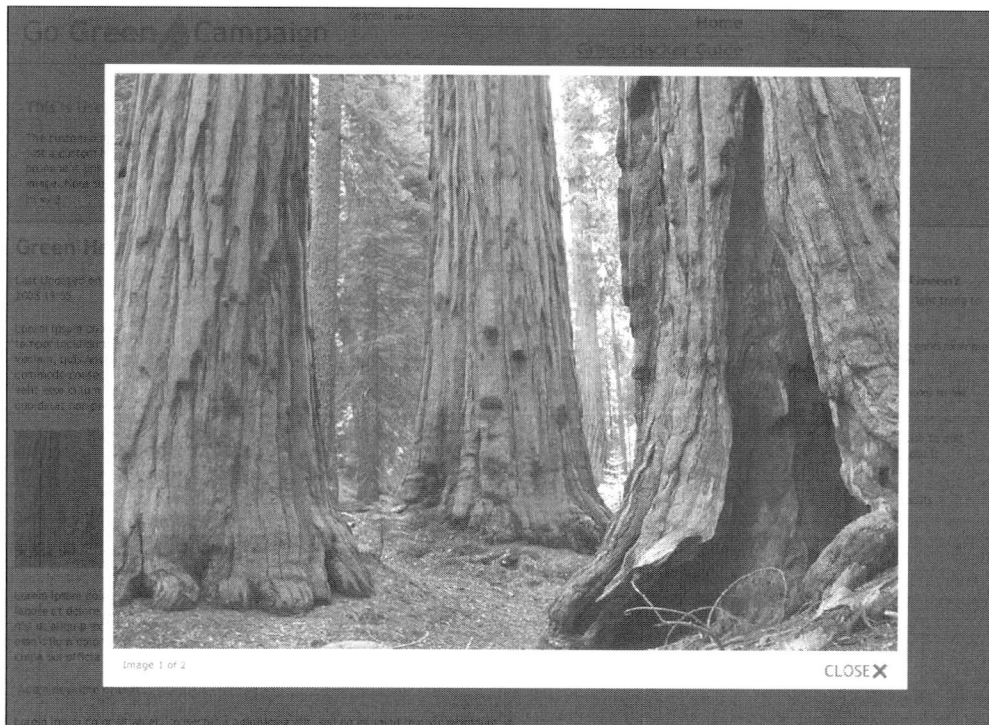

jQuery selectors: In order to make jQuery lightBox work well with your template, you should to understand selectors. Karl Swedberg has two excellent articles on targeting anything you want with jQuery selectors: `http://www.learningjquery.com/2006/12/how-to-get-anything-you-want-part-2`. You can also use jQuery's reference guide: `http://docs.jquery.com/Selectors`.

There's also jQuery's ThickBox: ThickBox installs and works very similar to jQuery lightBox. However, in addition to handling images similar to Lightbox JS, it can *also handle* in-line content, iFrame content, and AJAX content (be sure to check out the examples on the Thickbox page): `http://jquery.com/demo/thickbox/`.

The downside: ThickBox requires that you add a special `class="thickbox"` to your `<a href` tag markup. The good news is, TinyMCE doesn't strip this out, but you'll need to have content editors that know how to add that class to their content with the WYSIWYG editor turned off. ThickBox also doesn't do that "smooth" animation that jQuery lightbox does when images are different sizes. This is a trade-off I've made when I've occasionally decided it's important to be able to display more than just images in a layout design or Jooma! template.

Summary

In this chapter we reviewed a few ways to take advantage of AJAX on your Joomla! site. We downloaded and installed a handful of useful extensions and looked at using jQuery and jQuery lightBox to enhance post and page content. Up next: let's take a look at offering your users some Administration panel control over your template by creating a `params.ini` file. We'll touch on editing template override files to get more CSS control, and lastly, we'll cover some final design tips for working with Joomla!

9

Advanced Enhancements and Design Tips for Joomla! 1.5

In this final chapter, we'll be enabling our template to make administrative users have some control over its appearance. We'll then take a look at working with template overrides and setting up custom class suffixes so that we can further control and tweak our layout. Lastly, we'll go over some great tips and tricks for designing your Joomla! 1.5 templates.

Giving users control

Template parameters are new for Joomla! 1.5. They're great in that they allow you to pass variables (parameters) to your template via XHTML forms that can be chosen from the Administrative panel.

We'll set up a very simple parameter function in four steps. You'll quickly see how to adapt this technique to any additional parameters you'd like your template's administrators to have control over:

Time for action: **Adding a basic parameter to your Joomla! template**

Let's take a look at setting up a basic parameter in Joomla!'s template system:

1. In your `templateDetails.xml` file, add the following to the `<params>` tag section of the file. Within the XML file, you can use XHTML to create forms, such as drop-down select lists, radio buttons, check boxes, and input fields. We'll create a simple drop-down select list and input field:

```
<params>
<param name="logoType" type="list" default="image" label="Logo
                            type" description="Type of Logo">
        <option value="graphicHead">Graphic</option>
        <option value="textHead">Text</option>
```

```
    </param>
    <param name="logoText" type="text" default="" size="50"
         label="Logo text" description="Your Logo Text" />
    <param name="sloganText" type="text" default="" size="50"
           label="Slogan" description="Your Slogan Text" />
    </params>
```

2. Create a file called `params.ini`. Make sure it is set to be "writeable" (**chmod 755**). This file can be a blank file, but we're going to add the following default parameter to it: `logoType=graphicHead`.

   Note how `logoType` matches the param `name` and `graphicHead` matches the `value` of that param. You can now see the parameters are available in the Administration panel's **Extensions | TemplateManager—go_green** template page:

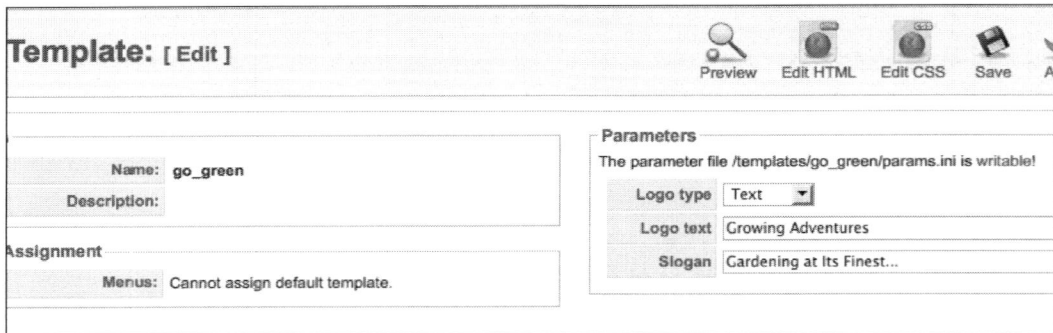

3. In your template's `index.php` file, you can now use the PHP function `$this->params->get("logoType");` to pull what we want from the user's selection into the template. Doing this allows us to determine what CSS class rule to apply to the container background and header, so that either the Go Green graphic (great for the Go Green Campaign) or plain text shows up if an administrator chooses to add his/her own text-based logo to the template. This is great when the Go Green Campaign shares its template with some other association that needs to put its name into the site.

   ° First, let's add the `get('logoType')` param call to the `container` id div and the `header` id div:

   ```
       . . .
       <div id="container" class="<?php echo $this->params-
                                   >get("logoType"); ?>">
       . . .
   ```

```
...
<div id="header" class="<?php echo $this->params-
                        >get("logoType"); ?>">
...
```

- Then, let's add the `get('logoText')` and `get('sloganText')` param call to the `header` div's `h1` and `h4` tags by replacing our "hard-coded" Go Green Campaign site name and slogan with the following:

```
...
<h1><?php echo $this->params->get("logoText"); ?></h1>
<h4><?php echo $this->params->get("sloganText"); ?></h4>
...
```

- When you refresh your site and look at the source code, you should see your `container` and `header` id divs now have either the `textHead` or the `graphicHead` class added. For example:

```
...
<div id="container" class="textHead"><!--container goes
                                            here-->
...
```

- The `h1` and `h4` tags inside the `header` should have whatever text you typed into the Administration panel input fields and then saved:

```
...
<h1>Growing Adventures</h1>
<h4>Gardening at Its Finest...</h4>
...
```

4. Lastly, you'll need a new "logo-less" header graphic, and then you'll need to update your CSS to accommodate the new CSS `id` and text that your parameters can pass to the template. You'll recall from *Chapter 2*, we set most text items in the header to `display: none`. We'll want the new CSS to make those items display if **Text** has been selected.

   - First, we'll go into Photoshop and save out a background that doesn't have the Go Green Campaigning logo in it. (I moved the leaf over a bit as well so that it can "accent" the new text logo.)

The following screenshot illustrates creating the blank
header background:

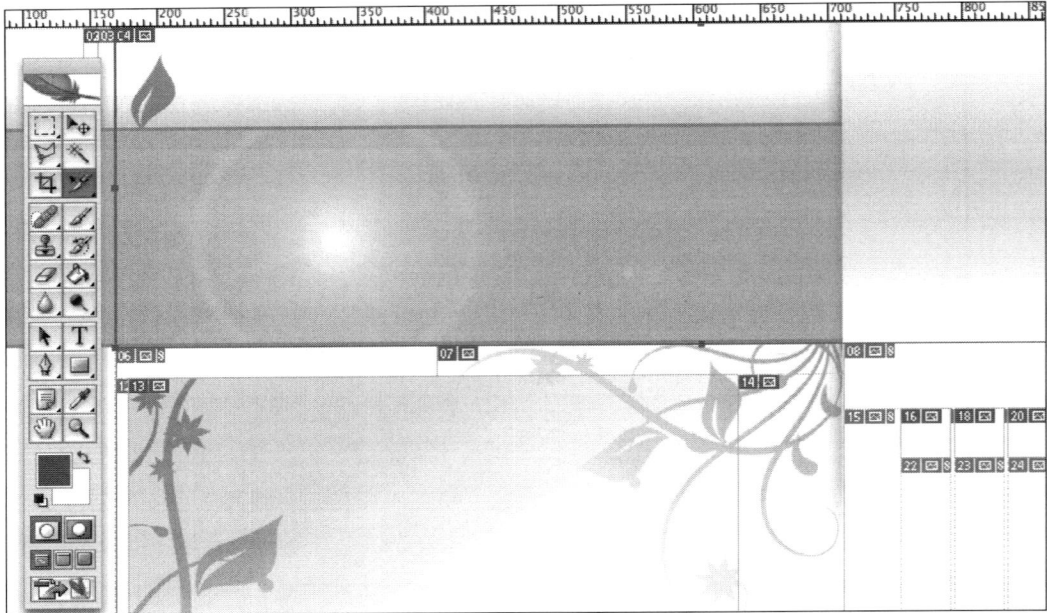

- Next, after slicing and exporting the new `gogreen_txtheader.
  jpg`, we'll remove the background image property from the
  `container` id rule and create two more rules that control that
  background property. Our `container` rule and new rules now
  look like this:

```
...
#container {
    margin: 0 auto;
    width: 1000px;
    /*border: 1px solid #666666;*/
    font-family: "Trebuchet MS", Verdana, Arial, Helvetica,
                                              sans-serif;
    font-size: 12px;
    line-height:16px;
}

#container.graphicHead{
    background: url("../images/gogreen_header.jpg") no-
                                    repeat top left;
}
```

```
#container.textHead{
    background: url("../images/gogreen_txtheader.jpg") no-
                                      repeat top left;
}
...
```

○ Lastly, we'll update our `header` id rules to accommodate the
`.textHead` and `.graphicHead` classes. We'll also be sure to
update our `user1` and `user2` id rules, as turning the text on
changes their positioning needs.

```
...
#header {
    height: 236px;
    padding-top: 0px;
}

#header.graphicHead h1, #header.graphicHead h4{
    display: none;
}

#header.textHead h1{
    margin-top: 10px;
    margin-left: 45px;
    font-size: 26px;
    color: #006633;
    line-height: 18px;
}

#header.textHead h4{
    margin-left: 55px;
    line-height: 10px;
    font-size: 16px;
}

.graphicHead #user1{
    margin-top: 90px;
    width: 250px;
    float: left;
}

.graphicHead #user2{
    margin-top: 60px;
    width: 250px;
    float: right;
}

.textHead #user1{
    margin-top: 0px;
```

```
      width: 250px;
      float: left;
}
.textHead #user2{
      margin-top: 0px;
      width: 250px;
      float: right;
}
...
```

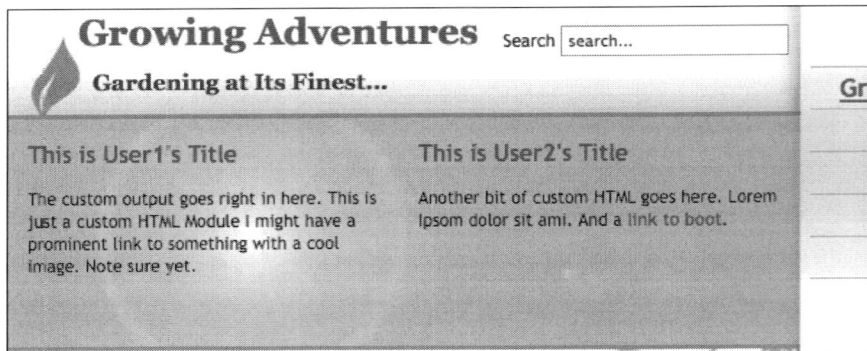

As you can see, the possibilities of control you can hand over to your user are endless. If you take a look at other Joomla! 1.5 templates, you'll find that commercial templates tend to offer lots of control to users using this method (something you'll want to do if you want to get a little extra income from creating Joomla! templates). You can use the above technique to offer control over the width of the design, different built-in color schemes and different column layouts, just to name a few popular options administrators like to see.

Editing a template override

In this book so far, our template development has been using the Beez template overrides that we implemented in *Chapter 3*. These have been working out well; I'm very happy with the table-less output. However, I'm concerned that the Go Green Campaign might not like that every page that happens to have a href-wrapped images now triggers the lightBox effect that we installed in *Chapter 8*.

The campaign may want to set up a special page or section that has gallery pages in it, and all other pages that won't trigger the jQuery lightBox no matter what the markup is.

To accomplish this, we just need to set up a page class suffix in Joomla! on the page (or pages) that we want to be our gallery (will get to that in a bit). But, I happen to already know that the Beez template doesn't contain the overall `contentpaneopen` class around the content area. The Beez template creators did put in the `contentheading` header, which can be "suffix-ized" by the page suffix preference in the Administration panel.

The easiest way to fix that is to delve into the Beez template override view for articles and touch it up.

Time for action: Editing a template override

1. First up, we'll need to find the proper template override view. Views are specific files that directly handle individual component and module aspects, determining how they appear in your template. We're interested in updating the article view. To locate it, in your `theme` folder, go into `com_content/article/default.php` through the `html` folder.

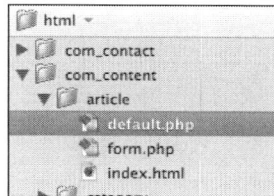

2. Next, we'll search through the code looking for anything containing the `contentheading` class so that we can see how the code that enables page suffixes is structured. I find this example on line **20** or **21** of the `default.php` file:

```
...
<h2 class="contentheading<?php echo $this->params-
                          >get('pageclass_sfx'); ?>">
...
```

3. Using that syntax, let's move down the page, noting where the `buttonheading` class paragraph tag is and where, just below that, the content display code starts after the closing paragraph tag (which is around line **72**). We don't need to understand everything in this file, but it's pretty obvious the PHP code that starts with `if (($this->params->get('show_section')` `&&...` is where our content will start. Right above that code, around line **74**, let's add this bit of markup:

```
...
<div class="contentpaneopen<?php echo $this->params-
                           >get('pageclass_sfx'); ?>">
...
```

4. Of course, we'll need to close that `div` tag. We'll do that at the bottom of the page around line **124.**

```
. . .
</div>
. . .
```

> **Why** `contentpaneopen`? You're right, we could have made the hard-coded class anything we wanted. However, even though this book's case study is pretty customized, I'm assuming a lot of you out there want to make commercial templates that are easy for people to use and tweak to their taste. By using the `contentpaneopen` class name, which is what Joomla's native core outputs, you'll be creating a template that is easier for another administrator (or even yourself in the future) to tweak via CSS by knowing what standard Joomla! class outputs to look for.

If you now return to an article page on your site and right-click and select **View Page Source**, you'll note that the content paragraphs are now wrapped in a `contentpaneopen` div. This is great because we can now create a custom page suffix to further tweak the styling of specific, individual article pages, or target them using our jQuery selectors for the jQuery lightBox plugin. We'll take a look at how to make that happen in the next section.

Adding suffixes to modules and pages

Now that we've added that bit of code to our template override article view, we can take advantage of it. While *Chapter 6* has a rundown of the main classes that Joomla! outputs, suppose you want to get granular control over a specific module or special article page. In that case, you can easily set up class suffixes for modules and pages in Joomla.

Page suffixes

Let's create a page suffix.

Time for action: Creating a page suffix

To create a page suffix, you have to address the page through the **Menu** module.

1. In your Administration panel, go to **Menu | Main Menu** (or, in case of multiple menus, the menu name that has the page you're addressing), and select the content page you wish to target.

2. On the right, under the **Parameters (System)** panel, there is a field called **Page Class Suffix.** There, you'll add your suffix name. In my case, I'll add a space and the new class name: `lightBox2`. (I've added 2 to my class name

just in case the jQuery lighBox CSS file we included in our template already has the obvious class name of `lightBox`.)

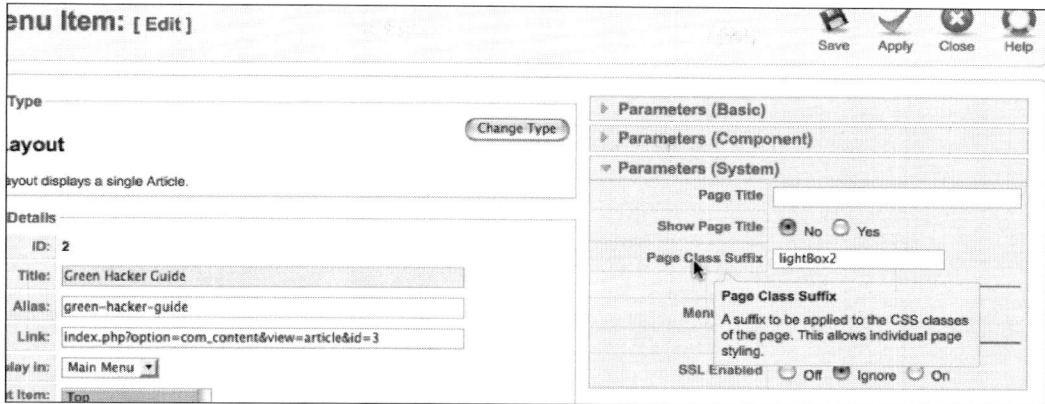

The following screenshot shows the article page now has the `contentpaneopen` class applied to a `div` with our page suffix added to it.

Module suffixes

Let's see how to create module suffixes.

Time for action: **Create a Module Class Suffix**

The Module Class Suffix works much the same way. You simply use the Module Manager to select the specific module you'd like to modify.

1. In your Administration panel, go to **Extensions** | **Module Manager**, and select the **Log In** module (or again, any module you want to modify)

2. Again, on the right, under **Module Parameters**, you'll find the **Module Class Suffix** field. There, you can add your dash/underscore suffix, or a space, and your new class name: `logIn`.

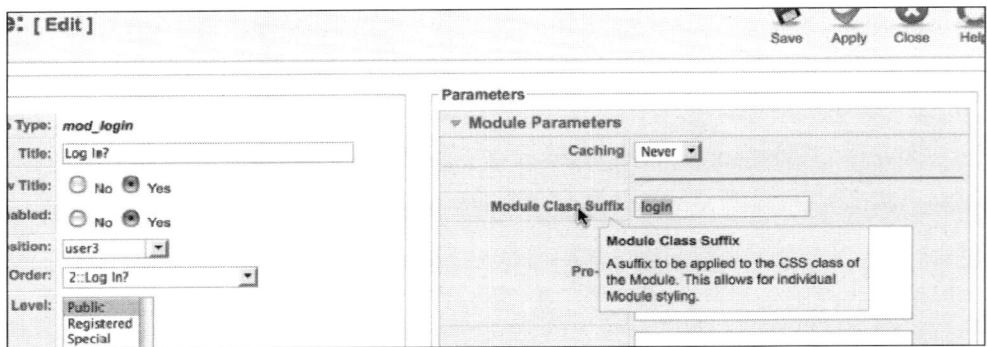

The trick

Here's a CSS productivity trick: while you can just use a dash or underscore to create a whole new CSS class to target (and sometimes, that is exactly what you'd want to do), notice that in the instances above, I didn't add a `-suffixName` or `_sufixName` into the field, but instead placed a space `className` in there.

You can have multiple classes listed in the class attribute as long as they're separated by spaces. This means that I don't have to go in and add a whole new additional class for this one instance that often has to reinclude a lot of information from the original class.

A lot of the time, you'll find that you want your page or module to be enhanced with some additional styling but still inherit the basic styles already assigned to all the other modules or pages. By using a space and creating a new independent class name, the instance inherits the original class, and all you have to do is add a new class that modifies what's needed (such as, most importantly, being able to change my jQuery selector path to only affect images that are wrapped in `hrefs` only inside this particular class only).

Assign more than one class rule to an XHTML markup object?

Yes, you can see by our sample above, you can assign more than one class rule to a markup object. Simply separate each class rule with a space (not a comma); for example, class="rule1 rule2". This comes in handy when you need to customize many elements yet don't want to repeatedly copy similar properties across all of them (plus, you can easily change the main properties in just one spot, instead of having to fix them all). This only works with CSS class rules, and not id rules.

Think whether or not this technique will work for you. After all, you'll recall from *Chapter 7*, to amend our main menu with the Suckerfish drop down, we set the **Module Class Suffix** to _sf, creating an all-new class that would affect only our main menu and no other menu items we may want Joomla! to output, so sometimes you don't want to use the space.

Design tips and tricks

Alright, for the last bit of this final chapter, let's sum things up by giving you a few final design tips, tricks, and troubleshooting ideas to take with you into your future Joomla! template designs. As we've gone through this book, there are quite a few tips that have been given to you along the way. Here are the top four to remember:

- **Create and keep lists**: Check lists, color lists, font lists, image treatment lists. Keep all of these handy from your initial design phase. You'll find them to be useful and excellent inspiration for designs to come.

- **Design for FireFox first, then fix for IE (and your other browsers)**: Firefox is more than a browser preference; it's a true web designer and developer's tool. Use the Web Developer Toolbar!

- **Validate your XHTML and CSS, often**: The more stable your markup and CSS is, the less hacks and fixes you'll need to make.

- **Consider usability issues when implementing site enhancements**: Steve Krug is a cool guy. Moreover, good usability naturally lends itself to great design.

With that said, let's go over a few final design techniques that any good designer wants in his/her arsenal these days.

The cool factor essentials

Next I'll go through what I feel are the most popular tricks used in web site design today. Most of these design techniques are easily incorporated into Joomla!, as they're handled 100% via CSS. A few items will require you to think and plan ahead, as you'll need to make sure the Joomla! template code accommodates the effect. The best thing is, if you can implement these techniques into a Joomla! template, you can implement them into any web site.

First off, this book's case study has already looked at several "cool factor" techniques that are very popular in web design today. Among these techniques are using the CSS `float` property to create a three-column layout. And we've also covered styling an unordered list vertically and using the CSS `hover` property for our Suckerfish drop-down menus, which could be applied to text or used with images for a rollover effect without the use (or with minimal use) of JavaScript.

If you want to be able to do whatever you want in a site's design, get a handle on these top five techniques, which we'll go over in further detail:

- **Backgrounds**: If you haven't already realized this by now, about 98% of the CSS that makes your Joomla! template look great is dependent on how creative you get with the CSS `background` properties of your XHTML objects, classes, and id rules.

- **Lists**: You need to know how to style them horizontally and vertically as well as about using background images.

- **Rounded corners**: We'll cover a couple of ways to tackle this. Again, it all centers around knowing the `background` property.

- **Text image replacement**: And yet again, like the rounded corner technique, the more you understand about the `background` property, the better.

- **Learn your image editor inside and out**: OK, this is not a specific "web technique", but it is what will set you apart. Whichever your editor of choice is, Photoshop, Fireworks, GIMP, Illustrator, or Inkscape, once you have a handle on controlling your layout with XHTML and CSS, the real factor that will make your Joomla! templates pop off the screen is how good you are at creating all those graphics that get loaded in via the `background` property.

Let's go over each of these techniques in detail:

Backgrounds

From your page header image background to data table spruce ups, rounded corners, and fancy replaced text (which you'll find out about in a minute), knowing how to really control and manipulate background colors and images via CSS is key. Check out `http://w3schools.com/CSS/CSS_background.asp` to learn the ins and outs of this CSS property.

You'll want to pay special attention to setting background images, controlling the vertical and horizontal repeat of these images, as well as controlling the positioning of the image. (This is great for using CSS sprite techniques for rollovers.) For a great article on using CSS sprites, check out `http://www.alistapart.com/articles/sprites/`.

The most common CSS shorthand of the `background` property that I often use is:

```
...
    background: #fff url("images/imageName.jpg") no-repeat left
                                                             top;
...
```

The first item in the "pile" or "stack" is of course a hex color; you can then add an image URL. After that, you can set the horizontal "x" (`repeat-x`) or vertical "y" (`repeat-y`) of an image or set it to `no-repeat`. Lastly, I like to set the position. The default position is `left`, `top`. You can set it to `right`, `top` or `left`, `bottom` or `right`, `bottom`, which is what you'll do with rounded corners. You can also set the exact pixel positioning (which works from the left and top), so `20px`, `20px` would be 20 pixels in from the left and down from the top.

The next most useful property I often use is `background-position`:

```
...
background-position: 0px -20px;
...
```

This applied to a `class` or `id` with an `a:hover` amendment would move the image loaded in with previous background shorthand back to the left by 20 pixels (because it goes from 20px to 0px) and up by a total of 40 pixels (because it moves from 20px to -20pixels for a total of 40 pixels up). This is key for using the CSS sprites technique for rollovers or just aiding in pre-loading images without JavaScript.

CSS shorthand

CSS shorthand has been mentioned a few times in this book. It allows you to use a more general property name and then pile or stack on the various properties for a CSS element, separating each with a space, without having to set up all the individual properties; that is, setting a `background-color`, a `background-image`, a `background-postion`, and so on. Most elements of CSS do have a shorthand property name, especially if there are multiple variances of a property. Learning how to use these will greatly enhance your style sheet's flow. However, be careful! It's easy to mess up a property and not clearly be able to see where the syntax is wrong. IE requires the "piling" or "stacking" to be specific, whereas other browsers can recognize the properties no matter what order you place them in. So be sure to note the proper stacking order of shorthand properties. A good place to check your shorthand in the correct order is to review the syntax of the specific property you're working with on W3Schools site: `http://www.w3schools.com/css/css_syntax.asp`.

Lists

In *Chapters 2* and *3*, we created a vertically-styled list and then amended it to handle Suckerfish drop downs. There are specific list properties that can help you control your lists to display vertically and horizontally. For an overview of all the list properties, check out `http://w3schools.com/CSS/css_list.asp`.

My most important list properties are controlling the `list-style`:

```
list-style: none;
```

More than just properties, for lists, you really need to know how to structure CSS rules that will target the various list elements properly. For instance:

```
.menu_sf ul{
```

Will target our main unordered list with that class assignment whereas

```
.menu_sf li ul {
```

Will allow us to target the styles of any nested unordered lists.

See it in action

Most importantly, it just really helps to often see and use good working sample list code. Listamatic is a great place where you can see all sorts of list manipulation techniques. You can find it here: `http://css.maxdesign.com.au/listamatic/`.

The Listamatic examples I find I reference most are:

- **For vertical lists**: *A List Apart's Taming lists* (`http://css.maxdesign.com.au/listamatic/vertical10.htm`) and *Eric Meyer's Simple Separators* (`http://css.maxdesign.com.au/listamatic/vertical06.htm`—which you'll find influenced this book's case study design's main menu)
- **For horizontal lists**: *Eric Meyer's tabbed navbar* (`http://css.maxdesign.com.au/listamatic/horizontal05.htm`)

If you want to have infinitely scalable tabbed horizontal navs, you'll want to check out the "sliding door" technique from (of course) *A LIST apart*: `http://www.alistapart.com/articles/slidingdoors/`.

Rounded corners

Rounded corners have been pretty popular the past few years, to the point that many sites have been accused of incorporating them just so that they seem "Web 2.0-ish". Fads aside, rounded corners are occasionally just going to work well with a design. (They're great for implying "happy-friendly-ish" tones and/or retro styles.) So you might as well know how to incorporate them into your Joomla! template.

The classic: All four corners

Joomla! already assumes that you'd like to have rounded corners that are flexible enough to scale vertically and horizontally. In *Chapter 3*, I had you set this book's case study module position tags to `style="xhtml"`. However, you can take advantage of a style called `rounded`, which will help you easily implement this technique.

Really understanding rounded corners in a table-less design: If you haven't noticed by now, I'm a huge fan of alistapart.com, so I'll leave it to these trusted experts to give you the complete low down on the ins and outs of making rounded corner boxes with CSS: `http://www.alistapart.com/articles/customcorners/`.

Also, there are many rounded corner generator sites out there that will do a lot of the work for you. If you're getting comfortable with CSS and XHTML markup, you'll be able to take the generated code from one of these sites and "massage" the CSS into your Joomla! `style.css`. roundedcornr.com is my favorite: `http://www.roundedcornr.com/`.

Time for action: Adding rounded corner images via CSS

Let's take a look at using Joomla!'s `jdoc include` attribute, `style=rounded`, to help us create rounded corners.

1. To start, in your `index.php` file, change the `style` attribute in the module position `jdoc` tags from `xhtml"` to `rounded"`. For example:

```
...
<jdoc:include type="modules" name="top" style="rounded" />
...
```

2. Now, just make four rounded corner images named `left-bot.gif`, `right-bot.gif`, `left-top.gif`, `right-top.gif` (or generate them at roundedcornr.com). And using a class name called `.module` (change this to whatever the output is, if you're using a class suffix as we discussed above to target a specific module), reference the images via `background` parameters in your CSS, like so:

```
...
.module {
    background: #cccccc;
    background: url(../images/left-top.gif) no-repeat top left;
    /*be sure to set your preferred font requirements*/
}
.module div {
    background: url(../images/right-top.gif) no-repeat top right;
}
.module div div {
    background: url(../images/left-bot.gif) no-repeat bottom left;

}
.module div div div {
    background: url(roundedcornr_170953_br.gif) no-repeat bottom
                                                          right;
}
.module div div div, .moduletable div div, .moduletable div,
                                                    .module{
    width: 100%;
    height: 30px;
    font-size: 1px;
}
.moduletable {
    margin: 0 30px;
}
...
```

Here's an example of the markup that Joomla! will spit out for a module:

```
...
<div class="module"> <!--//left-top.gif-->
<div> <!--//right-top.gif-->
    <div> <!--//left-bot.gif-->
        <div> <!--//right-bot.gif-->
            <h3>Header</h3>
                Content the module outputs goes in here
        </div>
    </div>
</div>
</div>
...
```

Your end result should be something that looks like the following:

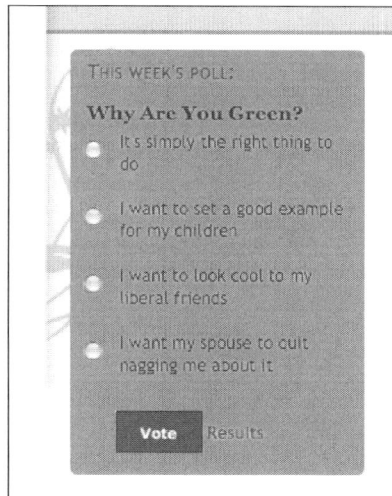

The two image cheat

I'll be honest; I'm on the cheater's band wagon when it comes to rounded corners. I often create locked-width designs. So, I always know exactly how much room my columns can take up, and they only need to be able to expand vertically. Plus, I already use enough `div` tags for containing and positioning elements. The fewer I can get away with, the better. I like this technique because it means I can leave my module position `style` attribute set to `xhtml` and only output a clean `div` with a .`moduletable` class (for some reason, Joomla! outputs .`module` when the style is set to `rounded` and .`moduletable` when it's set to `xhtml`) and an `h3` header tag inside.

More A List apart: Again alistapart.com comes in with a great take on this two image process, along with some great tips for creating the corners in your favorite graphic program: http://www.alistapart.com/articles/mountaintop/.

This rounded corner fix only works for a set width with a variable height. That means, no matter how wide you make your graphic, it is as wide as your outer div should be. So, if you know the width of your columns and just need the height to expand, you can do this two image cheat by only making a top image and an extended bottom image, like so:

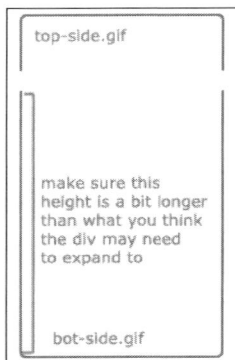

```
top-side.gif



make sure this
height is a bit longer
than what you think
the div may need
to expand to



bot-side.gif
```

Test this technique

In the last graphic, I mention that you need to **make sure this height is a big longer than what you think the div may need to expand to**. Once you have it implemented, try it out in different browsers and set your browser's default type to different sizes. If someone has his/her browser set to very large type, this effect can be easily broken.

Time for action: Adding rounded corner images via CSS

For this example, as I'm fairly confident that the majority of the site's users will be using IE7 and up, I've created two slightly transparent images (similar to the leadPost graphic I made in *Chapter 2* and implemented in *Chapter 3*, which shows up slightly transparent behind the lead story on the home page). Next, reference the images in your CSS (note how much simpler the CSS becomes):

```
...
.moduletable {
   margin:0 0 10px 0;
   padding:0 0 10px 0;
```

```
    width: 150px;
    background:url(../images/bot-side.png) bottom left no-repeat;
      /*be sure to set your preferred font requirements*/
}
.moduletable h3 {
    padding:8px 10px 6px 15px;
    margin-bottom:8px;
    /*be sure to set your
    preferred font requirements*/
    background:url(../images/top-side.png) top left no-repeat;
}
...
```

You'll see the XHTML markup is now greatly simplified because I take advantage of my header tag as well:

```
...
<div class="moduletable"> <!--//bot-side.png-->
    <h3>Header</h3><!--//top-side.png-->
    Content the Module's outputs goes in here
</div>
...
```

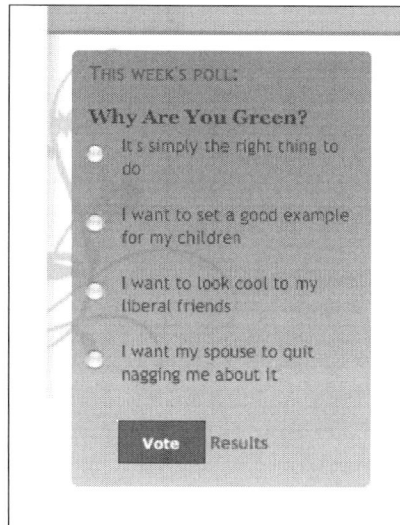

Great for block quotes

I also use this technique to handle custom block quotes that get used inside static pages and posts (a great way to spice up pages so that they look "magazine-ish"). Again, the block quotes must be of a set width. I only need to make sure I place in my `<blockquote>` and `<h3>` tags to have an effective style with minimal (and semantic) markup. Just replace the `.moduletable{...` above with `blockquote{...` (or make a special class to assign to your `<blockquote>` tag).

Text to image replacement

Now here's something that's a total pain that all web designers have had to deal with. As we discussed in detail in *Chapter 2*, there're really only three, maybe five, truly safe fonts for the Web, fonts that you can be fairly sure that every PC and Mac (and maybe Linux) computer has natively installed. And while being sure, you can stack your fonts as we discussed; only a handful of your audience may see your intended fonts and all other fonts tend to be off limits for web design. This is a shame, as typography is a huge element of great design. None-the-less, if you want these fonts, you have to create them as graphics and include the images into your layout.

The problem with using graphics instead of text is that it really messes with your site's semantics. Usually, it's the section headers that you want in the unique font. However, if you use in-line image tags, your semantic markup gets thrown off and your SEO will fall because search engine bots really like to find those h1, h2, and h3 header tags to help assess the real **keywords** in your page. Plus, if your style aesthetic changes, you have to not only change the template but also update individual posts and pages with new images from within Joomla!'s Administration panel.

The solution is to use text in your header tags, yet display unique fonts as images by setting up custom classes in your stylesheet. This CSS technique will move the text out of the way and insert your graphic font as a background image.

Again, as we mentioned in *Chapter 4*, search engine bots generally view your pages as if the stylesheet has been turned off. Therefore, search engine bots and people using screen readers will keep flowing smoothly over pure text, whereas the rest of us get to see your sweet design and nice font selection. The bonus: when the site design changes, all your images are handled via the CSS sheet, so you won't have to touch individual post and static pages.

My Joomla! template makes use of HandWriting - Dakota font in the header. I'd love to use it for my section headers, but the problem is, too many people don't have HandWriting - Dakota on their computers. Even if my user has HandWriting - Dakota on his/her machine, I think the font looks best when it's anti-aliased. While Mac users would then see it OK in Safari or Firefox, PC users using Windows XP might not be able to do it. I've created graphics of my headers using HandWriting - Dakota and while I'm at it, I decided I might as well add a little "flourish". I'll set up my header tags with classes to move the XHTML text out of the way and use my new background images.

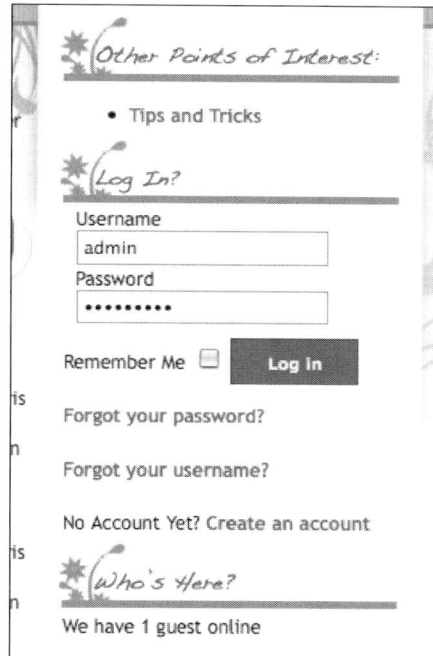

The drawback

Try to keep track of the bandwidth your site needs to load. The more images and the bigger they are, the longer, of course, it will take to load. By switching my headers from pure XHTML text to a full non-repeating image, I added about 4k to 10k per graphic. On the whole it's no big deal, especially in this day and age of broadband, but still something to keep in mind as you try to assess what elements of your design will use pure XHTML and CSS, and what will be images.

As an example, in your CSS page, set up the following class rules for the module header and the class called `.textMove`:

```
...
.textMove, .moduletabel h3{ /*this is your standard for each header*/
    height: 23px;
    margin-top:10px;
    width: 145px;
    text-indent: -2000px;/*This pushes your text back so it's
                                                    invisible*/
}
.specificTextName{ /*specific header-text that you set in the
                                                    moduleimage*/
    background: url("../images/specificText.jpg") no-repeat left top;
}
...
```

The resulting output should look like this, where the class `logIn` would replace the above `specificTextName` class example. (You can refer to the *Adding suffixes to modules and pages* techniques given earlier in this chapter, for examples on how to set up two class calls in a class attribute):

```
<div class="moduletable logIn">
    <h3>Log In?</h3>
```

Now, after giving each of your modules an additional specific class name, you can replace the headers. If you'd like to do the same thing in your template's content pages that contain the text you'd like to apply this technique to, you'll apply the appropriate classes to the header(s) that you'd like to use your graphic text image in (again, if you're in the Administration panel, turn off the TinyMCE editor or use the **HTML** view).

```
...
<h2 class="textMove specificTextName">Section Header</h2>
...
```

Note the multiple class rules assigned to an object again. In the case of graphic text headers, I like to make one rule that handles pushing the text out of the way and sets the height and margins for my header images. All my other class rules just handle the background image name; for example, `class="textMove graphicText"`. Remember that this trick only works with CSS `class` rules, not `id` rules.

Extra credit: Use PHP to make graphic headers easy

Above, I made custom images as it was only three headers and I really wanted to add a little green flourish as well. But for sites where I just need the font against a solid background color, I like to simplify this process by using a simple PHP script with a local **TTF (TrueType font)** to help me quickly generate my header graphics. I can then simply include them into my CSS sheet, dynamically setting up the text that the header needs to display.

This technique is very useful if your site is going to be mainly controlled by clients, as they'll probably have to let you know every time they make a new header that needs to be a graphic loaded in via CSS. You'll be able to accommodate them on-the-fly (or even better, teach them how to do it), as opposed to having them wait for you to generate the graphic with PhotoShop or Gimp, then implement the CSS.

> **Heads up**: This PHP code requires the standard ImageGD library to be installed with your PHP configuration. This library has been on most shared/virtual hosting companies I've used, but to be safe, contact your web site host administrator to ensure the ImageGD library is installed.

You can place this script's file anywhere you'd like. I usually place it in my template's image directory, as I will be referencing it as an image (as always, when adding a new file, update your `templateDetails.xml` file).

`imgtxt.php:`

```php
<?PHP
/*Basic JPG creator by Tessa Blakeley Silver.
Free to use and change. No warranty.
Author assumes no liability, use at own risk.*/
header("Content-type: image/jpeg");
$xspan = $_REQUEST['xspan'];//if you want to adjust the width
$wrd = $_REQUEST['wrd'];//what the text is
if (!$xspan){//set a default width
   $xspan = 145;
}
$height = 20;//set a default height
$image = imagecreate($xspan, $height);
//Set your background color.
//set to what ever rgb color you want
if(!$bckCol){
   $bckCol = imagecolorallocate($image, 255, 255, 255);
}
```

```
//make text color, again set to what ever rgb color you want
if (!$txtCol){
   $txtCol = imagecolorallocate($image, 20, 50, 150);
}
//fill background
imagefilledrectangle($image, 0, 0, $xspan, $height, $bckCol);
//set the font size on the 2nd parameter in
//set the server path (not the url path!) to the font location at the
                                                  7th parameter in:
imagettftext($image, 15, 0, 0, 16, $txtCol, "home/user/sitename/
                       fonts/PLANE___.TTF", "$wrd");//add text
imagejpeg($image,'',80);//the last number sets the jpg compression
//free up the memory allocated for the image.
imagedestroy($image);

?>
```

This script only works with TrueType fonts. Upload the TrueType font
and directory location you referenced in the script to the matching
location on the server. Also, my script is very basic, no drop shadows or
reflections. It only creates a JPG with a solid background color, TrueType
font, font size, and solid font color. If you're comfortable with PHP, you
can perform a Google search on the Web for PHP image scripts that allow
you to do more with your text image; that is, add gradient backgrounds
or generate transparent PNGs, or overlay other images on top of or
behind your text. Also, be aware that if you include TrueType fonts with
your template for distribution, licensing issues may apply, which you'll
need to sort out with the creator of the font.

From here on out, you'll only need to reference this PHP script in your CSS by
passing your text to it via a query string instead of the images you were generating.
(For your information, referencing the PHP script as an image does keep your CSS
file valid with W3C's validator:)

```
.specificText {
   background: url("../images/imgtxt.php?xspan=300&wrd=This Is My New
                                   Text") no-repeat left top;
}
```

- The xspan variable is optional. If you don't include it, the default in the script
  is set to 145 pixels wide. If your custom text will be longer than 145 pixels,
  you can set it to the pixel width you desire. (In the example above, I have it
  set to 300. Be sure your width doesn't conflict with your div widths.)

- The wrd variable is where you'll set your custom text. (Be aware that some
  characters may not come over, as the string will be URL encoded.)

Each time you have a new graphic to generate, you can do it entirely via the template's stylesheet. The following is a screenshot from my professional site, which uses the above PHP script to generate header fonts.

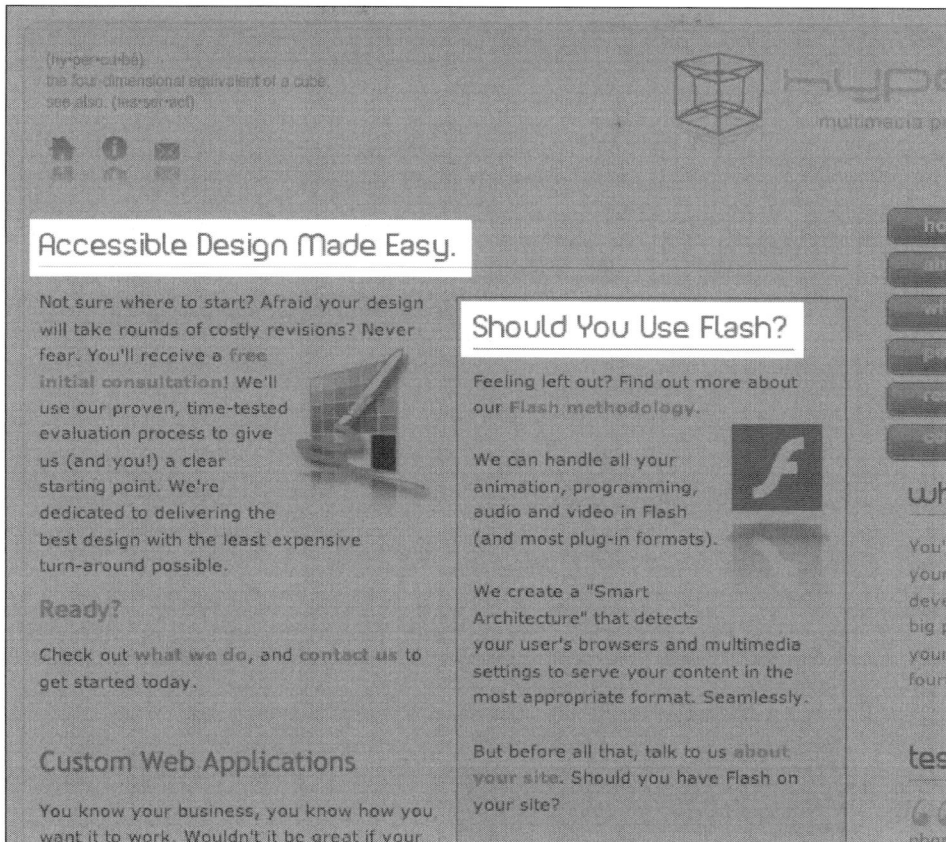

More extra credit: Make unique fonts even easier with the sIFR technique

Recently, a new technique called **sIFR (Scalable Inman Flash Replacement)** has emerged, which takes advantage of the Flash player to display unique fonts ("Inman" is a nod to Shaun Inman who originally conceived of a DOM text replacement method that inspired Mike Davidson's sIFR method). The sIFR method degrades very nicely in that if people don't have the Flash player installed, they see a CSS-styled, plain text alternative, and while it's working, unlike with image replacement, the text is fully selectable and accessible at all times.

sFIR is a good technique to try out if:

- You're familiar with Flash and understand how to use the Flash authoring environment to embed custom fonts into a dynamic Flash text field

- If you're more interested in just displaying the unique font rather than displaying the font and enhancing it with a graphic

- It's important to you that people be able to select all your text, even the headers

If you qualify these three points, it's easy enough to implement the sIFR files directly into your template on your own. You'll want to download it from Mike Davidson's site and then follow his instructions for updating the .swf file and installing the JavaScripts and CSS into your template (after installing the jQuery lightBox in the last chapter, this task should be about the same process). You can download the sIFR package and learn all about it from here: http://www. mikeindustries.com/blog/sifr/.

> **Even more easy**: Don't want to futz and fiddle with adding JavaScripts and CSS sheets to your template? Of course, there's a Joomla! 1.5 extension: http://extensions.joomla.org/extensions/style-&-design/typography/6081/details.

Learn all about your image editor and keep tabs on current design trends

If you look at the best Joomla! commercial template sites out there, their layouts are not all that unique that often. Many can be broken down into a header and footer with three columns in between, just the same as this book's case study.

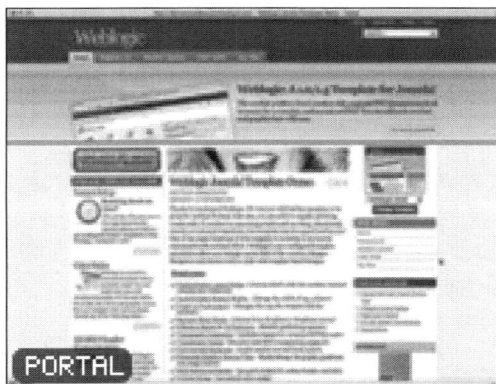

What sets these great templates apart are the slick background images that load in via CSS. For example, the main background seems to glow around the edges of the content area—there are subtle gradients, and shiny, funeye-catching icons. These are all effects created in image editing programs.

In addition to rounded corners, there're some fairly common graphic interface techniques that seem to define those trendy "2.0" sites. They include:

- **Gradients and glows**: But remember, it's all about being subtle (nothing says "1997 – 2000" better than a harsh gradient with a bevelled edge and bulky drop shadow).

- **Reflections**: Again, just be subtle.

- **Vector images and creative drop shadows**: A drop shadow doesn't have to look like your object is merely floating a few pixels off the page. Give your page a feeling of "space" with more three-dimensional shadows. The following image collage depicts subtle reflection and shadows from iomega. com, vector flowers and subtle gradients from verywildflowers.com, and glow effect from psdtuts.com

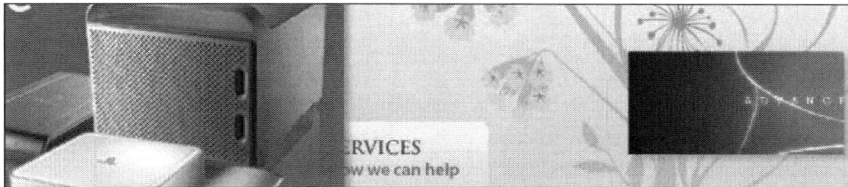

- **Thin, diagonally striped backgrounds**: It could be for just header delineation and not necessarily the whole site's background.

- **Glass or jelly buttons and star-burst stickers**: You can get stripes from kaushalsheth.com and sticker icons from psdtuts.com (just use their search form to find "stickers").

- **Grunge-organic**: This emerged in its hey-day of print design in the early 90's, but it's quickly becoming the new "Shiney, Clean, and Bright" of Web 2.0 sites—paper-looking photos, X-file-ish folder/messy desk layouts, decaying/misprinted fonts, natural edges and liberal (but again, subtle) doses of various spills, drips, and drops that we usually encounter in creative life. The following image collage depicts photo edge from glassburycourt.com/coldspring, torn edges from adventuretrekking.com, and misprinted type with spills from lataka.com

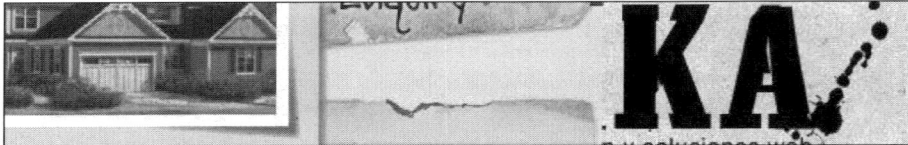

- **Breaking the boundaries**: This is a great way to get your template to "pop". It's usually a purely graphical trick with a CSS background, but it gives the impression that pieces of a layout are breaking the rules of a layout, or otherwise, lifting off the page or pushing out of "the grid". This book's case study design achieves this with the "paper bridge" that supports the main menu. Many other templates like to have an item that seems to hang or jump out to the side of the margins or fall down below the header into the content area. The following image collage shows examples of boundary breaking from the Go Green Campaign—Revolution's Vertigo Template:

Design trends come and go. While the above effects are popular today, they'll become "old hat" soon enough (and start to look like those harsh gradients, beveled edges, and drop shadows of the 90's). Take note of and bookmark leading sites and blogs of designers, web programmers, and key contributors to the web field. Visit these sites often (the good ones update their interface at least once a year. Most are constantly tweaking their interface, adding new things little by little). By keeping your finger on this "design pulse", you'll be able to recognize new trends as they start emerging and then think about how you can creatively leverage them into your own template designs. You'll probably find yourself inventing your own unique interface looks that other people start adopting.

Once you start recognizing the trends, you'll need to learn the ins and outs of how to use your image editing software. Right now, a large part of these design trends are graphics loaded in via CSS. To get those great designs into your template, you'll need to understand CSS, and as I've already mentioned, to know how to effectively (and sometimes creatively) use the `background` property in your CSS rules.

PSDTuts and **VectorTuts** focus on Adobe Photoshop and Illustrator, and are great sites for picking up a little quick "how to" knowledge for current design techniques (VectorTuts has some Inkscape tutorials as well). Both sites are definitely worth a look through. They both have special sections for interfaces and web design that cover how to create many design trends and visual effects: `http://psdtuts.com/category/interface-tutorials/`.

GIMP users will like this site: `http://gimp-tutorials.net/`. And if VectorTuts doesn't have enough for you Inkscape users, check out `http://inkscapetutorials.wordpress.com/`.

Stylegala and **SmashingMagazine** (`http://smashingmagazine.com`) are a few other good sources for keeping up on web design trends. Stylegala also has a great, clear, concise *CSS Reference* chart that I've found very useful from time to time (`http://www.stylegala.com/features/css-reference/`).

Before & After magazine: This is a paid subscription, but for 24 dollars, you get to download 32 beautifully produced PDFs that let you build a great reference library you can keep forever. I have to say, I'm a bit of a cheap-skate myself, but I've been a subscriber for years and continually find my B&A library useful for all sorts of projects, with tips for creating great design using all sorts of trends and techniques: `http://www.bamagazine.com/`.

Good design isn't always visual: Looking at SEO

At this point, you've gone through the trouble to create a semantic, user-friendly, accessible XHTML template, and one of the benefits of that structure is it helps with **SEO (Search Engine Optimization**, if you haven't guessed by now). You might as well go all out and take the time to set up a few more optimizations.

Search-engine-friendly URLs

Joomla's URLs by default are dynamic, which means they are a query string off the `index.php` page; for example, `http://mysite.com/index.php?option=com_conte nt&view=article&id=3&Itemid=2`.

In the past, dynamic URLs had been known to break search engine bots who either didn't know what to do when they hit a question mark or ampersand and/or started indexing entire sites as "duplicate content" because everything looked like it was coming from the same page (usually the `index.php` page).

Generally, this is no longer the case, at least not with the "big boy" search engines such as Google. But you never know who is searching for you and using what service.

Also, by changing the dynamic string URL to a more **SEF (Search Engine Friendly)** URL, it's a little harder for people to directly manipulate your URLs, because they can't clearly see what variable they're changing once it's in a search-engine-friendly URL.

Joomla! has this SEF URL feature built in, but only if you're running PHP on Apache.

In your Administrator panel, go to **Site | Global Configuration**, and on the right side of the page, under **SEO Settings**, set **Search Engine Friendly URLS** to **Yes**.

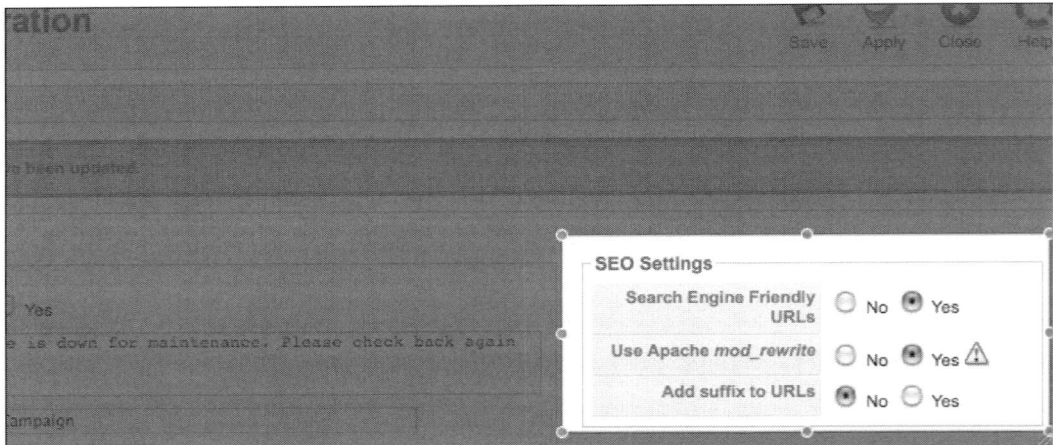

That's it! When you switch back to your site, you'll note that the URLs now appear to reflect your content based on the **Alias** you gave them in the **Menu Module** or other appropriate module; that is, `http://sitename.com/green-hacker-guide`.

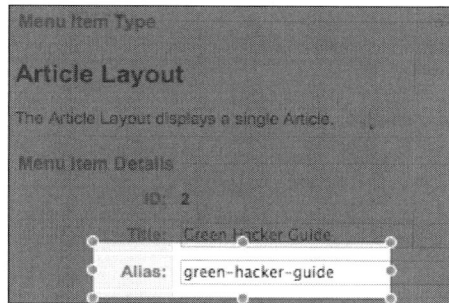

Search engine bots will "think" the forward slashes are directories and not freak out about question marks and ampersands or assume that everything on your site is really the same page.

Forget the search-engine-friendly URLs! What about people-friendly URLs?

In the past, Joomla! 1.0 simply changed the dynamic URL to a parsed up version of itself. Although, this removed the question marks and ampersands and duplicate content issues, it still provided URLs that were not very intuitive to read. Joomla! 1.5 has finally gotten great at people-friendly URLs. Sometimes, you're in a situation where you just can't copy and paste your link over to your browser. It's great to have lunch with your friend and be able to verbally give her the URL to your latest web rant and know that she'll easily remember it: `http://myurl.com/rants/newrant`. Also, clearly named URLs greatly boost your "link trust" (that's what I call it anyway). If the relevant link you've emailed to people or posted in your site or as a comment on someone else's article or blog doesn't appear to clearly have any indication of what you promised is in it, people are much less likely to click on it. (Do you like clicking on long strings of odd numbers and cryptic variable names?) And, while the impact of **keywords** in URLs seems to be waning, there are SEO experts who still swear that your URLs should contain the top **keywords** in your document. If you haven't done so already, be sure to take advantage of this great feature in Joomla! 1.5.

Keywords and descriptions

Although the effectiveness of placing keywords into your meta tags is now widely disputed (especially as there's even speculation that perhaps the big search engines don't reference this meta tag at all anymore), I find it's still wise to place your major keywords for each article into a meta tag (again, if nothing else, the smaller, lesser-known search engines may still use them). I'm not so big on targeting misspellings anymore; search engines compensate for misspellings, but some still say it's important. (Don't you just love the "exact science" of SEO?)

Beyond keywords, well-written meta descriptions are useful, as it seems search engines may randomly chose to display your meta description instead of the relevant bit of text on the page that pertains to the keyword search someone just performed. When it comes to these two meta tags, I'm an advocate of "less is more". Do not drop two hundred keywords and a four paragraph description into your meta tags. Simply put in the top five to ten keywords used in your article or page (note the words you used in your headers) as well as a one-sentence description (maybe two sentences tops) that also uses at least three to five of those keywords in it. Anything more than that, and I believe the "Google Monster" will assume you're trying to pull some "SEO-blackhat" stunt and ignore fully indexing your pages.

Unlike some CMSs, Joomla! has always allowed you to add custom, individual keyword and description meta tags for each content type you create for your site. You may have noticed in your Joomla! Administrator's panel, when you edit or create a new content page (be it an article, static page, or even a wrapper), there's a side panel off to the right. If you click the **Metadata Information** tab, you'll have two places to include your content page's description and keywords.

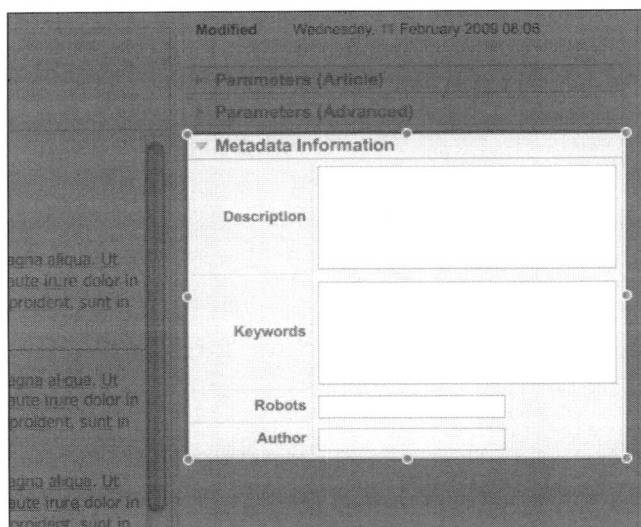

Summary

We've learned how to implement parameters into the **Template Manager** so that your administrators can have some control over your template. We also took a look at tweaking a template override. In addition, we reviewed how to add module and page class suffixes to your site for precise control via CSS. Lastly, we reviewed the main design tips you should have picked up from the previous chapters, covered some key tips for easily implementing today's coolest CSS and graphic design techniques into your template, as well as looked at a few final SEO tips to enhance your site once you really start putting content into it or turn the site over to the content editors.

I hope you've enjoyed this book and found it useful in aiding your Joomla! 1.5 template creations.

Index

M

menu output options 159
menu style
  legacy - flat list 161
  legacy - horizontal 161
  legacy - vertical 160
  list 160
Mobile Safari browser 131
module chrome
  about 8, 87, 163
  working 163, 164
module class suffix 236
module overrides 161, 162
module position styles
  about 157
  Joomla! 1.0 to 1.5 159
module position tags
  about 156
  module position styles 157
modules 20

N

Nvu 14

O

ObjectSwap method 199
ObjectSwap script 200

P

page suffix
  about 234
  creating 234
pagination 166
PHP 12
PHP if/else conditional statements
  about 180
  code, adding 180-184
PHP syntax 180
PHP variable
  passing through swf file 198
plug-ins 21
positions 25

Q

QorSMode bookmarklet 131
quirks mode 116

R

rapid design comping
  about 23
  overview 23, 24

S

sandbox 73
Satay method 195
Scalable Inman Flash Replacement. *See* sIFR
Search Engine Optimization. *See* SEO
semantic XHTML structure 34
  about 34
  basic style sheet, adding 32
  CSS file, attaching 32
  DOCTYPE 30
  DOCTYPE, adding 31
  strict DOCTYPE 30
  translational DOCTYPE 30
  XHTML file requirements, adding 31
SEO
  about 255
  keywords 258
  meta description 258
  search-engine-friendly URLs 256, 257
sIFR 41
sIFR method 251, 252
site header information tag
  about 156
  Joomla! 1.0 to 1.5 conversion 156
SmashingMagazine
  breaking the boundaries 255
standard parameter types
  calendar display 175
  hidden variable 175
  list 174
  radio buttons 174
  text 174
strict DOCTYPE
  about 31

U

Universal Description and Discovery
Information. *See*

V

validation
  about 122
  advanced validation 126
  mobile browsers, optimizing 131
  text browsers, optimizing 131
  work, checking in IE 130
validation, checking in IE
  IE Developer Toolbar 131
  multiple versions of IE, running 130
  QorSMode bookmarklet 131

W

W3Cs CSS validator 122
Web Developer Toolbar 128
weblog. *See* blog

X

XHTML
  about 12
  validating 122, 124
XHTML comments 95

Z

Zipping 148

Packt Open Source Project Royalties

When we sell a book written on an Open Source project, we pay a royalty directly to that project. Therefore by purchasing Joomla! 1.5 Template Design, Packt will have given some of the money received to the Joomla! Project.

In the long term, we see ourselves and you — customers and readers of our books — as part of the Open Source ecosystem, providing sustainable revenue for the projects we publish on. Our aim at Packt is to establish publishing royalties as an essential part of the service and support a business model that sustains Open Source.

If you're working with an Open Source project that you would like us to publish on, and subsequently pay royalties to, please get in touch with us.

Writing for Packt

We welcome all inquiries from people who are interested in authoring. Book proposals should be sent to authors@packtpub.com. If your book idea is still at an early stage and you would like to discuss it first before writing a formal book proposal, contact us; one of our commissioning editors will get in touch with you.

We're not just looking for published authors; if you have strong technical skills but no writing experience, our experienced editors can help you develop a writing career, or simply get some additional reward for your expertise.

About Packt Publishing

Packt, pronounced 'packed', published its first book "Mastering phpMyAdmin for Effective MySQL Management" in April 2004 and subsequently continued to specialize in publishing highly focused books on specific technologies and solutions.

Our books and publications share the experiences of your fellow IT professionals in adapting and customizing today's systems, applications, and frameworks. Our solution-based books give you the knowledge and power to customize the software and technologies you're using to get the job done. Packt books are more specific and less general than the IT books you have seen in the past. Our unique business model allows us to bring you more focused information, giving you more of what you need to know, and less of what you don't.

Packt is a modern, yet unique publishing company, which focuses on producing quality, cutting-edge books for communities of developers, administrators, and newbies alike. For more information, please visit our website: www.PacktPub.com.

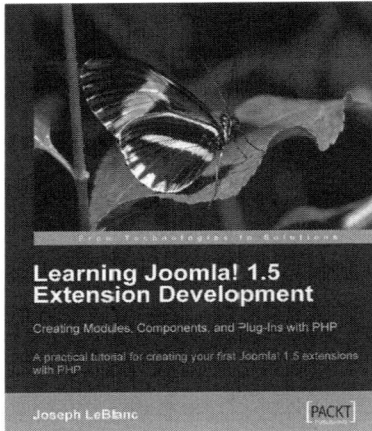

Learning Joomla! 1.5 Extension Development

ISBN: 978-1-847191-30-4   Paperback: 200 pages

A practical tutorial for creating your first Joomla! 1.5 extensions with PHP

1. Program your own extensions to Joomla!

2. Create new, self-contained components with both back-end and front-end functionality

3. Create configurable site modules to show information on every page

4. Distribute your extensions to other Joomla! users

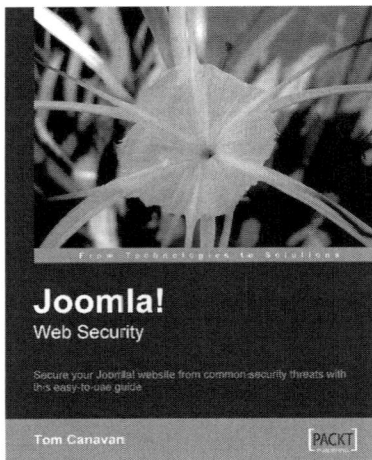

Joomla! Web Security

ISBN: 978-1-847194-88-6   Paperback: 264 pages

Secure your Joomla! website from common security threats with this easy-to-use gu

1. Learn how to secure your Joomla! websites

2. Real-world tools to protect against hacks on your site

3. Implement disaster recovery features

4. Set up SSL on your site

5. Covers Joomla! 1.0 as well as 1.5

Please check **www.PacktPub.com** for information on our titles

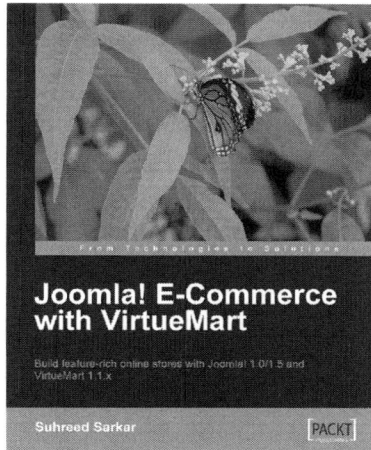

Joomla! E-Commerce with VirtueMart

ISBN: 978-1-847196-74-3   Paperback: 476 pages

Build feature-rich online stores with Joomla! 1.0/1.5 and VirtueMart 1.1.x

1. Build your own e-commerce web site from scratch by adding features step-by-step to an example e-commerce web site

2. Configure the shop, build product catalogues, configure user registration settings for VirtueMart to take orders from around the world

3. Manage customers, orders, and a variety of currencies to provide the best customer service

4. Handle shipping in all situations and deal with sales tax rules

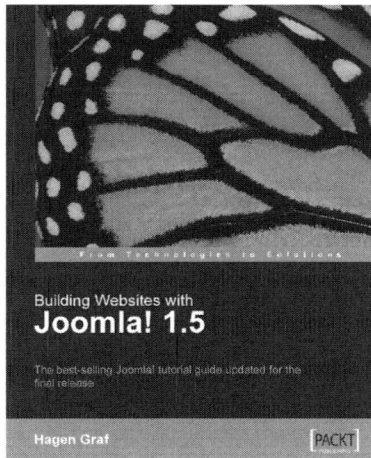

Building Websites with Joomla! 1.5

ISBN: 978-1-847195-30-2   Paperback: 384 pages

The best-selling Joomla! tutorial guide updated for the latest 1.5 release

1. Learn Joomla! 1.5 features

2. Install and customize Joomla! 1.5

3. Configure Joomla! administration

4. Create your own Joomla! templates

5. Extend Joomla! with new components, modules, and plug-ins